THE EMERGENCE OF THE GLOBAL POLITICAL ECONOMY

Given the current fascination with globalization and its possible implications, it is worth keeping in mind that the processes associated with globalization have been ongoing for centuries. They are not entirely novel or recent in origin. The book focuses on the emergence of a global political economy as early as the sixteenth century although even this development had been preceded by centuries of changes leading up to a closer economic integration of eastern and western Eurasia. Several themes are addressed. The political economic dynamics for the global system can be generalized but they are not timeless. Circumstances helped create a global political economy and, once created, it continues to evolve and undergo transformation. Some west Europeans played an important part in the emergence of the system but the ascendance of western Eurasia in the system cannot easily be attributed primarily to various "superior" attributes of western Europe. The major exceptions to this generalization are naval technology and military weaponry but it is also easy to exaggerate the role played by military superiority. A number of other factors were just as critical, if not more so. Once the system was created, a major dynamic for political change focused on a process of challenge developed. Although we do not always recognize the continuity of this process, the major wars of the past 500 years have been caught up and focused on questions of leadership succession in the global political economy. While we cannot assume that this process will go on forever, it is possible to sketch out its general parameters, and to use the historical tendencies to speculate about the future of the global political economy. The argument is not simply that the system is or has been governed by a cycle of periods of economic-political-military primacy, and leadership succession attempts, although that has been the case, but also that there are aspects of the dynamics that suggest a potential for further fundamental transformation of the global political economy.

William R. Thompson is Professor of Political Science at Indiana University and a former co-editor of *International Studies Quarterly* (1994–98). He has previously taught at the University of California, Riverside, Claremont Graduate University, and Florida State University with visiting appointments at the Universities of Arizona and Minnesota.

INTERNATIONAL RELATIONS AND
HISTORY SERIES
Edited by Jeremy Black

How states operate internationally, the nature of conflicts that divide them, the instruments they employ to pursue their ideals and secure their interests are of paramount importance to historians and the study of history.

The *International Relations and History* series explores the international system and international relations between countries and nation states from antiquity to the twentieth century. The series investigates themes such as the structure of international society, notions of statehood, national interest and the practicalities of conflict, competition and co-operation.

Forthcoming titles:

POST-WAR PEACE MAKING
Philip Towle

CODE OF CONDUCT: THE RULES OF
INTERNATIONAL RELATIONS
Ralph Menning

FROM STATE FORMATION TO GLOBALIZATION
Roland Axtmann

THE AMERICAN CENTURY: THE FOREIGN RELATIONS
OF THE UNITED STATES, 1900–2000
Nigel J. Ashton

THE UNITED STATES AND LATIN AMERICA
Joseph Smith

THE EMERGENCE
OF THE GLOBAL
POLITICAL ECONOMY

William R. Thompson

London and New York

First published 2000
by Routledge
11 New Fetter Lane, London EC4P 4EE

Simultaneously published in the USA and Canada by Routledge
29 West 35th Street, New York, NY 10001

Routledge is an imprint of the Taylor & Francis Group

© 2000 William R. Thompson

Typeset in Garamond
by Steven Gardiner Ltd, Cambridge
Printed and bound in Great Britain by TJ International Ltd, Padstow, Cornwall

British Library Cataloguing in Publication Data
A catalogue record for this book is available
from the British Library

Library of Congress Cataloging in Publication Data
A catalog record for this book has been requested

ISBN 0-415-214-521 (hb)
ISBN 0-415-214-53X (pb)

CONTENTS

FIGURES

TABLES

PREFACE

Book projects tend to have multiple origins and reflect several impulses. This one is no exception. It is my seventh book (counting authored, coauthored, and edited volumes) on the subject of world system development. Path dependencies being what they are, it should come as no surprise that I am continuing to work in this area. There is so much yet to be done that I doubt very much that it will be my last book on the subject. A second source, though, was Jeremy Black's kind invitation to write something for this new series on historical topics. I think Jeremy thought it would be interesting to see if I could do a book without numbers in it. On my part, as a non-historian, the idea of getting a more direct access to historians and their students certainly had appeal. A third source can be laid at Jack Levy's doorstep. Sometime around 1994, he invited me to do a paper commemorating the 500th anniversary of 1495 for an International Studies Association panel. The year 1495 did not mean too much to me but it was close enough to 1494, which did have meaning, for me to go along. Not only did it turn out that I was the only one to go along on the "1495" panel (everybody else on the panel wrote about something else), I ended up with a very long paper that I would either have to extend even further or else walk away from it altogether. That paper became the core of chapters 3 and 4 and, a few years later, encouraged me to try my hand at the related subject of chapter 5.

There are four other sources. One was an aborted, coauthored project on the idea of challenges and challengers from the early 1990s that somehow never proceeded very far. Again, I had written a very long paper for my part of the project but the other chapters were never quite forthcoming. After a few of these situations, you begin to identify with the first man out of a World War I trench who chances to look behind him and sees that no one else is following. The rational thing to do is to get back to the trench as fast as possible. I'm afraid my inclination is to keep charging the "enemy," with or without company. Chapters 6, 7, and 8 stem from that project.

George Modelski has been trying to educate me for thirty years so far. I hope he does not abandon the project. His latest innovation has been in moving toward the development of an evolutionary paradigm for international politics. I find that I tend to resist his arguments at first and then ultimately become convinced that he was right all along. Speaking, no doubt, to the question of to whether some people are teachable, I can at least say that the time between initial resistance and ultimate conversion has decreased over time. I was fortunate to attend two conferences in Seattle that he hosted on this subject. I have since hosted a third in Bloomington. Parts of chapters 1, 2, and 8 were linked directly to the Seattle conferences. Chapter 11 is a more indirect product of thinking from an evolutionary perspective.

Chapter 9 emerged from another innovative attempt to bridge the chasm between historians and political scientists that was realized in a meeting held in Tempe, Arizona and hosted by Colin and Miriam Elman of Arizona State University. This was the third such conference I had attended but the first one in which some explicit effort was actually made to span the inter-disciplinary gap. It did not work for me in the sense that I felt any great desire to switch "sides." At the same time, I am no more prepared to ignore the work of historians than I was before. Like some voyages, though, it may be the travel to some destination that is often more rewarding than the actual arrival. I hope that we can at least continue to argue about our differences of interpretation and opinion – even if few conversions should be anticipated (as explained, I think, in the chapter).

Finally, chapter 10 comes out of a collaborative project on great power rivalries in which I assigned myself the Anglo-American rivalry. That rivalry is interesting for a variety of reasons. It was selected initially because it was a rich case for the study of rivalry escalation and deescalation. But it has other payoffs – one of which is that it is revealing about transitions between system leaders. Therefore, it seemed to add something worthwhile to the present mix of issues.

Given these multiple sources and their confluence, it is my contention (and, no doubt, conceit) that these various topics come together more or less coherently even if they were not explicitly planned to do so from the outset. I do not contend that they resolve fully the puzzles and controversies that they address. Hopefully, though, they make some dent in what should be an ongoing process of interpretation and explanation of the evolving world system and its constituent components.

I have benefited from the comments on individual chapters from various people: Jeremy Black, Terry Boswell, Claudio Cioffi-Revilla, Colin Elman, Miriam Elman, Suzanne Frederick, Barry Gills, Thomas Hall, Edward Ingram, David Kelly, Jack Levy, Joel Migdal, George Modelski, David Rapkin, Richard Rosecrance, and John Vasquez. I do not wish to give the impression that any of them agreed with anything I have argued. They are not to blame. Nor have I always heeded their advice. But I have appreciated the invaluable criticism. If someone must be blamed, there are always my wife, Karen, and my daughters, Cam and lLieu. But since they conspire to keep me away from writing books – and most of the time I would not have it any other way – it would hardly be fair to blame them either.

Parts of Chapters 1, 2, and 8 were presented at two conferences on evolutionary paradigms in international relations held in Seattle and hosted by George Modelski. Parts of Chapters 3, 4, and 11 were presented at International Studies Association meetings in Chicago and Toronto. Chapter 5 was meant to be presented at a London meeting of the Anglo-American Historians but, regretfully, I was forced to withdraw at the last minute – something about which I still feel guilty. Chapter 9 was first aired in Tempe at a conference on bridging the gaps between history and political science put together by Colin and Miriam Elman. Chapter 10 was first presented at a rivalry conference at Indiana University that I hosted. An earlier version of Chapter 11 was presented at Emory University thanks to an invitation from Terry Boswell. I certainly gained general feedback on these occasions that also proved to be quite useful.

I am grateful for permission to reprint revised versions of Chapter 1 which first appeared as "K-Waves, Leadership Cycles, and Global War: A Form of World System Analysis Without the Hyphen" in Thomas D. Hall, *The World-Systems Reader: New Perspectives on Gender, urbanism, Cultures, Indigenous Peoples and Ecology* (Lanham, Md.: Rowman and Littlefield, 1999); Chapter 5 which first appeared as "The Military Superiority Thesis and the Ascendancy of Western Eurasia and the World System," in *Journal of World History* 10 (Spring, 1999); 143–78; Chapter 8 which first appeared as "The Evolution of Political–Economic Challenges in the Active Zone," *Review of International Political Economy* 4 (Summer, 1997): 286–318; Chapter 9 which first appeared as "Venusian and Martian Perspectives on International Relations: Britain as System Leader in the Nineteenth and Twentieth Centuries," in Colin Elman and Miriam Fendius Elman, eds., *International History and International Relations Theory: Bridges and Boundaries* (Cambridge, Ma.: MIT Press, 1999); and Chapter 10 which first appeared as "The Evolution of the Anglo-American Rivalry," in William R. Thompson, ed., *Great Power Rivalries* (Columbia: University of South Carolina Press, 1999).

Part I

INTRODUCTION
AND OVERVIEW

1

K-WAVES, LEADERSHIP
CYCLES, AND GLOBAL WAR

An orientation

We tend to think of international political economy as a recent arrived phenomenon. Prior to the early 1970s, and especially the first oil shock in 1973–1974, academics had not shown a great deal of interest in the subject although, of course, people had been talking about political economy processes for some time. But as the study of international political economy (IPE) became increasingly fashionable, it also took on a marked preoccupation with current events. Since it was economic deterioration and recession on a world-wide scale that had galvanized concern with the subject perhaps that is not altogether surprising. The study of international relations, in general, is hardly immune to the same emphasis on "currentism", but there are clear costs in treating these questions and processes ahistorically. The greatest cost is that it is quite difficult to make sense of processes that have been underway for centuries if we choose to look only at the most recent tail end. That is not to say that no one examines international political economy questions while paying sufficient attention to historical matters. There are a number of analysts who do pay attention to the origins of the processes they study. The point remains, however, that the central tendency is still one of assuming that history does not matter all that much.

One of the theses of this study is that history does matter a great deal to the study of international political economy. It does not matter for history's sake alone. History matters in this case because current processes have been developing and evolving for a considerable period. To know how things work in the current world, we need to know their origins and how they have become structured with the passage of time. At the same time, these structures are not carved in stone. They change. We need to know what causes them to change. All these concerns advise against an exclusive preoccupation with the present.

The main thrust of this study is that the current global political economy began to take shape around 1500 and that some of the present's key processes were already dimly perceivable several hundred years ago. The adjective "global" has a special meaning here. "Global" is not merely another synonym for "international" or "world". The term "global" as used here refers to interregional transactions. Technically, interregional transactions have actually been going on for many thousands of years. It is possible, for instance, to study the evolution of a Eurasian or Afro-Eurasian political economy since around 4000 BCE. The current global political economy thus was not born in or around 1500 CE. It had been shaped by more than 5000 years of history prior to that time.

This is not the time or place to take on a maximal history of political-economic transactions across regions. We are still only beginning to flesh out our understanding of how to do 6000-year histories. For the most part, a 500-year emphasis will be stressed here instead for several reasons. One is that the scale of global political economy began to encompass the entire planet about this time. A second reason is that western Europe began to become increasingly central to the operations of a global political economy some 500 years ago. Note that there is a difference between "began to become" and "became." A third reason, not unrelated to the first two, is that some of the current system's principal processes began to emerge between the end of the fifteenth and the early seventeenth centuries. Nevertheless, some processes require longer perspectives because they began to take shape long before 1500. Where necessary, a 1000-year vantage point will be assumed, especially in terms of the emergence of "modern" economic growth.

As long as we do not fall into the mental trap of thinking modern history began around 1500 and as long as there are specific reasons for looking at specific important changes, the questions that are adopted as central will tend to dictate the time period examined. Hence, the temporal focus of this study will emphasize historical processes of the late fifteenth through the early twentieth centuries, even though it will not be restricted to these same centuries in all instances. That is because three sets of questions will be examined. The first question set has to do with the ascent of western Europe or, more accurately, some parts of western Europe to a position of political-economic centrality. Why and how did this happen? These questions are explored in Chapters 3, 4, and 5.

A second set of questions pertains to the sequence of leadership and challenge that has become a hallmark of transitional changes in the global political economy. A singular leader emerges, is preeminent for a while, and then enters into a phase of relative decline. The leadership of the global political economy is then contested by a variable number of challengers who seek to supplant the incumbent system leader. We have gone through a number of iterations of this process and, therefore, it is possible to advance some generalizations about how the challenge process works. Who challenges whom, when, and to what effect? These questions are examined in Chapters 6, 7, and 8.

The third set of questions focuses on puzzles about structural change. The approach adopted here is highly structural. Chapter 9 reexamines the wisdom of this emphasis by looking at (and rebutting) the criticisms of historians who rebel at the notion that Britain was the leader of a global political economy in the nineteenth century. Chapter 10 looks more closely at one of the more curious elements of the challenge process. Why is it that the most successful challenger ends up defending the declining system leader against other challengers and then ascends almost by default? Chapter 10 examines the British–US transition up to the point at which their nineteenth-century rivalry ended. It might be thought this topic belongs to the second set of questions but its placement in the third set should become more clear in the context of Chapter 11's scrutiny of long-term changes in the way system leaders are interrelated over time. The pattern is highly suggestive of fundamental changes in the organization of the global political economy's management principles. Just because a process began to take shape 500 years ago does not imply that the shape assumed will remain unaltered into the future. The global political economy is evolving constantly. The trick is to decipher in what direction it is evolving.

There are certainly other questions to ask about the historical functioning of the global political economy but these three sets will have to suffice for one book. Prior to tackling them, though, some preliminary material needs first to be considered. Chapters 1 and 2 provide an overview of the main features of the global political economy as they have unfolded over the past few centuries. These two preliminary chapters also discuss many of the assumptions that will reappear in attempting to answer the three sets of questions described above.

AN ORIENTATION ON THE DEVELOPMENT OF THE GLOBAL POLITICAL ECONOMY

Some of the most central questions in the study of the global political economy include:

- Why do preeminent states, and their associated political orders, rise and fall?
- Why are some types of economic activity more critical at some times than at others?
- Why do some parts of the world economy seem more central to economic operations at some times than at others?
- Why is economic growth intermittent rather than continuous, and what difference does it make?
- What relationships link intermittent processes of economic growth to such ostensibly political phenomena as war, domestic stability, and state-making?

These are all important questions. They address the basic rhythms of political-economic life; they are very much about how the world works. These questions are also closely related because of the rise and fall dynamics, the shifting centrality of the world economy, and the discontinuities of growth share roots in a thousand-year old, evolutionary process of long-run economic growth and structural change.

Among the core dynamics of these processes are long, Kondratieff waves (K-waves) of innovation and even longer cycles of politico-military preeminence and order (leadership long cycles). The shape of these processes are not perfectly uniform throughout time. Their periodicities are less than precise. They have a specific historical genealogy in the sense that their operations and transitions can be traced back roughly over the last millennium in a continuous fashion and seemingly no further, at least in a continuous fashion. Nor did they emerge abruptly with all of the characteristics that K-waves and leadership long cycles possess currently. On the contrary, almost 500 years went by before these processes began to assume the attributes associated with their contemporary manifestations. Similarly, we should not assume that these core dynamics must continue forever. They may but it is most unlikely that they will do so without undergoing substantial modification, just as they already have done in the past.

The remainder of this chapter will focus on providing an overview of the interdependence between long-term economic growth, global political leadership, and global war and how that interdependence has evolved over the past millennium. The arguments that are advanced constitute a type of world-systems analysis that does not embrace the central tenets of Wallersteinian "world-systems" analysis. While this interpretation shares an interest in macrostructures and their impact on microprocesses, the concern of the present focus is not oriented primarily toward the processes of capital accumulation, capitalism, and core-periphery divisions of labor. Rather, and perhaps betraying a disciplinary origin in political science, the focus is on waves of political leadership, order, and large-scale violence closely linked to processes of long-term economic growth. Thus, in the end, we arrive at a classical world-systems position: "economic" and "political" processes are tightly intertwined and reciprocally interdependent. However, our initial assumptions are not the same as those associated with world-systems analyses with a hyphen.

At the same time, these assumptions are hardly congruent with most historical and political science approaches to interstate conflict and international political economy. While there are certainly many different approaches to interpretation in the literature on international relations, mainstream approaches are reluctant to embrace the notions of systemic structures, high degrees of economic and military concentration, and historically patterned fluctuations in long-term economic growth and its variable impacts. Mainstream international relations prefers to stress the role of nation states as the principal actors in world politics. Many analysts argue that nation states are entirely free from structural constraints and opportunities. Movement to and from bipolarity and multipolarity are conceivable, even though the probable outcome is disputed, while unipolarity is deemed beyond the pale of likelihood. Short-term economic growth is the preferred province of economists and political economists alike. The operating attitude is that in the long term, we are all dead, so why worry about the ephemeral? The idea that some of those long-term patterns even exist and/or might influence behavior in the long- and short-term is more often ridiculed than examined empirically.

THE DOUBLE HELIX OF K-WAVES AND LONG CYCLES

K-waves represent surges of radical innovations that peak and decay over durations of approximately 50–60 years. Long cycles are periods of variable politico-military leadership reflecting the initially ascending and then eroding primacy of a single world power over durations of approximately 100 years. Each world power's order is tied to a specific pair of K-waves. The first wave in the set helps to propel a new systemic leader to preeminence. The second wave follows a period of intense conflict and is made more likely by the nature of the conflict. The period of intense conflict, in its own turn, is made more probable by the destabilizing, politico-economic outcomes of the first K-wave which catapults one or more states ahead of its competitors. The subsequent politico-military leadership is very much dependent on the nature of the struggle and the outcome of the intensive competition. Each set of four shocks (two innovation surges, one period of intense conflict, and the development of politico-military preeminence) thus define a distinctive era organized around the finite salience of a single state – the "world power" or the lead actor in the global politics and economy of its time.

Especially critical to this interpretation is the distinction between global and nonglobal activity. The global adjective is not used as a synonym for world or international political and economic activities. Global activities refer to interregional, long-distance transactions which, of course, have become increasingly salient. A principal question is when did a global system specializing in the political management of interregional transactions begin to emerge? To answer this question, it is not simply a matter of finding the first recorded instance of interregional transactions and commencing our history of the global system from that point on. Interregional transactions have been around for quite a long time but they were also characterized by a great deal of intermittence in ancient times. The question, then, is if we work back from our own time, how far back can the perceived continuity of the contemporary system be traced?

Modelski and Thompson (1996) find nine sequentially related sets of innovation-based leadership between 930 and 1973: two Chinese (Northern and Southern Sung), two Italian (Genoese and Venetian), one Portuguese, one Dutch, two British (Britain I and II) and, so far, one American.[1] The scope of these instances of leadership have become increasingly "global" and, therefore, focused on the management of interregional transactions. For a variety of reasons, conditions (population scale, urbanization, marketization, and maritime commerce) came together propitiously in tenth-century China to begin a continuous sequence of innovation-driven, long-term, surges of economic growth. The expansion of maritime trade (in the South China Sea and Indian Ocean) and the revived use of the Silk Roads on land facilitated the emergence of competing trading empires in the eastern Mediterranean that helped to transplant-transmit the growth surges and the innovation-based sequence of paired K-waves to the other end of Eurasia. At the end of the twentieth century and after several more geographical shifts in location, we appear to be in the process of entering a tenth K-wave set that may or may not assume a US leadership identity. It is too soon to tell for sure. Too many degrees of freedom remain open to human agency.

Table 1.1 lists the leaders and the chronological pattern of political and economic leadership. Each long cycle is characterized by four phases that can be interpreted in two different ways. If we wish to emphasize the rise of a new leader, the appropriate

Table 1.1 Long cycles in global politics: learning and leadership patterns

Long Cycle Mode	Phases			
Learning ("rise")	Agenda-setting	Coalition-building	Macro-decision	Execution
Leadership ("decline")	Delegitimation	Deconcentration	Global war	World power
	starting in			
	(Chinese/Italian Renaissance)			
Northern Sung/Southern Sung	930	990	1060	1120
Genoa/ Venice	1190	1250	1300	1355
	(west European)			
Portugal	1430	1460	1494	1516
Dutch Republic	1540	1560	1580	1609
Britain I	1640	1660	1688	1714
Britain II	1740	1763	1792	1815
	(post-European)			
United States	1850	1873	1914	1945
	1973	2000	2030	2050

Source: Modelski and Thompson (1996)

sequence of phases is agenda-setting, coalition-building, macrodecision, and execution. To emphasize the decline of an incumbent leader, the phase sequence is global war, world power, delegitimation, and deconcentration. Each phase delineates different types of behavior. The macrodecision/global war phase determines the identity of the next system leader or world power. The post-war execution/world power phase is the period of peak economic and politico-military leadership. Agenda-setting delegitimation is a period in which leadership declines and challenges to the existing world order become increasingly noticeable. New problems emerge that demand innovative responses. Finally, coalition-building/deconcentration is a period marked by competitive preparations for developing new versions of world order and succession to systemic leadership.

The political processes of the leadership long cycle, it is argued, have coevolved with the economic processes of the K-wave. There are at least three reasons why this might be so:

1 Political leadership and waging global wars are expensive propositions that depend on adequate economic resources. Economic fluctuations, therefore, are likely to influence the exercise of political leadership.
2 The world economy's activities are dependent on a minimal level of stability and security. Intensive conflicts within the political system are likely to influence the functioning of the world economy.

3   To emerge as the world's politico-military leader requires technological leader-
    ship. Technological leadership, in turn, is predicated on the development of
    innovation in commerce and industry. Once some level of technological leader-
    ship is attained, politico-military leadership, or its pursuit in global war, can be
    quite useful in expanding the edge associated with technological leadership and
    protecting the consequent accumulation of wealth.

The economic carriers of these interdependent processes are the rise and decline of
leading sectors or clusters of basic innovations that periodically restructure economic
activities. The innovations are Schumpeterian in the sense that they encompass new
ways of production, the opening of new markets and sources of raw materials, as well
as new forms of business organization. They are also Schumpeterian in the sense that
many of the old ways of doing things tend to be destroyed by the ascendance of new
leading sectors. The innovations that fuel these long waves of economic growth may
be limited to one or more of the various types of change but their implications for
economic restructuring must be substantially more than merely routine increments
to existing practices and activities. They revolutionize commerce and/or industrial
production. They are not the only source of long-term growth (for example, population growth is another important source) but new technology does constitute one
of the more significant sources.

Why should this pattern characterize long-term economic growth? Innovations are
responses to problems encountered by economic (and political) agents. As commercial
routes or industrial profits become increasingly unpredictable or unattainable, the
search for new routes and production possibilities is quite likely. For instance,
Europeans began searching for a way around the Moslem–Mameluke lock on the
east–west flow of spices some 300 years before they finally found a route around
Africa in the late fifteenth century. Or, looking for a way to deal with water in mines
led to the development of steam engines with subsequent implications for railroads,
the iron industry, and the transportation of agricultural goods to markets (and
soldiers to battle).

Once a sufficiently radical innovation or complex of innovations is launched, its
potential for facilitating economic growth is finite. Just how finite depends on
the specific nature of the innovation, the rate of diffusion, the number of new
competitors, demand elasticities, and impacts on supply. One good example is
pepper and its long life as a leading sector of growth for Genoa, Venice, Portugal, and
the Dutch – each of which discovered new ways of supplying this commodity to
European markets. The various commercial innovations relating to the pepper trade
each had their own growth curves, but in the process of innovating new ways of
supplying pepper, each new leader managed also to increase the supply. Prices and
profits fell as the pepper trade became routinized and lost its ability to function as a
leading sector. Attention shifted, partially as a consequence but also in accordance
with concomitant changes in supply and demand, to other drugs (in the seventeenth
century, sugar and tobacco).

Not coincidentally, the shift in leading sector commodity emphasis favored the

9

English who controlled a good number of what were to become the prime North American production sites over the Dutch who had been more successful in the Asian trades than in acquiring territory in Brazil and in North America. The paths to success in the world economy changed in the mid-to-late seventeenth century. The overcommitment of the incumbent lead economy (in this case, the Dutch) to earlier paths created an opportunity for new sources of entrepreneurial innovation.

The rise and decline of leading sectors are thus concentrated in both time and space. Fifty to sixty years are needed for what is initially revolutionary to become either routine or to be superseded by some new way of doing things. The innovations tend also to be monopolized initially by entrepreneurs in one national economy. Gradually, the innovations spread to other (but not all) economies. The K-wave sources of long-term economic growth are thus highly concentrated spatially and subject to processes of diffusion in which some other economies catch up to the leading positions first established by the economic pioneers.

Keying on the timing of a rising leader (see Table 1.1), we should expect these growth surges or K-waves to peak immediately before and after phases of global war if the politico-military and economic processes are as truly interdependent as argued earlier. This is not a matter of working backwards and saying that since we know there have been K-waves, leaders, and global wars that they must all somehow be related. Rather, the causal logic begins with the notion that new, rising leaders require an appropriate economic foundation to ascend in the political-economic hierarchy. However, the relatively abrupt development of the economic innovations (suggested in Table 1.2) that support this foundation is destabilizing for the system. The positions of some rivals may be advantaged by the new ways of doing things. Other rivals will perceive themselves as falling behind. The incumbent, declining (that is to say, falling behind) leadership is particularly apt to feel threatened by changes it can no longer harness for its own purposes. Intensive conflict thus becomes more probable.[2] The innovative edge of the rising leader makes its victory in this conflict more probable. Waging the conflict and winning it also improves the probability of another postwar growth surge. For these reasons, we expect the innovation surges to cluster in the temporal vicinity of the global wars.

It is also reasonable to expect some preliminary, start-up activities for each K-wave that precedes the peak in the growth of the new ways of doing things. More precisely, K-wave peaks are anticipated to fall within the phases of coalition-building and execution – the two phases immediately adjacent to the macrodecision/global war phase. Start-up phases are linked to the phases that precede the peak growth phases – agenda-setting and macrodecision respectively. Since leadership long-cycle theory links global wars to the attainment of military-political leadership, we should also expect that some appropriate leadership threshold is achieved, if at all, after the first and before the second K-wave peak.

Keep in mind that the temporal sequence displayed in Table 1.1 was developed well in advance (by more than a decade) of the construction of the three hypotheses about the timing of K-wave peaks and the attainment of politico-military leadership. This permits us to pinpoint the anticipated timing of these phenomena within two or

Table 1.2 The hypothesized relationship between the learning long-cycle and global lead industries

Learning long cycle	Global lead industries	Predicted "start-up"	Predicted "high-growth"
LC1 Northern Sung			
K1	Printing and paper industry	930– 960	960– 990
K2	National market; Champa rice, iron casting, paper currency	990–1030	1030–1060
LC2 Southern Sung			
K3	Admininstration reform	1060–1090	1090–1120
K4	Maritime trade; navigation (compass)	1120–1160	1160–1190
LC3 Genoa			
K5	Champagne fairs	1190–1220	1220–1250
K6	Black Sea/Atlantic trade	1250–1280	1280–1300
LC4 Venice			
K7	Galley fleets	1300–1320	1320–1355
K8	Pepper	1355–1385	1385–1420
LC5 Portuguese			
K9	Guinea gold	1430–1460	1460–1494
K10	Indian pepper	1492–1516	1516–1540
LC6 Dutch			
K11	Baltic and Atlantic trades	1540–1560	1560–1580
K12	Eastern trade	1580–1609	1609–1640
LC7 Britain I			
K13	Amerasian trade (especially sugar)	1640–1660	1660–1688
K14	Amerasian trade	1688–1713	1713–1740
LC8 Britain II			
K15	Cotton, iron	1740–1763	1763–1792
K16	Railroads, steam	1792–1815	1815–1850
LC9 United States			
K17	Steel, chemicals, electric power	1850–1873	1873–1914
K18	motor vehicles, aviation, electronics	1914–1945	1945–1973
LC10 ?			
K19	Information industries	1973–2000	2000–2026
K20		2026–2050	2050–2080

Source: Modelski and Thompson (1996)

three decades without biasing the test outcome with post-*hoc* knowledge of how things worked out historically. The question then becomes just how accurate are the predictions in specifying the timing of long-term economic growth and systemic leadership.

Table 1.3 Predicted versus observed growth peaks in global lead Industries

Learning long cycle	Global lead industry indicators	Predicted "high growth"	Observed growth peak[a]
LC1 Northern Sung			
K1	None	960– 990	[b]
K2	None	1030–1060	[b]
LC2 Southern Sung			
K3	None	1090–1120	[b]
K4	None	1160–1190	[b]
LC3 Genoa			
K5	Champagne fair	1220–1250	*b. 1250*
K6	Genoan trade	1280–1300	*1290s*
LC4 Venice			
K7	Romanian galleys	1320–1355	*1330s*
K8	Levantine galleys	1385–1420	*1390s*
LC5 Portuguese			
K9	Guinea gold	1460–1492	*1480s*
K10	Indian pepper	1516–1540	*1510s*
LC6 Dutch			
K11	Baltic trade	1560–1580	*1560s*
K12	Asian trade	1609–1640	*1630s*
LC7 Britain I			
K13	Tobacco, sugar, Indian textiles	1660–1680	*1670s*
K14	Tobacco, sugar, textiles, tea, Indian textiles	1714–1740	*1710s*
LC8 Britain II			
K15	Cotton consumption, pig iron production	1763–1792	*1780s*
K16	Railroad track laid (absolute amount and per square kilometer)	1815–1850	*1830s*
LC9 United States			
K17	Steel, sulphuric acid, electricity production	1873–1914	*1870s/1900s*
K18	Motor vehicle production, aerospace sales, and semi-conductor production	1945–1973	*1950s*

Notes:

a Observed growth rate peaks are italicized if they fall within the predicted window

b While no empirical indicator series are available for the Chinese cases, the appropriate literature appears to support the hypothesized periodicity. The data and the appropriate sources are listed in Modelski and Thompson (1996)

In every case, as demonstrated in Table 1.3, the growth peak of the first K-wave in each pair is located within the coalition-building phase. Moreover, the peak is usually observed immediately prior to the decade in which the macrodecision/global war phase commenced. The second K-wave peak also follows the macrodecision phase.

However, its precise timing – even though it does consistently fall within the predicted execution/world power window – varies. Sometimes, the peak occurs right at the end of the macrodecision conflict. Sometimes, it is located toward the end of the execution/world power phase. But since these phase windows are fairly short, we probably should not make too much of these slight variations in timing.

GLOBAL WAR

Within this macrocontext of fluctuations in long-term economic growth and political leadership, we see global war as an outcome of the combination of processes of concentration and deconcentration operating at both the global and key regional levels of analysis. That is, a focus solely fixed on global structures and processes will miss an important part of the puzzle in explaining why the world system periodically erupts into large-scale violence. Global and regional processes move in and out of synch with one another, but not all regions are equally important. For much of the past 500 years, western Europe has been the key region of the world system. When the European and global processes became fused, the probability of a global war breaking out was greatly enhanced.

Global concentration processes

From a systemic perspective, the global political economy is characterized by undulating patterns of capability concentration, followed by deconcentration, and then followed again by reconcentration. We attribute this pattern primarily to the emergence and relative decline of lead economies. The linkage to global war is straightforward. When the global political economy is highly concentrated, the out-break of a global war is unlikely. After the global political economy has experienced considerable deconcentration, the outbreak of a global war becomes more probable because global wars, inherently, can be seen as succession struggles over which economy will replace the incumbent as the global system's military-political center. In fact, we designate as global wars only those intensive conflicts that lead to a new phase of significant reconcentration and global military-political and economic leadership. In this respect, we admit to being more interested in these wars' roles in the concentration–deconcentration process than we are in their identities as increasingly lethal wars among major powers. That is, we think global wars merit special attention as a distinctive set of wars that are a critical part of the global political economy's functioning.

The tendency toward concentration, deconcentration, and reconcentration is much older than the "institution" of global war. We can find instances of concentration and deconcentration since around 3500 BC and the Sumerians but, in the leadership long-cycle perspective, the concentration–deconcentration–reconcentration sequence only emerged as a continuous process with the advent of Sung Chinese economic and maritime innovations a millennium ago. In the period

13

Table 1.4 Global war coalitions

Global war	Major participants
Italian and Indian Ocean Wars, 1494–1516	Portugal and Spain and (England) versus France
War of Dutch Independence, 1580–1608	Netherlands and England and France versus Spain
Wars of the Grand Alliance, 1688–1713	Britain and Netherlands versus France and (Spain)
French Revolutionary and Napoleonic Wars, 1792–1815 1792–1815	Britain and Russia versus France and (Netherlands, Spain)
World Wars I and II 1914–1945	United States and Britain and Russia/Soviet Union and France versus Germany and (Japan)

Source: Based on Rasler and Thompson (1994: 17)

roughly between 1000 and 1500, we can trace early, transitional versions of successive lead economies in the global, transcontinental sense (Northern and Southern Sung, Genoa, Venice, Portugal). Their fluctuations in relative prosperity appear to be associated with periods of intense conflict that intervene between the twin peaks of economic growth described earlier but they do not take on the form of the global wars with which we have become more familiar in the twentieth century. After 1494 the global war institution began to emerge in its modern form. It is assumed that this emergence reflects an evolving system experiencing environmental change. The global political economy evolved in such a way that it became increasingly susceptible to intermittent fusion with European regional politics. Global wars are one of the consequences of that evolutionary change.

We return to both the regional dimensions of global war and the implications for system transformation in later sections. Next, we need to focus on further elaborating the global processes that are most important. Five global wars are identified: the Italian and Indian Ocean Wars (1494–1516), the Dutch-Spanish Wars (1580–1608), the Wars of the Grand Alliance (1688–1713), the French Revolutionary and Napoleonic Wars (1792–1815), and World Wars I and II (1914–1945). These wars were fought by coalitions of global and other types of powers, as identified in Table 1.4.

The pattern is essentially one of the incumbent global system leader and its allies arrayed against a principal challenger and its allies. So far, the challenger has never won. On the other hand, the incumbent leader may also lose its status to one of its allies if the most active economic zone (that is, where the new leading sectors are emerging) has shifted away from the old leader's control. In both the Dutch–British and British–American transitions, the political-military shifts in relative status took place during the respective global wars. The junior partner going into the war emerged as the senior partner and the new system leader.

In this respect, we should emphasize that the structure of conflict is more complicated than a simple challenger versus incumbent situation. Declining incumbents select, to some extent, which challengers they will fight and with whom they will ally to meet the intensive challenge. The selection process is primarily a function of four variables: maritime-commercial orientation, proximity, similarity (regime type, culture, ideology, and race), and innovative nature. The threats that are seen as most dangerous are those associated with explicitly premeditated challenges that come from dissimilar types of states with fundamentally different strategic orientations. States with strategic foci on utilizing land forces to expand territorial control have found it difficult to compete with sea powers other than via attempts at direct conquest. Nearby challengers are less easy to ignore than those located farther away. The more "alien" the challenger, the greater is the likely level of suspicion and misperception in divining motivations and intentions. A challenger and incumbent leader are also more likely to fight if their economic competition is based on similar commercial-technological commodities. If the challenger perceives that the leader will thwart any peaceful positional encroachments, a nonpeaceful competition is more probable.

Similarly, potential challengers adopt different strategies of confrontation. The most traditional approach can be referred to as "capture-the-center," in which the challenger attempts to seize control of the lead economy and its commercial networks. An alternative approach is to avoid attacking the leader on its home ground and to focus instead on attacks on its farflung commercial networks and the development of alternative networks, as demonstrated by warfare among Portugal, Spain, England, France, and the Netherlands in Asian and US waters. A third strategy involves creating a relatively autonomous subsystem within the world economy that excludes economic competition with the system leader. Napoleon's Continental system, German *Mitteleuropa* aspirations, Japan's co-prosperity sphere and the communist international system of the second half of the twentieth century are all illustrations of this third strategy. How threatening this strategy appears will depend on how coercive the subsystem creation and maintenance processes are and who suffers most from the exclusionary policies. The capture-the-center strategy has gradually lost much of its appeal. The flanking, alternative network approach became increasingly popular in the period that most focused on long-distance commerce while the exclusionary subsystemic approach has become more prevalent in the movement toward increased emphasis on industrial production.

Throughout the past 500 years, the global power élite has remained a small group: Portugal (1494–1580), Spain (1494–1808), England/Britain (1494–1945), France (1494–1945), the Netherlands (1579–1810), Russia/the Soviet Union/Russia (1714 to the present), the United States (1816 to the present), Germany (1871–1945), and Japan (1875–1945). Of this group, only four global powers have qualified as world powers: Portugal, the Netherlands, Britain, and the United States. To qualify for these designations, world powers must have exceeded control of over 50 percent or more of the global reach capabilities, which, historically, we equate with sea power. Global powers need to demonstrate sea power activity in more than one regional sea and control over at least 10 percent of global reach capabilities.

Table 1.5 Attainment of global leadership and the timing of K-waves

World power	First K-wave peak (observed)	Occasions for global leadership[a]	Naval threshold attained[b]	Second K-wave peak (observed)
Portugal	1480s	1494, 1499	1510	1530s
Netherlands	1560s	1601, 1608	1610	1620s
Britain I	1670s	1689, 1701	1715	1710s
Britain II	1780s	1793, 1815	1810	1830s
United States	1870s/1900s	1941, 1947	1945	1950s

Source: Modelski and Thompson (1996)
Notes:
a Modelski (1987: 42; Modelski and Modelski, 1988)
b Fifty percent share of capital warships of global power navies (Modelski and Thompson, 1988)

However, the development of these global reach capabilities do not take place in a vacuum. The military ascent of the world powers is very much geared to their economic fortunes. The Chinese and Italian leads were prototypical predecessors confined to less geographically ambitious theaters. Their economic activities were certainly linked to naval superiority but not on the planetary scale achieved after the 1490s. Nevertheless, the observed pattern after the 1490s, shown in Table 1.5, is remarkably consistent. In four cases, the Portuguese, Dutch, Britain II, and the United States, naval leadership was clearly attained prior to the second K-wave peak. Only in the case of Britain I did the naval threshold attainment occur at about the same time as the second K-wave peak. Hence, we conclude that naval leadership is a function in large part of sufficient resources to pay for the fleets (the first K-wave) and a strong security incentive to expand one's arsenal of coercive maritime resources (participation in the global economy and global war).

While we are emphasizing the significance of naval capability in the leadership long cycle, it is, of course, assumed that the naval capability leadership is based upon economic leadership. We have earlier demonstrated empirically that this is the case for nineteenth- and twentieth-century data centered on the British and US leadership eras. Figure 1.1 summarizes the "causal" relationships that were found in time-series analyses. Rapid-leading sector growth leads to finite periods of economic leadership in those leading sectors and to somewhat longer-lasting naval power leads.

Figure 1.1 also connects innovation and global concentration processes to global warfare. Based on theoretical arguments and empirical findings (on nineteenth- and twentieth-century data), systemic warfare is seen as a product of economic innovation and leadership processes. In turn, systemic warfare influences innovation, economic concentration, and naval concentration. In this sense, long waves of economic and technological change, the political-military leadership long cycle, and warfare are all highly interdependent dynamics that lie at the heart of the global political economy's functioning.

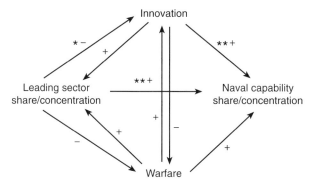

Key: *Britain only; ** United States only

Figure 1.1 Innovation, concentration and warfare

The intermittent fusion of global and regional processes

Nevertheless, an exclusive focus on global politics is inadequate for the global system is not an autonomous sphere of activity. On occasion, global politics have become tightly fused with regional politics. These fusions can take many forms. Ambitious states in any region may make coercive bids for regional leadership. Vietnam in southeast Asia or Iraq in the Middle East come to mind as recent examples. Just how dangerous these bids are depends in part on how salient is the region in which they occur. Regional concentration processes in more peripheral regions are apt to be less destabilizing than similar processes in more central regions. The appropriate comparison is between the Third Indochina War and the Gulf War versus, say, World War II. All three events were lethal but the first two contests were unlikely to become "globalized". The third one spread throughout the planet relatively quickly. They all began as subregional or regional contests. The difference is that World War II emerged in part from a contest over the control of Europe – still one of the most salient or central regions of that time.

It also mattered that the European region was the home base for a number of global powers. It is easier to remain aloof from more distant contests than ones that take place in our own backyards. Salience and proximity help explain why European regional international relations, on occasion, have been so explosive for the global political economy. This intermittent fusion of European regional and global politics is absolutely essential to our explanation of structural change and global war. A strong reliance on Dehio's (1962) interpretation of the history of European international relations should also be acknowledged.

Unlike other regions of the world, especially eastern Asia, no single power ever established hegemony over Europe for very long. The basic Dehioan insight is that this outcome was due to what appears to be a relatively unique geopolitical pattern. Before a would-be regional hegemon could unify Europe coercively, counterweights emerged from areas immediately adjacent to the region. Introducing extraregional resources, they were repeatedly able to block the creation of European hegemony.

The eastern counterweight supplied brute land force. The western counterweight increasingly specialized in sea power, that was, in turn, predicated on the development of specializations in the role of commercial intermediary among Europe, Asia, and America. When both counterweights were operative, an aspiring regional hegemon was forced to fight a resource draining-war on two fronts that it was likely to lose. The outcome was an intermittently renewed balance of European power that depended on the region remaining open to extraregional resources controlled by flanking states.

The regional motor of the balancing dynamic hinged on an intermittent rise of a hegemonic aspirant and the concentration of regional capabilities. France inaugurated this system in its 1494 attack on Italy. It was resisted by Spain primarily and then for a short time by a unified Hapsburg entity. A Franco-Ottoman coalition thwarted the second bid, this time on the part of the Hapsburgs. Both of these initial efforts preceded the emergence of a western maritime power capable of functioning as a counterweight. With some English assistance, the Netherlands provided the first maritime counterweight to Philip II's bid for supremacy. By the mid-seventeenth century, Spain had surrendered its regional lead to a restrengthened France. Louis XIV's late seventeenth-century activities came to be perceived as a direct threat to Europe and the global political economy. A second Anglo-Dutch coalition developed the first large-scale maritime blockade of the European continent and defeated the expanding navy of France in 1692. Between 1692 and the next destruction of the French fleet in 1805 at Trafalgar, the generally eroding, relative strength of the French kept the mid-century Anglo-French fighting from turning into a full-fledged struggle over either regional or global supremacy.

Unlike the earlier, more gradual bids for regional hegemony, the third French bid in 1792 emerged abruptly and was unusually successful for a few years before the Napoleonic variant was crushed in 1814 and 1815. After 1815, the main emphasis of global concern shifted away from the European region to the Russo-British sparring along their mutual Eurasian imperial boundaries. The British remained worried about the French potential for causing trouble in Europe for some time after 1815 but a fourth French bid, with hindsight, was increasingly unlikely. One reason was the emergence of a unified Germany.

Whether or not the ascending Germany of the late nineteenth century was merely seeking equality with other leading powers or European domination, a mixture of commercial and naval rivalries combined with geographical proximity increased the probability that Britain would identify Germany as its primary threat. In World War I, Germany then proceeded as if it were indeed seeking regional supremacy. By World War II, which can be seen as a continuation of World War I, both Germany and Japan had become more overt and ambitious about the extent of their regional aspirations. The end of that war led to the territorial dismemberment of the principal challenger (Germany). The division of the entire region into US and Soviet spheres completed the process of diminishing the regional autonomy of Europe and, presumably, some of its ability to generate local problems that could intrude into the functioning of the global political economy. While the significance of European economies for the global political economy remains high, a renewed, coercive bid for European regional domination seems unlikely.

From a regional perspective, the principal dynamic of this system has been the movement from a peak in the strength of the leading regional power through a long trough to next peak and so on. The long troughs were characterized by a leveling process. The regional leader that had peaked earlier was in gradual decline, thereby encouraging and facilitating the emergence of new regional contenders. During the troughs, relative power relationships and alignments were unstable. The troughs not only provided windows of opportunity for the emergence of new land powers. They also encouraged the upwardly mobile to challenge the regional status quo. At the same time, the strength of the western maritime powers should also be most concentrated during the troughs in regional concentration. The less the threat from adjacent land empires, the more the maritime powers could thrive.

The rhythms of two dissynchronized cycles or waves of power concentration, centered on two different types of major powers are thus envisioned. On land, the leading regional power waxed and waned. At sea, the leading global power ascended and declined. For the most part, the one declined as the other peaked, but not in a completely dissynchronized fashion. Declining global leaders encouraged would-be regional hegemons. Suppressing would-be regional hegemons galvanized new global leaders to emerge or, in the case of Britain, to reemerge. It is not too much of an exaggeration to say that regional and global powers represent two very different "species" of power, and, there was certainly an overlap. Some strong regional powers in Europe were also contenders in the global political economy. But they were never quite as successful as they might have been given their roots in regional/territorial orientations as opposed to maritime orientations. The leading regional powers rose to primacy on the basis of absolute autocracies, large armies and bureaucracies, and the success of expansionist foreign policies. Spain, France, and Germany were all created via coercive expansion within the region. Neighboring enemies could be beneficial in the sense that they provided rulers with incentives for developing military and economic strength. Global powers were more oriented toward long-distance trade than territorial expansion close to home. To varying degrees they were able to restrain their autocracies. Global powers had good reasons to favor navies over armies. They also led in the movement away from command bureaucracies toward more representative regimes for resource mobilization. Security depended on some type of geographic insularity, or at least the relative absence of proximate adversaries. Without some form of natural protection, they were likely to succumb to the superior military strength of adjacent, land-based empires, but the iterative introduction of extraregional resources could not be repeated infinitely. Drawing in the flanking powers and their resources increasingly reduced the ratio of power that could be mustered within the European region relative to what could be mobilized away from Europe. Eventually, challengers from the European region could no longer expect to compete with stronger states outside Europe.

This finite durability of the classical European regional system may have depended on a unique constellation of geohistorical factors. Would-be regional conquerors found themselves caught between offshore rocks and eastern hard places. Despite repeated attempts, European hegemons could not overcome the western and eastern flanks with much more access to the resources useful for war and economic growth. Regionally biased strategies to overcome these barriers to supremacy proved to be largely self-defeating. The European subsystem retained its pluralistic structure but, ultimately, at the expense of its onetime autonomy and salience. The Soviet–American Cold War subordinated the European region to a global contest after centuries of regional problems diverting global interests and resources.

Whither the future?

It has been the interaction between global and regional structural changes that have generated the contexts for the world's most significant and serious wars. From a regional vantage point, the relationship between concentration and the probability of global war is positive. Greater concentration leads to the greater likelihood of intensive conflict. From the global perspective, though, the relationship is reversed. High concentration leads to a decreased likelihood of intensive conflict. The problem has been that these structural rhythms have been out of synch with one another. Global concentration levels tend to be low when regional concentration levels are on the rise.

Very much at the risk of oversimplification, we can reduce future scenarios to two: one is pessimistic and the other is optimistic. Both scenarios assume that the K-wave and leadership cycle dynamics will continue to characterize global politics and economics. Both scenarios also assume that the salience of the European region has been greatly diminished, thereby "neutralizing" the possibility of lethal regional–global structural interactions. The pessimistic scenario transfers the salient region focus to eastern Asia which has some potential for reproducing some of the circumstances that characterized the period between 1494 and 1945. It is a multi-polar region in which predominance is likely to be contested (just as it has been contested in the past). The most likely challenger is China and, if an attempt at perceived regional hegemony were to be mounted in the twenty-first century, China could anticipate an opposing coalition of land and sea powers. The only difference might be that the directions would be reversed from the historical European pattern, with the land forces coming from the west (and northwest) and the sea powers from the east. While it seems difficult to imagine given the lethality of military capabilities, it is possible that some form of intensive conflict (global war) might reoccur around the mid-twenty-first century. This pessimistic scenario is then premised on a "more-of-the-same" assumption.

The optimistic scenario is predicated on an extinction of the historical pattern of intermittent fusion with regional hegemonic schemes. It is conceivable that no single region will ever reproduce the interaction between western Europe and the global system between 1494 and 1945. And, just as it took 500 years to bring together the elements that characterized global politics and economics for the next 500 years, there may be grounds to anticipate other types of fundamental parameter shifts. One possibility is that the K-wave/leadership cycle dynamics will sputter out as technological change comes so quickly that it is difficult to monopolize for very long. Technology and highly technological production has become increasingly multinationalized, therefore, it may also be increasingly difficult for one world power to monopolize leading sectors. Another possibility is that trends toward increasing democratization will fundamentally alter international relations. This "democratic peace" process (that is democratic states do not tend to go to war with other democratic states) is not entirely independent of the leadership long cycle. World powers have also been leaders in democratization and defending the democratized community. One way to look at democratization is to view it as an expansion of the group that has governed global politics and the global economy for the past half-millennium. The expansion of that group should permit more complex processes of governance to emerge. More complex governance processes would include less reliance on a single leader and primitive trial-by-combat succession techniques as well as increased participation by (other) global institutions. It should also decrease the size of the pool from which militarized challengers issue.

That the world system could proceed down either fork in the road underlines the inherently nondeterministic nature of the explanatory apparatus. Global politics and economics have evolved over the past millennium. We may be able to capture the basic parameters and their major transformations after the fact. However, we are not able to predict what will happen in the future. We can only presume that the system will continue to function as before unless it undergoes significant transformation in its operating parameters. These transformations have occurred before and they may again.

2

EVOLUTIONARY
AND COEVOLUTIONARY
CONSIDERATIONS

The perspective advanced in Chapter 1 simplifies the grand sweep, or at least some significant aspects of it, of the past millennium to a very specific pattern of politico-economic coevolution. The claims are not modest. No doubt, the assertions and related findings will be fiercely resisted, or, in some cases, they will be simply ignored by analysts who are more comfortable with much less structured views of the past. Cognitive dissonance is difficult to overcome. On the other hand, the argument and empirical support ultimately may turn out to be misconceived and misleading. That is a matter for further analysis to work out. Let us take the argument and the findings at face value for the moment and ask, if they have some validity, what are the implications for the study of international political economy?

First of all, history matters and it matters very much. The present state of the international political economy, of course, is a product of its past. The question is just what are the most important details of that past? Should we emphasize property rights, capitalism, demographic changes, or peripheral exploitation? Without an understanding of what the past has been about, just how long that past is and how that past has evolved, it is extremely difficult to make sense of the present. It is even more difficult to generate any expectations about the near future. More specifically, the argument outlined in Chapter 1 documents an unambiguous geohistorical past for the contemporary world economy and its interdependence with global politics. A remarkably regular rhythm can be traced back to roughly the middle of the tenth century and the eastern edge of the Eurasian continent. Some 200 years later, the primary source of the rhythm had migrated westward to the eastern Mediterranean. Another 200–300 years later, the focus had shifted further westward to the Atlantic edge of Eurasia, where it remained for some 350 years (albeit moving northward along the west European fringe) until it shifted across the Atlantic to North America. Whether the westward movement is continuing remains to be seen.

Other analysts have observed a long-term, western shift in the locus of central political-economic activity. No one else, to our knowledge, has been able to impose a fairly precise periodicity on the movement and, in addition, support the claims of a temporal pattern with empirical data encompassing over nine centuries. The testing is made possible, in part, because theoretical emphasis is not placed on economic growth or political power concentrations in general. Rather, a sequential pattern of very specific, long-term growth as manifested and realized through the development of leading economic sectors with fairly finite life cycles (periods of start-up, high growth, and decline) and shifting geographical loci is documented. Linked closely to this rhythm of long-term economic growth are periods of variable levels of global political leadership and organization. As the spatial focus of the economic growth has shifted, so, too, has the spatial focus of global political leadership.

Most studies of long economic waves assume that these 50–60 year fluctuations began with the British Industrial Revolution in the late eighteenth century. No doubt, this assumption combines a variety of auxiliary assumptions including the notion that the British Industrial Revolution was a unique watershed in economic history, that long waves were somehow linked to the nature of industrial production and the prices of commodities of the nineteenth and twentieth centuries, as well as the idea that appropriate data simply did not exist prior to the nineteenth century. All these assumptions, it is argued, are in error. Economic revolutions occur periodically with each new K-wave. We do not have to depreciate the significance of the British Industrial Revolution when it is observed that it fits into a sequence of 19 revolutions of varying magnitude over the past 10 centuries. Long economic waves have a continuous history of some 1000 years – not merely one or two centuries and, appropriate data encompassing roughly 900 years of leading sector activity support this interpretation.

Second, questions about long-term processes require different perspectives and answers than are generated customarily by the social sciences that are more usually concerned with short-term phenomena. Short-term analyses of economic growth and international politics are likely to miss or misinterpret the nature of coevolving world economies and global politics. It also means that analysts interested in long-term processes must be prepared to cross disciplinary boundaries as necessary to grasp coevolutionary dynamics.

Third, there is an extensive literature on the interactions between international politics and economics. Modelski and Thompson (1996) found as many as 14 different conceptualizations of the causal relationship between war and prosperity. Most of them are asymmetrical. Either economic conditions increase the probability of war or it is the other way around – war increases the probability of economic conditions. Only a small number of interpretations envision a genuinely continuous process of interaction. Those that do tend to see a relatively uniform pattern – a downswing or upswing producing war which, in turn, produces a downswing or upswing. Chapter 1 suggests a unique and more complicated pattern. The first of a set of K-wave surges impacts on war by destabilizing the political-military pecking order and generating new resources for martial activities. The first growth surge also increases the probability of a second surge in long-term economic growth. The intervening war impacts on the probability of the second surge but the second surge does not lead back to more war. Nor can it be assumed that the second surge will increase the probability of a third growth surge and, even if it does, the next growth surge will not necessarily take place in the same economy.

Fourth, the international political economy literature tends to speak of economic and political interactions in the generic sense. Chapter 1's argument spells out a very specific application that concerns only a few states and their economies directly and everybody else indirectly. The technological sources of long-term economic growth are initially highly concentrated and only gradually diffuse. It is also a very specific and rare type of war (global war) that is involved in this central coevolutionary process. Nevertheless, the form of systemic crisis associated with the macrodecision phase only gradually took on the form of global war. There were no global wars between 930 and 1493. Other factors had to develop that made global wars more likely. It may be that these "other factors" have continued to evolve in such a fashion that future macrodecision phases will also not take the form of global wars.

Fifth, in addition to providing an explanation of the macrocontours of the last 1000 years, a theory that integrates K-waves and long leadership cycles helps to explain what we are currently experiencing in terms of the transition difficulties as we move from one K-wave engine to another. Long-term economic growth moves in discontinuous jerks. The world economy currently (and more or less for the past two decades) has been stuck between the jerks as one technological paradigm erodes and the next one has yet to realize its full growth potential.

We can observe the impact and creative destruction of information technology (IT) all around us. Unemployment has increased with changes in uses of labor. Once powerful corporations have declined in economic significance as new corporations have moved into the lead as producers of the latest leading sectors. The transition has affected the spatial world economy differentially. The Soviet Union is no more. Europe continues to suffer high unemployment. A few parts of the Third World have developed production niches that exploit the coming of IT but most of the southern hemisphere is more familiar with the economic dislocations of a K-wave downturn than the benefits of a new upturn.

Not coincidentally, the comparatively more prosperous zones in the world economy tend to be associated with the development of the national carriers of the next economic paradigm – the United States and Japan. Their national economies are in competition to become the world's next lead economy. Exactly how this competition will play itself out is not predictable based on the last 1000 years of information. It cannot even be predicted that only one of the two rivals will emerge as the clear leader. That has been the pattern in the past but the nature of technological change may favor less of an emphasis on traditional national economies and more of a focus on transnational corporations and their interfirm alliances. Alternatively, should the historical pattern continue along previous lines, we might expect the early stages of the emergence of new global political leadership. The spatial location of that leadership will shift only if the spatial locus of the K-wave shifts and/or if the significance of national economies should erode.

Finally, there are a vast number of implications for the study of history, political science, economics, international political economy, and international relations. Many of these implications will take some time to work out. One of the more obvious ones, however, has to do with the place of an evolutionary paradigm in the analysis of phenomena such as history, economic growth, and world politics. This is the focus of the second portion of this chapter.

SOME IMPLICATIONS FOR THE QUESTION OF EVOLUTIONARY PARADIGMS

Raising the question of evolutionary paradigms immediately invokes auxiliary questions. The most salient one is what type of evolution one has in mind. If, by evolution, all that is meant is change over time – seemingly the most minimal meaning of evolution – the findings on global economic and political coevolution have obvious implications. If, on the other hand, we have in mind adopting features of the evolutionary research program in biology for the study of the social sciences, implications exist but they are more debatable.

Beginning first with the more minimalist approach, it is clear that an emphasis on change over time is inescapable in the study of the interdependent macroevolution of global politics and the world economy. How else are we to comprehend the serial discontinuities and tectonic shifts associated with innovation, long-term economic growth, global war, and the production of world orders. Granted, there are alternative ways to interpret the processes which are being discussed but the only way to suppress the critical element of change over time is to ignore altogether such phenomena as leadership, systemic crises, and variable amounts of anarchy/order.

As inescapable as this emphasis on change over time may be, we have managed to create social science disciplines that do escape the obvious. Political science and economics, the two disciplines most closely related to the study of world politics and the world economy, are dominated by rather static approaches to very short-run phenomena. For example, the currently prestigious neorealist school in political science assumes that there has been very little structural change in international relations over the last 300 years. At best, the structural change that is recognized is restricted to the 1945 switch from multipolarity to bipolarity and, more recently, a change if not back to multipolarity at least away from bipolarity. Unipolarity as a conceptual category and empirical possibility is brushed aside as an unimaginable, empty cell. The possibility that polar situations in which actors are more or less equal in capability might lead to different behavior than in polar situations in which actors are more or less unequal in capability is rarely explored. Nor is the related idea that shifting inequalities within polar types might make some difference frequently examined.

Economics has been even more successful in creating a discipline that is characterized by an ahistorical fixation on short-run equilibria problems. Several authors have attributed this approach to the imitation of metaphors and techniques found in eighteenth and nineteenth century physics. England (1994: 194) suggests that the most prominent features found in the perceived mechanics of physics and economics, especially models of economic growth, include:

1   A world believed to be inherently simple.
2   Trajectories and relationships that are reversible.
3   Lawful and deterministic behavior.
4   Generalizations that are universal in spatiotemporal scope.
5   The operation of systemic wholes that are unaffected by the movement of
     constituent parts (systemic movement without friction).

We might add that simplicity, reversible relationships, and universal generalizations
are all incompatible with the notion that history can be significant in shaping
behavior (David, 1993; Snooks, 1993a; Snooks, 1993b). Thus, a sixth strongly
ahistorical feature might be added at the risk of some redundancy. Less redundant is
a seventh feature that emphasizes stability and equilibrium states as the modal entry
point for analysis.

   The hybrid study of international political economy is in a somewhat better shape
on the subject of change over time. There are at least pockets of analysis in which
change is a principal focus. Yet there is also a peculiar tendency for this hybrid field
to assimilate many of the errors of the major disciplines to which the development of
the hybrid field is supposedly a correction. Political scientists who study international
political economy phenomena often adopt the professional stances of economists.
By disciplinary definition, this means an emphasis on the static short run and the
application of a variety of microeconomic tools and theories to ostensibly political
subjects. It also means that disciplinary boundaries are given too much respect.
For many political economists, there are "economic" processes that have "political"
consequences. The point is that political scientists who study political economy are
expected (and are usually content) to focus on the consequences and take the
antecedent processes as given to be explained by somebody else. Thus, the original
boundaries are oddly recreated even within a supposedly interdisciplinary field.

   Economists who study international political economy (IPE) are often like the
"new" economic historians. They are microeconomic imperialists exploring territory
off the reservation with a tendency to bend their subjects to fit within conventional
disciplinary toolboxes. The new economic historians choose to look at old topics with
contemporary outlooks and concepts. Economists who choose to look at international topics with political overtones tend to bring with them much the same types
of assumptions that they might bring to domestic topics with or without recognized
political overtones.

   The general outcome for international political economy is much less emphasis on
history, processes of change, and "complete" causal chains than the subject matter
demands and deserves. Economics has been a discipline in which history and change
have been suppressed for the convenience of mechanistic ontological assumptions,
theory construction and methodological advancement. Political science has also been
a discipline in which change and history have been suppressed for similar reasons,
if less evident success. The marriage of the two fields within the IPE rubric, too
frequently, has meant a carryover – and sometimes even a compounding – of these
"bad" habits.

If we accept the charge that the suppression of history and change are indeed bad habits, then an increased focus on the evolution of structure and processes should be a beneficial corrective. In that minimal sense, we very much need more evolutionary emphases in the paradigms of social science. Far too many of those same structures and processes are path-dependent phenomena with histories that make critical differences in comprehending how they operate to proceed otherwise.

But what about the more maximal approach? Should we make the effort to adopt the assumptions, vocabulary, and hypotheses of evolutionary biology in the social sciences? Biologists, after all, have been specializing in evolutionary questions for nearly 150 years. One of the problems, however, is that biologists have and have had a large number of ideas about evolution. These ideas have experienced evolution over the past 200 years, and, presumably, their efforts to explain biological evolution will continue to evolve. They also have distinctive problems to explain, such as the diversity represented by a million types of insects, that appear unlike problems encountered in the social sciences. With the exception of physical anthropology, the social sciences do not analyze changes in the human species *per se* but rather changes in the behavior of humans. In comparison to other species, humans have developed an increasingly greater collective capacity to both modify their environment and their own behavior – and to do so rather quickly. Adaptation to environmental change need not work in quite the same way as tribolytes, marsupials, or pandas which must slowly mutate and reproduce in order to evolve. Moreover, the intermittent intensity of competition within the human species appears to be unusually savage at times. There may well be idiosyncratic features associated with the particular species on which social science inquiry specializes.[1] So, if we are to borrow or contemplate borrowing from biology, just what is it that we should focus upon?

Mayr (1991: 36–37) suggests that the Darwinian evolutionary paradigm can be reduced to five theories:

1   Evolution – the world is constantly changing and organisms are transformed over time.
2   Common descent – every group of organisms descended from a common organism and that all organisms go back to a single origin.
3   Multiplication of species – organic diversity is due to subdivisions and the development of new species made possible by geographical isolation.
4   Gradualism – evolutionary change takes place through gradual change.
5   Natural selection – evolutionary change comes about through a combination of genetic variation, competition survival, and the endurance of well-adapted characteristics in subsequent generations.

If these five components are the crux of the Darwinian paradigm, it seems unlikely that the social sciences can borrow the paradigm without modification and substantial elaboration. The basic idea of constant change and transformation is fine as a first assumption but it may prove to be no more useful than the opposite argument for the absence of change and transformation. Some combination of change and stasis, a combination that is not unknown to biology, seems a preferable starting point. In contrast, the ideas of common descent and multiplication of species seem rather alien to social science concerns. The conceptual payoff involved in borrowing them are not clear.

Gradualism is an argument that is being contested within biology by punctuated equilibria arguments (Eldredge, 1985: Gould, 1987). If we perceive long-term economic growth as being dependent on a series of discontinuous, radical innovations, as envisioned in K-wave arguments, punctuated equilibria arguments and the notion that change can be sudden are quite appealing. The easy-to-accept compromise is the generalization that different processes can be characterized by different rates of change. Some processes change rapidly while others change slowly. Processes such as long-term economic growth are characterized by both gradual and abrupt changes.

The idea of natural selection has an unfortunate ideological history – social Darwinism and the survival of the fittest – that gives one pause in contemplating the adoption of the fifth component. Nevertheless, it is a metaphor with some utility in explaining the rise and decline of successive leaders in world politics and economics. Actors in competition respond to (and create) fluctuations in the politico-economic environment in different ways. Actors who develop new ways of doing things tend to cope best with the opportunities and problems associated with macrochange. The process is not random although it may entail substantial trial and error. It involves the creation and destruction of economic techniques and political regimes. Success can also be attributed to the uneven distribution of actor (genetic) characteristics, such as societal openness and geographical location.

Modelski (1990) has elsewhere argued that global war is a basic selection mechanism for leadership in world politics. The war's winning coalition and its policy agenda and preferences are selected by the war from a field of competing approaches to governing global interactions. Once the war is over, the winning coalition is in a position to organize the next long leadership cycle. Variation is thus seen in terms of multiple and competing interpretations of political problem-solving. In world politics, selection involves intense combat and leads to reorganization.

Much the same metaphor can be applied to economic innovation. There may be an infinite number of ways of solving economic problems, whether it be pumping water from mines (the origin of steam engines), reducing transportation costs (railroads), or finding replacements for diminishing energy supplies (nuclear power). Some inventions are selected from a field of competing approaches to become innovations that transform the way economic interactions work and the way the economy is organized. Schumpeter's (1939) "gales of creative destruction," as manifested in K-wave dynamics is the analogous selection mechanism at the national and international economy levels. Unsuccessful firms are likely to die (or merge), not unlike the extinction of species in biology, as new economic paradigms emerge. Those economies that are most successful in adopting, and adapting to, the new paradigms, reorganize the world economy to their own advantage.

Creative actors and actors capable of learning new ways of doing things (problem-solving) have opportunities to survive and flourish. Variation exists in learning/creative capabilities just as it does in the range of solutions available for problems. Selection mechanisms in global politics and the world economy also exist. But Allen (1988: 98) cautions us about making too much of this selection metaphor:

> The image that this presents is one of evolution as a "blind watchmaker", where the intricate machinery of the world is comparable to that of a watch, whose cogs and bearings are the fruit of the selection, in the past, of unspecified trials. Behind this is the idea of evolution as an optimizing "force", which has led to the retention of the individuals and organizations we see because of their functional superiority. In this way, the classical theories of economics, of evolutionary biology and of anthropological interpretation have been permeated by the mechanical paradigm of classical physics. Carried deep within this is the idea of "progress", of the rightful "survival of the fittest", and of a natural "justice" which must characterize the long-term evolution of a complex system.

To the extent that Allen is right, there is considerable irony in rejecting one paradigm as too mechanical for another that is equally so, if only more subtle. Moreover, selective borrowing from the Darwinian paradigm suggests a focus on processes that experience change over time, at different rates, and that are governed by natural selection. But all that is meant by "natural selection" is that actors that cope best with change are most likely to survive the competition for scarce resources. Paradigmatically speaking, these principles may sound like thin gruel indeed. But, perhaps we should evaluate them in comparison to alternative paradigmatic foundations. They begin to look more appealing when contrasted with the foundations of the prevailing paradigms in economics and political science.

Still, it is equally clear that any evolutionary paradigms in the social sciences will need more foundational work than merely an emphasis on variation, differential rates of change and selection processes. Nor does it seem probable that a single evolutionary paradigm for the social sciences is likely to emerge in the near future, even though one might be desirable. There are certainly advantages to divisions of labor when confronted with complexity. There will also be a wide range of units of analysis and *problematiques* preferred by different strategies of social science inquiry. Yet we may be forced to develop a cadre of analysts who specialize in the long-term interdependencies among the principal subsystems. Otherwise, developing an understanding of their processes may be an excessively long-term process in its own right.

Should we move toward genuinely evolutionary perspectives, the most substantial payoff may be found in adopting the conceptual implications of coevolving processes. Species do not simply react to environmental change and thereby evolve. Their environment is evolving concurrently. The consequent emphasis is not on explaining a special reaction to change. Rather, the conceptual problem is one of tracking and

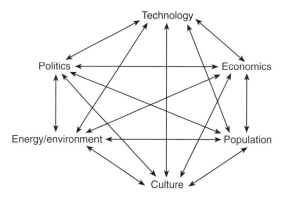

Figure 2.1 Coevolving parts of the whole

explaining sometimes parallel and sometimes disequilibrated changes in different spheres or subsystems and their consequences.

In the case of the world economy and global politics, the Chapter 1 story envisions substantial interaction and reciprocity in the two realms. Radical change in economic innovation leads to intensive conflict and radical change in global politics which, in turn, facilitates further radical change in economic innovation. Significant hierarchies in both the world economy and world politics are created as a consequence. The probability of imposing some semblance of order in world politics and the probability of economic development (mobility within the economic hierarchy) in the world economy, two consequences of the hierarchies, are governed by the timing and nature of these changes.

Yet consider the complexities involved if the notion of coevolution is extended, as it should be, to the realms of population, energy, and the environment. Politics and economics coevolve with each other but they also coevolve, separately and together, with changes and continuities in population, energy supply, and the environment. We can complicate the situation even further by acknowledging, as in Figure 2.1, that a technology (military and nonmilitary) subsystem should be differentiated from economic dynamics. Another realm engaged in coevolution with the other six is culture. The placement of culture at the bottom of Figure 2.1 is not meant to imply necessarily any hierarchy in the arrangement of the subsystems.[2]

One way to illustrate some of the intra-subsystemic interactions is to consider the application of air conditioning in the southern United States. The innovation of air conditioning technology and its dependence on the development of new energy sources had a range of interconnected implications for economic development, population migration (and certainly death rates if not birth rates), environmental modification (and deterioration), and, ultimately, political, and cultural change. While it is unlikely that anyone who has resided in a tropical or semitropical climate would deny the significance of air conditioning to life in general, tracing the myriad impacts and feedbacks with any degree of precision would be a more challenging task.

Still another complicating feature of interaction (not shown in Figure 2.1) is that it goes on at different levels of analysis. Biology has its organisms, species, and eco-systems. Politics goes on at global, regional, national, and local levels. There is a world economy, some regional economies, many national economies, and a host of local economies. The dynamics that characterize any single level may be generalizable to other levels but one should be careful to investigate whether this assumption is really valid. The multiple levels of analysis, also, further compound the complexities associated with a (co)evolutionary perspective.[3]

Perhaps ameliorating some of the complexity, however, it seems likely that each subsystem, depending on the focus of the analyst, will be represented by one or more prominent processes. Innovation and diffusion would most likely be the main foci of the culture and technology (commercial, industrial, agricultural, and military) subsystems. Birth and death rates and migration should be salient in the population subsystem. Energy supply and environmental deterioration (ranging from ice ages through fish stocks' depletion to famine and plagues) will loom large in the energy/environment subsystem. Growth and inequality are the première processes in the economic subsystem. Similarly, leadership should be a major feature of the political subsystem. However, no doubt displaying the biases of the author, a host of other processes come to mind, for example global war and order, democratization, or even political realignment.

We have a great deal to learn about how the six clusters of processes have coevolved in the past and how they are interacting in the present. Unfortunately, merely invoking the concept of coevolution does not tell us much about the specific macro-processes of "coordination" that may be involved, but at least the concept alerts us to the need to search for nested processes of change and the principles that govern how the nesting proceeds.

It is possible to go beyond merely sketching vague interconnections between analytical subsystems and the equally ambiguous hypothesis that they all somehow coevolve. It should be possible to outline a paradigmatic template for analyzing coevolutionary processes that would have more value as a research guide than simply borrowing selected metaphors from biology.[4] Such a template would include the following principles:

1 Social interaction can be organized analytically as the ongoing mutual adjust-ments of a number of subsystemic parts with their own histories and variable amounts of autonomy.

2 Each subsystem represents a complex cluster of dynamics that is likely to be related to all of the other subsystems. Causal chains are apt to be long and complex. Each subsystem is characterized by a mix of change and continuity that affects the mixtures of change and continuity in the other subsystems. The evolution of any single subsystem, therefore, is likely to be influenced by the evolution of both the other subsystems and the system as a whole. Yet the impact on other subsystems of change in one subsystem is neither automatic nor mechanical.

3   Each subsystem may be characterized by additional, within-subsystem levels of complexity based on distinctions made about individual actors and aggregated combinations of interacting actors. The strong possibility of different types of relationships operating between levels of analysis within subsystems and across subsystems further complicates the analytical undertaking.

4   Change is ubiquitous and more normal than stasis and equilibrium, although the extent to which this generalization holds should remain a theoretical and empirical question. Potential sources of change are multiple and may be pre-meditated or accidental. Intrasubsystemic and intersubsystemic relationships tend to be characterized by variable levels of flux. Behavioral laws with extremely long-term validity are likely to be rare. Spatiotemporal qualifications are apt to be obligatory.

5   Non-reciprocal relationships between subsystems are unlikely. It is far more likely that subsystems will reciprocally shape and modify one another than it is that one subsystem will determine the nature of the other clusters of activity. Nevertheless, there is no need to assume that each subsystem is equal in causal significance to every other subsystem. There may well be prime movers but it is equally possible that the identities of the prime movers will not remain stable for long periods of time.

6   Processes tend to be both path-dependent and open-ended. Historical trajectories are significant factors in shaping subsequent processes and outcomes and futures, due to complexity and contingency, are difficult to forecast very far into the future with any precision.

7   Processes are characterized by a mix of continuities and discontinuities. Over time, some processes may be characterized by cyclical behavior while others trend and still others do both. It should not be assumed that either cyclical or trending behavior must continue forever or that cycles and trends must extend indefinitely into the past.

8   Actors are faced with problems that require variable degrees of resolution. As a consequence, actors are not simply moved hither and yon by vague systemic forces. Actors are constrained (and empowered) by structural factors but they are also capable of reshaping their structural constraints. While actors will attempt to intervene in their complex environments (via problem solving efforts), they are unlikely to be entirely successful in either fully conceptualizing what is at stake or controlling simultaneously the multiple sets of dynamics that may be involved. Unintended and unforeseen consequences, therefore, are quite probable.

9   The sheer complexity of the interacting subsystems will also tend to overwhelm actor attempts at optimizing choices. Actors are not hyperrational. They operate with imperfect information, and have hazy ideas about their own values and preference schedules. They do not necessarily weigh all options and then proceed with the least costly, most advantageous alternative. Policy formulation and execution is likely to be a process of trial and error in which policies emerge after a number of experimental probes in different directions. Just which direction will

be privileged is not always clear. Moreover, preferences, procedures, and choices are constrained and empowered by path dependencies and the system of inter-acting parts. The open-ended nature of interactions, on the other hand, permits challenges to the constraints and lock-in effects associated with path dependency. In general, though, the inherent complexities argue against reducing behavior to optimizing agents, even solely for the purposes of modeling. This is particularly the case for long-term processes but, it may not be as critical for short-term processes. Thus, perspectives on processes of long-term coevolution and short-term rational choice need not be inherently incompatible as long as appropriate divisions of analytical labor can be realized.

10   However, because competition and evolution are continuing processes, actors who are capable of adapting to changing circumstances, learning new things, and taking creative advantage of new opportunities will be favored by the selection mechanisms operating in different subsystems. No matter how scarce problem-solving creativity is, multiple approaches (variation) to solving problems (strategies) will exist. This is the very crux of an evolutionary paradigm. Many things are capable of evolution but a particular emphasis on the evolution of actor strategies is most pertinent for situations involving social (as opposed to biological) evolution. Changes in environments and in actors with decision-making influence will lead to greater probabilities that old strategies will be abandoned by at least some actors and new strategies either innovated or "taken off the shelf". The question then becomes whether the new strategies survive and are copied by other actors. Selection mechanisms will privilege some strategies over others. As new strategies are selected and become predominant, the sub-systems in Figure 2.1 (co)evolve. Whether the successive outcomes of these variations and selection processes are judged to be progressive remains as open-ended a question as the future evolution of the system and its reciprocally interdependent parts.

More succinctly, the primary *problematique* of (co)evolutionary analyses is explaining change and its pervasive impacts in overdetermined systems. Preferences for units of analysis will vary according to the substantive question(s) at hand and the mix of subsystems brought into the analysis. However, the focus on tracking process and processes within fairly complex contexts (in terms of history and the relative density of possibly significant relationships) should be a consistent and predominant emphasis. Historical change, interactive processes, and complexity, with or without genes, are the defining criteria of a (co)evolutionary paradigm. Equally important, however, is the idea introduced above that in each subsystem there are ongoing and interacting processes of variation, innovation and selection. Strategies or responses to problems are chosen from a range of possible solutions. How the solutions are chosen, which ones are chosen, and with what subsequent impact are the defining criteria of a (co)evolutionary paradigm.

Some might argue that explanatory paralysis is another characteristic of a coevolutionary paradigm. If analysts are enjoined to avoid oversimplification and if everything does turn out to be interrelated, how is it possible to develop any explanations? A coevolutionary perspective does indeed counsel considerable humility in developing generalizations about how processes work. But it does not mean, except perhaps for our most dedicated postmodernist colleagues, that empirical answers to theoretically justified research questions are impossible or even that our strategies of inquiry must be altered fundamentally. We have no choice but to proceed with foci on specific processes, delimited versions of reality, and attempts to assess the degree of correspondence between our interpretations and whatever portion of observed reality we can grasp. The complexity assumption leaves little choice. The specific burden that a coevolutionary analyst assumes, however, is greater sensitivity to the possible (and probable) existence of long-term feedback possibilities and the likelihood that whatever processes are being investigated are apt to be embedded within a complex, path-dependent, and open-ended context. If nothing else, these sensitivities suggest skepticism about many prevailing disciplinary assumptions, exclusive emphases on short-term processes, and the wisdom of respecting too much academic boundaries in the pursuit of an understanding of long-term processes of change.

Perhaps what we should do is to plunge immediately into the coevolutionary vortex and attempt to juggle analytically all the important subsystemic bundles of processes simultaneously. An alternative strategy is to enter the vortex more gingerly. The remaining eight chapters in this study clearly approximate the latter strategy more than they do the former. Three sets of questions are examined. The first one is a classic puzzle. Why did some Europeans ascend to the apex of the global political economy several hundred years ago? If one had been forced to predict which corner of the world would next be preeminent in 1400, 1500, 1600, or maybe even 1700, it is not clear that western Europe would have been a consensus selection. Yet western Europe did ascend, and with critical consequences for shaping the structure of the global political economy.

As noted, why Europeans ascended when they did is a classic puzzle. The explanations are numerous and can be related to processes at work in any and all of the subsystems identified in Figure 2.1. The next three chapters do not attempt to resolve this puzzle definitively. Instead, the focus is on narrowing the range of explanations that are most pertinent. Western Europe did have some advantageous attributes but they are not necessarily the ones that have received the most attention. Western Europeans did not succeed primarily because they possessed Protestant cultures, less governmental interference, lower birthrates, better access to South America, or bigger guns. Some of these attributes were certainly facilitative but the main reason had to do with European strategic variation. Five hundred years or so ago, western Europe fostered more variation than any other region. As a consequence, it also facilitated the emergence of more innovation but not necessarily on a European-wide basis. A mixture of technological, military, and political innovations were the ticket to ascent in the global political economy, and they remain so today.

But these bundles of innovations are not inherent to any given region or group of people. Only some actors in Europe stumbled onto the trick of bringing these innovations together in the mid-second millennium. They were facilitated in doing so by a regional environment that offered them sufficient space to survive. Yet that same regional environment was not always so facilitative. Over long periods of time, opportunity space for doing new things opens and closes. People can choose to take advantage of these opportunities or not but only some will achieve success. The point remains that situations involving the opening and closing of opportunity spaces and variation in actor propensities and capabilities of doing something about them are not monopolized by any geographical location or their inhabitants. We need to look for opportunities, variation and trial-and-error strategy evolution, not for people who are thought to be superior to others on the basis of some inherent attribute thought to be important.

The second question, tackled in Chapters 6–8, pertains to one of the consequences of the European ascent. One of the byproducts of the Europeanization of the global political economy was the development of a particular and rather primitive succession process. As old leaders lost their competitiveness, would-be successors challenged the old leaders and their rivals for the opportunity to be the ultimate shaper of the global regime. The challenge process can be traced back in very crude form to its east Asian roots but the contemporary version really began to take shape first in the eastern Mediterranean and then along the coasts of the Atlantic Ocean. As a moderately old process that has been around for hundreds of years, it possesses some characteristics that are stable and generalizable, as well as others that have been experiencing change over time. While one might think that such an important process would be well known, it is not. We know the descriptive history surrounding the challenge process, but the recognition that this descriptive history is about a generalizable process remains restricted. The questions to address, then, are how does the challenge process work?, who is most likely to challenge?, who wins?, who loses? A related question addressed in Chapter 8 is why is it that the eventual successor was not the most violent challenger of the old order? In fact, the most violent challengers have always lost, at least after 1494. The winners have tended to be aligned with the declining incumbent leaders and inherit the leadership prize almost by default.

The third question has two faces. One face relates to a form of reality check. Is all this talk about millennium-long and/or half-millennium-long processes of global political economy a product of overwrought academic imaginations? Chapter 9 examines and rebuts the criticisms of historians who deny much, if any, role for structural continuities. The specific focus is in the context of the nineteenth-century British systemic leadership era.

The other face of this third question (is a long-term, structural interpretation truly advantageous and if so, how?) has to do with observing the possibility of changes in the way the global political economy operates. Neither a 500- or a 1000-year history implies that the key processes must persist. On the contrary, it has taken quite a few years for these same key processes to emerge in the present form. Continuing metamorphosis or evolution is to be expected. One of the advantages of a long-term perspective is that it is sometimes possible to see subtle changes underway that might be otherwise missed or, more likely, not fully identified. There seems to be just such a change underway in the nature of the global political economy's leadership and its core membership. The change(s) has hardly gone unrecognized. Observers frequently point to ongoing processes of democratization, globalization, interdependence, and technological change as fundamentally altering the global political economy. Perhaps this is so. But if it is the case, the developments are not entirely novel. They have been building momentum for several hundred years, if not longer. They need to be addressed as longitudinal processes, and not as abruptly novel changes, in the way we do things in the global political economy. Chapters 10 and 11 take on these tasks in different but related ways by looking at the deescalation of British–US hostility (Chapter 10) and the system leader lineage (Chapter 11).

Part II

THE ASCENDANCE OF
WESTERN EUROPE

3

THE 1490s

A question of evolutionary (dis)continuity?

From time to time, dramatic events in world politics give the impression that something new is taking place. The old ways of doing things are being discarded in favor of the construction of novel patterns. We refer to these periods as breakpoints or watersheds because they demarcate significant discontinuities in otherwise continuous processes. The destruction of the Berlin Wall in 1989 seemed to signify the end of the Cold War which presumably made an opportunity for creating a "New World Order". Earlier, the late eighteenth-century British Industrial Revolution is commonly viewed as an economic breakthrough demarcating the advent of a new, more industrialized economic world. And even earlier, the 1490s (1492, 1494, 1495, or 1498) are thought to have encompassed the "Discoveries", the emergence of capitalism, and the birth of the European state system.

Breakpoints are always easier to see after they occur. But, frequently, their perception depends very much on assumptions about what processes are most important and how these important processes function. How else are we to differentiate between genuine watersheds and minor hiccups in ongoing rhythms? When our interpretation of what processes are most important or how they work change, we need to reexamine the accuracy of the discontinuities that we have come to take for granted. It may be that what was once an obvious breakpoint will diminish in significance when viewed from a different vantage point. The 1490s are a case in point. How that decade is viewed depends very much on the Eurocentricity of one's perspective. A less Eurocentric interpretation not only scales down the overall significance of the decade, it also facilitates our understanding of a host of related topics. In this chapter this revisionist agenda will be pursued with a specific focus on long-term economic growth (especially what is referred to as the "European Miracle"), the dynamics of international relations, and their interaction. In assessing the breakpoint status of the 1490s, it will be necessary to scan more than 2000 years of development and developments. The end result will be a conclusion that the 1490s were not quite as discontinuous as is widely perceived.

SOME PRELIMINARY ASSUMPTIONS

Modelski and Thompson (1996) contend that the process of long-term economic growth has a continuous history since the tenth century. The pattern is one of highly concentrated surges in innovation every 50 years or so leading to high rates of growth in leading economic sectors and the emergence of transitory hot zones of leading economic activity. Northern and Southern Sung China initiated the pattern and the chain was then extended through Genoa, Venice, Portugal, the Netherlands, Britain and the United States in 18–19 long waves of growth. Each growth leader was associated with at least one twin-peaked, paired set of productivity surges.[1] Thus, the origins of long-term growth initially are highly concentrated sectorally, spatially, and temporally. Gradually, the advantages associated with pioneering new ways of doing things erode as the new ways become relatively routine and as they diffuse to other parts of the world economy. Another dimension of the basic pattern is the timing of system crisis/warfare which intervenes between the pair of growth peaks. A newly emerging growth leadership increases the probability of intense conflict. It also supplies the material base for defeating opponents. Victory, in turn, makes a second growth peak more likely.

The focus of Modelski and Thompson (1996) is on delineating the pattern theoretically and historically, while at the same time empirically testing several major hypotheses with data spanning the millennium in question.[2] One question that receives little attention in the Modelski and Thompson (1996) inquiry is the early shift from Sung China to the Italians operating in the eastern Mediterranean. Why did the shift move from east to west? What are the implications of its occurrence? What can it tell us about other longstanding questions of interest to students of world history/politics and macrochange?

One of the more overt implications of such a perspective has to do with the post-1500 rise of Europe to a position of predominance over the rest of the world. The nature of this ascendance remains hotly contested because it touches on a number of important assumptions and arguments about the sources of long-term economic growth.[3] If we can explain the European ascent, we should have a better handle on a host of questions on growth and related queries about inequality, divisions of labor, dependency, and exchange. Another implication has to do with the emergence of a European "interstate" system after 1494. We tend to assume that world politics and regional European international relations are synonymous. Moreover, we refer to post-1494 international relations as "modern," which suggests a fundamental discontinuity with what took place before 1494 and a fair amount of continuity characterizing what transpired afterwards. There is also more than a whiff of progress associated with the "modern" concept. What exactly is it, then, that differentiates the premodern from the modern? Or, just how much (dis)continuity in world politics is exhibited before and after the 1490s, and in what spheres should we expect to find it? Moreover, what, if anything, do these (dis)continuities in world politics have to do with long-term patterns of economic growth?

These are not simple questions and it is probably safe to say that they cannot be answered adequately in a few pages. Still, the initial question, which is not all that much more simple, deserves to be addressed first: why did leadership in economic growth pass from one end of Eurasia to the other? The answer to that question should be revealing and suggestive for the larger questions. But before the question can be answered, we need to turn first to a consideration of the 1490s and arguments about the rise of Europe. The initial conclusion is that authors tend to emphasize either endogenous or exogenous emphases, but these alternative interpretations are not necessarily incompatible. They need greater integration and balance within the context of long-distance trade and related institutions and strategies. Next, nine general principles of long-distance trade are delineated and applied to the history of Afro-Eurasian political economy. Third, a comparison of the (co)evolution of the east Asian and western European regional subsystems is undertaken to show how processes of economic growth, long-distance trade, and grand strategies need to be interwoven in order to explain why one region supplanted the other at the center of the world political economy.

THE 1490s AND THE "EUROPEAN MIRACLE"

In retrospect, the 1490s, now some 50 decades past, seem to have constituted one of the basic turning points in world politics. Columbus sailed the wrong way and established European contact with the Americas. Vasco da Gama sailed the right way around Africa and pioneered a new European path to the Indian Ocean, the maritime heart of the Afro-Eurasian world economy. These "discoveries" were also associated with an upsurge in capitalistic economic practices that were gradually diffused throughout the rest of the world. In other spheres of activity, the territorial consolidations of Spain and France had more or less peaked after centuries of gradual movement and intermittent setbacks. Both states quickly found themselves clashing over the control of Italy, thereby ushering in a new era of periodic general wars in Europe and the full-fledged emergence of a European state system. Thus, in one decade western Europe seems to have annexed the new world, captured the center of the old world, shaken free of feudalism and initiated the diffusion of capitalism throughout the world, and developed a distinctive system of international relations at home. Would any of these changes have seemed very likely in the 1480s?

If this interpretation of the 1490s as an abrupt and major watershed is correct, we need to understand why the discontinuities emerged and why the activities of the 1490s were so discontinuous in effect. After all, major breakpoints, not unlike miracles, are presumably rare yet highly significant in their impacts. These appear to have been fundamentally responsible for shaping the basic parameters of the current world. Therefore, whether one is interested in international politics, international political economy, or the mysteries of economic growth, the roots of the present would appear to be traceable to events seemingly encapsulated in a singular decade 500 hundred years ago. Or are they? Is it possible that the conventional view is in error? If the 1490s were less discontinuous than is often thought, our search for the roots of the present system might be fixated on the wrong time period. More seriously, we might also be grossly misinterpreting what did take place by emphasizing discontinuities at the expense of even more basic continuities.

The author's position on this question approximates, with some qualification, the latter position spelled out above. The 1490s did constitute a breakpoint for several facets of international activities. But, we have exaggerated the extent to which it marked a fundamental change in the way the world worked then and continues to work now. In doing so, we have not fully appreciated the formative influences of processes operating prior to the 1490s. Nor have we fully appreciated important clues to such questions as how does one account for the "European Miracle" in economic growth or how should one go about distinguishing between the international relations of the European region as opposed to those of the world system or other regions.

These questions are hardly small. To address them appropriately requires the interpretation of information encompassing one or two millennia of time and events and behavior throughout the world. Those who have attempted such undertakings will admit to some dizziness from time to time in attempts to keep the names and societies straight, in avoiding being overwhelmed by the trees in search of some semblance of a forest, and, ultimately, simply evading information overload. Fortunately, a large number of very capable people have worked within this analytical arena in the past. Whether or not it is necessary to climb on their shoulders, it does make a great deal of difference that many scholars have been interested in the phenomenal rise of Europe to a position of political, economic, and cultural predominance. If nothing else, it makes it easier to assess the relative explanatory utilities of the various and multiple tangents that have been explored. And even if it may seem that everything possible under the sun has already been said by somebody, it does not mean that the components of different arguments and treatments, and their implications, cannot be reassembled to yield an improved explanatory package.

The key to this undertaking revolves around an explanation of the "European Miracle" – a reference to the seemingly low probability development of a complete dependency reversal on the part of one of the more underdeveloped corners of Eurasia. How other things fall into place will revolve around the interpretation placed on this central process. Nevertheless, the constraints of time and space preclude a detailed survey of all the previous efforts to explain the ascent of Europe. Instead, we suggest that most can be captured parsimoniously within a two-by-two table that juxtaposes an emphasis on endogeneity/exogeneity of the processes involved versus the uniqueness/non-uniqueness of the western periphery of Eurasia.[4] Various authors can be located within three of the four cells of the table, as is demonstrated in Table 3.1. The most heavily populated category is located in the upper left cell (endogenous processes/European uniqueness). Weber (1958), North and Thomas (1973), early Jones (1981), Hall (1985, 1988) and Mann (1986, 1988), are all representative of this school of thought. Essentially, the argument is that only in Europe was it possible for the ingredients necessary for the emergence of a dominant position vis-à-vis the rest of the world. Various ingredients are favored: Protestant

Table 3.1 Endogeneity/exogeneity and the uniqueness of Europe in representative
explanations of European ascendancy

	Endogenous emphases	*Exogenous emphases*
Unique Europe	Weber (1958)	
	North/Thomas (1973)	Abu-Lughod (1989)
	Jones (1981)	Diamond (1997)
	Mann (1986, 1988)	Chase-Dunn/Hall (1997)
	Hall (1985, 1988)	
	Rosenberg/Birdzell (1986)	
	Landes (1998)	
Non-unique Europe	Jones (1988)	Blaut (1992, 1993)
	Powelson(1994)	Gills/Frank (1993)
	Snooks (1996)	
		Frank (1998)

ethics, a competitive interstate system, property rights, rain-based irrigation (and ample rain), or the ability to avoid reliance on extensive irrigation projects, agricultural innovations, birth control techniques, and so forth. The bottom line of these arguments is that Europe and the Europeans were different and that it was the way(s) in which they differed from the rest of the world that was (were) responsible for what transpired after the 1490s.

In marked contrast, the lower right cell combines exogenous processes and the nonuniqueness of the Europeans. Blaut (1992, 1993) is the most outspoken exemplar of this point of view. He maintains that there was virtually nothing taking place in Europe that could not also be found going on somewhere else in Afro-Eurasia. Therefore, to give credit to the uniqueness of European conditions is entirely wrong. What the Europeans did, thanks to their locational advantage, was to stumble into the silver mines of South America before other Eurasians did. The exploitation of these resources were critical in acquiring increasing control over the Afro-Eurasian political economy. Thus, the Europeans were in the right place at the right time and took advantage of their good fortune at the expense of the rest of the world.

Frank (1998) shares this position and would stress in addition that the Europeans were unable to displace Chinese centrality in the world economy prior to the nineteenth century. Hence, the European ascent is easy to exaggerate, and was due more to industrialization after the late eighteenth century, and was also a very brief phenomena, with China bidding to reoccupy its traditional place in the twenty-first century. More generally, Gills and Frank (1993a, 1993b) have led the way in opening up these sorts of questions to much longer time perspectives and wider geographical applications as part of their argument that the world system has a 5000-year history as opposed to a 500-year one. Economic growth and expansion have cropped up intermittently at various times and places during that 5000-year interval, thereby rendering the uniqueness of Europe a matter more simply of analytical myopia.

In the upper right cell (exogenous processes/European uniqueness), the argument tends to boil down to the position that whatever unique attributes Europe possessed and which may have proved facilitative for the ascent to hegemony, the major reason the Europeans were triumphant was a matter of timing and the state of affairs outside of Europe. The Middle East was in decline. India was lethargic. China, after demonstrating its capability of establishing naval supremacy 100 years before the arrival of the Portuguese, had retreated into isolation. The Europeans thus stumbled into an Indian Ocean-based trading system that they were able to take over by force and largely by default. In the 1490s and into the next century, the Europeans met with little effective resistance. If they had come earlier or later, it might have been a different story. Abu-Lughod (1989) currently is the most prominent representative of this perspective.

Chase-Dunn and Hall's (1997) more complicated version places western Europe in a Eurasian political economy with at least a two-millennia history of exchange in ideas and goods. European peripherality combined to create incentives for a hybrid strategy for overcoming its weakness and moving up in the system. A mixture of military technology and capitalist institutions were harnessed to bring about European hegemony. While they emphasize a Europe embedded on the margins of a larger world, a European uniqueness quality emerges in the form of coercive capitalism which becomes the predominant style of the world economy thanks to European expansion.

In contrast, the Diamond (1997) position is parsimonious. His primary interest lies in explaining why the Eurasian environment produced more wealth and complexity than most non-Eurasian settings. But he briefly considers the European question – that is, why, within Eurasia, did the Europeans become dominant? Diamond's (1997: 409–416) answer is that the Fertile Crescent and China held enormous leads over Europe but lost them due, primarily and respectively, to an ecologically fragile environment (Fertile Crescent) and excessive unity (China). China's unity and Europe's "chronic disunity" are due to the geography of the two Eurasian ends with China coming to be dominated by a single core area and Europe inevitably characterized by many, relatively small states, none of whom could dominate the others for very long. The first condition, single core dominance, proved to be a handicap when the Ming were able to foreclose the possibility through imperial edict in the fifteenth century. Something similar could never have happened in Europe and, in fact, did not – as best exemplified by Columbus seeking patronage from a succession of royal courts before making his connection.

The lower left cell (endogenous processes/the absence of European uniqueness) is not empty but it is not densely populated with many examples. Jones (1988) is about growth and economic change. As such, it does not really concentrate on European expansion *per se*. However, Jones (1988) is especially noteworthy in the sense that his 1988 argument largely repudiates his 1981 argument – often regarded as one of the exemplars of the endogenous/European unique genre. As Jones (1988: 67) states, an examination of economic history reveals "a world of **extensive** growth in which novelty repeatedly bubbled up and more than once boiled over into **intensive growth**". This insight leads Jones to argue that if growth is a natural phenomena, then the analyst should look for the constraints that are imposed on it. Where the constraints to growth are least powerful, other things being equal, is where one should find the economic growth success stories (Europe and Japan).

Powelson's (1994) argument is quite similar. His point is that economic growth is dependent on power diffusion among economic interest groups that leads to growth-promoting institutions. Prior to about the thirteenth century, power was concentrated all around the planet. But, about that time, northwestern Europe and Japan began to develop increasingly balanced domestic power distributions that ultimately led to a culture of compromise and a more equitable participation in economic processes. The roots of this development, Powelson suggests, can be traced to land scarcity and long-distance trade problems. But neither the roots nor how durable economic development precisely led to European expansion are not among Powelson's main concerns. He does note, though, that the northwest European attributes of compromise and relative equality were diffused to North America and Australia/New Zealand by northwestern European colonization, despite the absence of either land scarcity or trade problems.

Snooks (1996) is even more ambitious in that he seeks to explain change over a 70-million year period by focusing on individual decisions to maximize material advantages by recourse to a variety of strategies (family multiplication, technological change, commerce, and conquest). Oversimplifying a great deal, Snooks' model reduces to an argument that dominant strategies play themselves out. When they do, systems are in crisis until new strategies are adopted. The basic difference between China and Europe around 1500, then, was that the latter had long since moved away from the Roman Empire's emphasis on conquest while Ming China had not. Europe, therefore, was less constrained in experimenting with the commercial and techno-logical strategies that proved to be successful.

After forcing a number of other authors into these artificial analytical corners, it should be noted that there are certainly analysts who emphasize endogenous processes but who also recognize some role for exogenous processes and vice versa. Some of them are found in Table 3.1. This table is meant to summarize rival *emphases* and not to censure previous authors for various types of myopia. Having advanced that caveat, my conclusion is that all the schools of thought are partially right and partially wrong. That is to say that my own position does not fit readily within any of the cells of Table 3.1. The "European Miracle" was a product of both endogenous and exogenous developments and processes. One is hardpressed to emphasize one over the other. Europe possessed some relatively unique attributes that were critical but it also shared other attributes with other parts of the world that were also an important part of the puzzle. Moreover, developments outside of Europe were critical to the eventual ascent of the west Europeans. What is needed is a differentiation between conditions that promoted growth locally and factors that linked western Europe to the rest of the world's growth processes. There is no need to assume that they were one and the same once you begin with the major assumption that western Europe did not initiate the processes of "modern" or long-term economic growth. Instead, some Europeans, thanks only in part to local growth, were able to jump on a growth bandwagon initiated originally elsewhere in Afro-Eurasia.

The position taken here must then be located at the dead center of Table 3.1 at the point where the four cells converge. However, this disinclination to accept a place within preconstructed pigeonholes does not mean that it is impossible to pick and choose among the postulated ingredients. Some played more critical roles than others. In particular, the version to be emphasized in this chapter stresses the role of long-distance trade, institutional orientations toward long-distance trade, and the strategies chosen to deal with the problems and opportunities associated with long-distance trade. All three emphases focus on interactions between endogenous and exogenous factors. They also focus on interactions between parts of western Europe and the rest of Afro-Eurasia, for the most important unique elements were anything but common throughout Europe. Still, the fact that these elements (independent trading states controlled by trade-oriented élites) existed in the first place was relatively unique to the Europe of the late Middle Ages.

ASSERTIONS ABOUT THE ROLE OF LONG-DISTANCE TRADE

The historical role of trade and especially long-distance trade is underappreciated. There are several reasons for this lack of adequate recognition. One reason is the orthodox view that precontemporary trade was small in size, especially in comparison to the wealth obtained from domestic agrarian production. If gross national product (GNP) figures were available far into the past, the proportion of GNP allocated to the import and export categories would not be very impressive for most cases. The implication is that the proportions were much too small to influence overall economic growth. A second orthodoxy is that long-distance trade, in particular, entailed, almost by definition, the exchange of luxury items for consumption by an extremely restricted number of élites. Trade over long distances, given the inherent transportation problems and protection costs, specialized in items low in weight and high in profit. Luxury goods, thus, were unlikely to account even for much of the volume in what trade there was and any impact on consumers was apt to be limited only to the very wealthy.

The small numbers involved (proportion of GNP, proportion of overall trade, and number of consumers directly affected) need not be contested to suggest, however, that there are other ways to interpret the significance of long-distance trade. The production of foodstuffs surely will predominate in terms of bulk and volume in agrarian economies. Yet bulk and volume are not the only considerations of importance. On the contrary, the opposing point of view (Adams, 1974; Schneider, 1977; Curtin, 1984; McNeill, 1992; Gills, 1993) that depicts long-distance trade as one of the most critical factors in socioeconomic change stresses qualitative factors that are difficult to measure easily.

A central thesis, albeit one with several variations, in the arguments promoting the importance of long-distance trade pertains to the development of urban networks. Curtin (1984) argues that cities are concentrations of people doing different things. The more different things cities are able to do, the more less multifunctional places become dependent upon the more multifunctional settlements, thereby creating hierarchies of economic and political dependency. But these hierarchies of increasing complexity and dependency, in turn, are dependent upon exchange within a network of cities, as well as between cities and their hinterlands. Local and long-distance trade, then, is one of the foundations of urban network development.

Several authors (Fox, 1971; Hohenberg and Lees, 1985; Rasler and Thompson, 1989) take this notion one step farther. Two basic types of cities or systems of political economy are hypothesized: central place and network cities. Central place cities specialize in servicing a nearby, usually agrarian region by providing a convenient market for perishable foodstuffs and political administration. Whereas a central place city is oriented primarily toward its immediate rural hinterland, network cities are oriented toward other cities of a similar type and act as nodes in an interactive system of cities specializing in the cultivation of interregional trade and other commodities such as information and culture.

Specific cities may combine both dimensions but it is unlikely that they will do so equally. The point is that a few cities operate primarily as the links in long-distance trade routes. Their development is, therefore, highly contingent on trade fluctuations. Agrarian market towns are much less influenced by these external swings. Agrarian market towns are also more likely to be lower on Curtin's urban hierarchy while the long-distance trade hubs are apt to rate highly on the multifunctionality scale. Thus, the impact of long-distance trade is not only differentiable by the type of economic unit under consideration, the impact is also apt to be greatest on the most important cities.

If long-distance trade impacts selectively but at key points in urban exchange networks, what exactly is it that is influenced? Several plausible and ostensibly compatible answers are found in the literature:

1   Premodern trade was a function of three factors: (i) some communities had a technological advantage that could not be copied elsewhere; (ii) some communities controlled unique sources of supply; and (iii) consumer tastes placed variable premiums on specific commodities (Chaudhuri, 1985). To these three factors we might also add physical obstacles (deserts, mountains, oceans, jungles), all of which could be overcome given the appropriate incentives, and the disruptions of political turmoil, which usually led to shifts in trade routes and termini following paths of least resistance. Despite the attribution of these five factors to "premodern" trade, it is not clear that they have been made totally obsolete by more contemporary trading patterns.

2   While long-distance trading networks could and did expand outward from a single hegemonic source, network growth and persistence is more probable if there is growth and demand at more than one point in the network, and if these

same points offer different specializations in commodities made available to the network (Curtin, 1984). Seen from this perspective, long-distance trade operates on something like a gravity-flow principle except that, unlike gravity, the nodes of the network have to work hard at maintaining supply, demand, and sufficient internode order to make sustained trade conceivable. The prototypical "pre-modern" scenario, therefore, has the probability of long-distance trade being greatest when two or more geographically distant but successful and wealthy empires each have commodities desired by the other. Given this incentive, traders will find paths that will link directly or indirectly the two markets. However, it may be the case that relatively large and powerful empires are needed if only to create and maintain the necessary technology of communication and transportation (Sanderson, 1994: 94). The more extensive the trading network, the more powerful the empires involved need to be. Imperial decline at both or one end of the extended trade route, or serious disruptions along the way, should decrease the likelihood of long-distance trade persisting.

3   Generating an economic surplus is critical for sustaining politico-military, investment and cultural activities. Assuming some competitive capability, the less closed the collectivity to external goods, capital, technology, and ideas, the greater the opportunity to capture a greater share of the potential surplus. Openness to the costs and benefits of external competition should also serve as a stimulus for the development of competitive exports (Gills, 1993). More generally, cross-cultural trade (in addition to military conquest) has been the most important stimulus to changes in the arts, science, and technology (Curtin, 1984: 1).

4   Agrarian societies are subject to a variety of constraints on the extent to which they are capable of autonomous change or sustaining the development of increasing complexity. Overcoming these constraints becomes more conceivable to the extent that actors are connected to a larger world of resources, inventions, and technology. It takes time for extremely large areas characterized by a range of obstacles to interaction to be thoroughly interlinked by an urbanized commercial network. But as the interlinkages became more significant, any changes in how things are done would be increasingly more likely to be communicated throughout the entire system and to lead to new changes. Possibilities that had been for all practical purposes closed to earlier generations might be more open to later groups. Interregional commerce thus leads to cumulative growth which ultimately increases the probability of transcending the constraints faced by agrarian societies (Hodgson, 1993).

5   Maritime trade, in particular, has constituted the leading sector of commercial growth in the world economy, perhaps as early as the ninth century, but certainly between the fifteenth and nineteenth centuries (Curtin, 1984: 179).

6   Economic systems have tended toward two types: command and price systems. Both types of systems are capable of mobilizing goods and manpower but the price system tends to be less expensive, more efficient, and more capable of operating over longer distances than is the command system. Price systems thrive

in circumstances in which political intervention is careful not to interrupt needlessly the exchange of goods and services. When disruptive political interventions have been avoided or minimized, greater potentials for economic production, relying on regional specialization and economies of scale, have been realized. Moreover, long-distance trade, which is highly responsive to price incentives and extremely difficult to control from afar, has played a critical role in the gradual triumph of price over command systems (McNeill, 1992).

7   Cumulative growth and an expanding scope for economic interdependence implies that regional economies linked in some way to a long-distance trading network can benefit from surges in innovation, economic growth, production, and prosperity at some point in the network even though the affected regions may appear to be quite distant from the source of growth (Hodgson, 1974; McNeill, 1982). Participation in the long-distance network expands the opportunities for exogenous growth influences, and presumably with other things being equal, the greater the participation, the greater the opportunities for external influences.

8   The downside of cumulative growth and an expanding scope for economic interdependence is that problems such as depression, inflation and disease, once they are introduced somewhere in the network, are more likely to spread throughout the long-distance trade network than had hitherto been the case (Goldstone, 1991). While all economic systems have some familiarity with depression and inflation, the introduction of alien diseases to populations unprepared to resist them can be especially destructive (McNeill, 1976, 1992).

9   Merchants and cities, especially cities controlled by merchants have different interests and interests that are frequently incompatible from those espoused by warrior aristocracies. To simplify, the latter seek territorial aggrandizement while the former prefer to accumulate capital. Whose interests prevail in the long run will profoundly impact the types of states and empires created. Weak princes in conflict with rival princes and local aristocracies, for instance, were more likely to exchange rights and privileges for resources with wealthy cities (Blockmans, 1994). But stalemate between landed gentry and urban commercial interests could lead to militarized political solutions which were inherently unstable (Hodgson, 1974).

None of these nine sets of generalizations about the operation and implications of long-distance trade appear to be contradictory. What they suggest is that long-distance trade has been crucial to innovation, economic growth, the development of price incentives, modernization (for example, overcoming the limitations of agrarian economies), and the degree of autocracy retained by rulers. Whether it is due to the exposure to new ideas and growth elsewhere in the system or to the development of new competencies to better compete in the larger system, trade is an important handmaiden of change. In its absence, it is too easy to remain in an equilibrium trap (see Elvin, 1973). In its presence, it is difficult to fully control or manage the implications of interaction with alien goods, ideas, and viruses. As a consequence, more open societies tend to fare better in selecting optional courses of action from the variety of alternatives available. They have more options from which to choose. They are also more likely to develop mechanisms for self-correction when initially chosen paths prove less than desirable.

In addition, there is a cumulative effect that is crucial. Exposure to trade may be one thing; exposure to a very old and increasingly extensive trading system is something else. The wheel is less likely to need to be reinvented in some distant province because some more advanced part of the network has already established a lead in wheel innovation. Interdependence facilitates learning. Cumulative interdependence means that technology and participating economies have opportunities to become increasingly complex in that they can build on previous learning. Technological change is apt to be diffused farther and more quickly. So is prosperity. But then so are depressions and new diseases.

These generalizations are stated in the abstract. Do any or all apply to our interest in placing the rise of Europe within a larger Afro-Eurasian system? The answer lies definitely in the affirmative. Without a very strong emphasis on the roles played by long-distance trade, and especially maritime trade, it is difficult to make much sense of the rise of Europe. And once we begin to appreciate the significance of long-distance trade, a number of other topics become amenable to new interpretations.

AFRO-EURASIAN LONG-DISTANCE TRADE

The history of Afro-Eurasian long-distance trade can be quickly summarized. Initially concentrated in the Middle East, Eurasian trade developed primarily along an east–west axis, involving towns in places such as Mesopotamia and Egypt and later Mohenjo-Daro. Trade between India and China and China and Mesopotamia is traceable to roughly fourth-century BC. But the most familiar pattern began to develop concurrently with the rise of the Han empire (206 BC–220 CE) in northern China and the Roman empire (202 BC–c. 476) in the Mediterranean.[5] Both empires rose and declined at about the same time (with Rome hanging on a bit longer). They shared structural common denominators and they also traded with one another even though their borders were not directly adjacent. In this case, the health of the geographically intervening Mauryan and Parthian empires also played some role. After their mutual disintegrations (referring in the Roman case to what happened to the western manifestation of the empire) which may well have been closely related to commingled disease pools and restless nomads in central Eurasia pushing west, east and south, long-distance trade slumped until the rise of the Sui (589–618) and T'ang (618–907) dynasties in China and the Abbasids (750–1258) in the west. Time may also have been required to allow the impact of the new diseases to dissipate and the nomadic movement to stabilize.

Unlike their predecessors, the T'ang and Abbasid empires actually clashed but they also traded with one another – building on an already existing Persian–Chinese trade network of lesser volume. Each empire also developed extensive ancillary markets from Korea to Indonesia and on to Africa in the T'ang case and throughout the Mediterranean and north through Russia to the Baltic in the Arab case. The decline of the T'angs and the Abbasids again depressed long-distance trade, with possible repercussions as distant as increased Viking–Carolingian conflict in northern Europe (Hodges, 1982: 157; Hodges and Whitehouse, 1983: 164).

The revival of trade around 1000 AD was more asymmetrical in inspiration. The spectacular economic expansion of Sung China was unparalleled in the Muslim or Christian west. At the same time, it is inaccurate to say that the west was mired in economic depression. The Byzantines hung on, even though more and more precariously. The Abbasids were followed by Fatimids, Ayyubids, and Mamluks (although not exactly in the same places) without any major attempt at reunifying the Islamic Middle East and North Africa before the development of the Ottoman Empire. Western Europe was expanding to the east and the south, with the Crusades as one obtrusive indicator. Long-distance trade on land and sea was thus able to expand with western termini in the Byzantine Black Sea, Persia, and Egypt. Focusing initially on the Black Sea route and later more on the southern routes through the Persian Gulf and Red Sea, Italian city states were critical in linking or relinking western Europe to the now well-established Afro-Eurasian network(s).

The replacement of the Sung by the Mongols led to an even greater acceleration in the volume of east–west trade, thanks to the order imposed on central Eurasia and the land routes of the Silk Roads by the Pax Mongolia. The price for this increase in Eurasian economic integration was paid in the mid-fourteenth century. Plague, probably spread by Mongol armies that had attempted to invade Burma extended throughout first China, then central Eurasia, and on to the Black Sea, the Mediterranean, and the North Sea following the western routes of the long-distance trade networks. Economic depression appears to have preceded the advent of the Black Death but the two calamities compounded their impact and worked to disrupt trade and economic growth throughout Afro-Eurasia for nearly a century. As may have happened several times before, however, the plague's effects gradually wore off as the survivors developed immunities to the new viruses and improved their ways of coping with disease. Long-distance trade had never disappeared but it began to increase again in the second half of the fifteenth century. The 1490s constituted an initial crest in this resurgence in long-distance, east–west trade. It was not coincidental that the Iberian attempts to find more direct routes to the east at this time could be seen as the revival of Crusader projects in the first half of the thirteenth century (Lewis, 1988: 142) and Genoese projects of a similar nature in the 1290s. In the 1490s, as in the 1290s, the strategic goal became one of removing Muslim, and especially Egyptian, middlemen in the Afro-Eurasian trade network. This could be done by finding a maritime path around Africa and/or by interdicting the flow of eastern trade in the Indian Ocean. The Genoese attempted to do both in the 1290s and failed. The Portuguese were more successful in the 1490s, even though they ultimately failed to realize their goal for very long.

The point to emphasize here, nonetheless, is that the Genoese and the Portuguese attempts at coercively manipulating the Afro-Eurasian trade network were responding to incentives that had begun to be established 1000–1200 years earlier with the initial establishment of a Han–Roman commercial linkage. The commercial linkages that were made at that time proved to be intermittent, depending as it did on the rise and fall of imperial centers, and related fluctuations in population, wealth, and disease (Curtin, 1984; McNeill, 1992; Bentley, 1993). Still, the nature and shape of the economic trade structure maintained its basic format from its Han–Roman origins to at least the 1490s. The viability and comparative attractiveness of various routes fluctuated over the years. The Mongols reestablished the dominance of the Asian overland routes for a century but the superiority (in terms of lower transportation and protection costs) of the maritime routes of the Indian Ocean preceded the arrival of the Portuguese.

The discontinuities of the 1490s, *vis-à-vis* the Afro-Eurasian trading networks, were not existential in form. The Portuguese did not establish new networks so much as they seized bases within the old one. In actuality, they attempted to hijack (with only partial success for a limited period of time) a maritime trading system that had been in existence more or less for at least a millennium and a half. Attempts to profit from east–west trade were well-established. The discontinuities introduced by the Portuguese were more a matter of nationality and style. It had not been customary for Europeans to dominate east–west trade routes in the east although southern Europeans and their agents had certainly been active there on an intermittent basis long before the European arrival by sail. The Portuguese also introduced a great deal more Mediterranean-style coercion into the Indian Ocean maritime trade than had been customary.[6]

The coerciveness emulated earlier Italian practices learned in the Christian–Muslim battles over control of the Mediterranean. The rise of the Abbassids had turned the Mediterranean into a Muslim lake, while at the same time, reorienting the trade of the southern Mediterranean populations toward the Indian Ocean. Part of the European expansion at the end of the "Dark Ages" involved the reconquest of territory in the northern Mediterranean littoral that had been occupied by Muslims. Some of this activity took the form of maritime raids, especially in the eastern Mediterranean. The early maritime raiders evolved into maritime traders without discarding the militarization that had been necessary to regain access to the Mediterranean.[7] The early competition among Amalfi, Pisa, Venice, and Genoa for market share and monopolies, as well as their participation in the Crusades as providers of transportation and naval force, reaffirmed the perceived value of militarized, coercive trading patterns. Much later, the Portuguese entered the Indian Ocean market assuming that they would have to break into another Muslim trade monopoly. Therefore, the tactics learned and used a half-millennium earlier in a different context seemed perfectly applicable. But since the context was different (trade in the Indian Ocean operated on different principles than trade in the Mediterranean), the west European way of doing business with non-Europeans proved to be relatively novel. The coercion may also have been necessary given the few commodities the Portuguese had to offer in exchange.

To this short-list of discontinuities amidst a stream of continuities we must also add the Iberian incorporation of the Americas to the Afro-Eurasia network which, among other things, helped to finance the continued participation of the upstart Europeans in a long-distance trade to which they initially had little to offer in exchange aside from the threat of their offshore cannons. But even the incorporation of the Americas was not quite the discontinuity it might seem (unless seen from the perspective of a Caribe, an Aztec, or an Incan). The Iberian integration of the Americas into the old world network was a continuation or extension of the gravity-flow principle that had fueled Afro-Eurasian trade since at least the time of the Han and Roman empires, and no doubt even earlier. The territorial space encompassed by the networks had expanded but it had expanded before. Nor had the governing principles changed quite as much as is sometimes claimed. If all that was needed were guns and sails, US gold and silver would not have become quite as significant to the velocity of Asian trade as it did.

The discontinuities in trading style and nationality nevertheless were real. The Portuguese were not the first to use maritime force in the Indian Ocean but they did initiate a new "Columbian" era of growing European dominance throughout Afro-Eurasia and elsewhere. Initially, this dominance was intermittent and rarely extended beyond the coastline. Gradually, it penetrated deeper. Some 400 years later, Europeans were dominant throughout Afro-Eurasia. Exactly how this took place is not a topic that need be pursued at present. Why Europeans were able to initiate the movement from the periphery to the very center of the system, however, is very much of interest. Moreover, it will be argued that the style in which they did so is critical to an understanding of the ascent of Europe over the rest of the planet. But even this remarkable discontinuity had precedence in the history of the larger Afro-Eurasian political economy. For what the Europeans did was preceded by what the Chinese "almost" did in the half-millennium prior to the 1490s. If it can be shown that earlier developments at one end of Afro-Eurasia were similar in some respects to subsequent developments at the other end, aside from one or two critical differences, it should be possible to develop a better understanding of long-term economic growth processes, the associated historical role of regional international systems, and their interrelationships. It should also be possible to demonstrate just where the 1490s fit in this bigger picture. Chapter 4 continues this examination by focusing on the divergent coevolution of eastern and western Eurasia.

4

THE DIVERGENT
COEVOLUTION OF TWO
EURASIAN REGIONS

From the perspective of a student of international relations an underappreciated part of the "European Miracle" puzzle concerns the very different evolutionary patterns of long-term economic growth patterns, "interstate" politics in east Asia and western Europe, and their interaction.[1] This is not an oblique reference to the oft-mentioned acephalous multipolarity in the west as opposed to the Middle Kingdom's allegedly stultifying unipolarity as one of the critical factors affecting growth probabilities. In fact, both regions tended to cycle in and out of more centralized states of affairs and at various critical times the east Asian region was just as multipolar and acephalous as the western region. Rather, a combination of different ecologies, different centraliz-ation patterns – or at least, different rhythms in the capability concentration patterns, and different prevailing grand strategies led to very different outcomes – one of which was the eventual supremacy of the western region over the eastern region. Yet it was never simply a matter of one region asserting dominance over another region by brute force. Both regions were changing or evolving over the 1500–2000 years in which we are most interested. Their evolutionary paths were not completely independent but they certainly were not parallel either. As they coevolved along different tracks, the conjunction of situational factors and choices made in the east and in the west rendered the western supremacy the more probable development.

The metaphor is far too mechanistic but it is possible to envision an Afro-Eurasian political economy clockwise mechanism, with multiple subsystems of turning gears, some of which were (are) more or less temporarily independent of other components. The speed at which the gears turn in the different subsystems also varied over time, with some subsystems moving quickly at some times and relatively slowly at other times. While all of the subsystems may be affected by either slowdowns or acceler-ations located initially in one part of the mechanism, it is most unlikely that the entire mechanism would move at the same speed. The gears in different subsystems might operate on similar general principles but their structural arrangements are apt to vary, just as the degree to which they are linked to the operation of the whole mechanism is variable.

One area in which the metaphor especially breaks down is the expectation that a collection of loosely synchronized "gears" would be more or less moving in the same direction. However, when the (co)evolution of two or more regions is analyzed, it is better to assume that the subsystems are not evolving in the same direction or along the same path. They might well be but it may be more likely that they are not.[2] Moreover, they may also be operating on different general principles. Or, the interaction of different ecologies, types of actors, distributions of power and so forth may produce very different outcomes and/or diverging trends. Then again, one need not assume that all regions are changing continuously. One may reach a stationary plateau for a period of time while another continues to adapt to environmental flux. The point is that we need to be sure our choice of metaphors does not contaminate our analytical expectations or interpretations.

If Afro-Eurasia was the whole, the parts were located in places such as east Asia, southeast Asia, south Asia, central Asia, the Middle East, Russia, eastern Europe, western Europe, north Africa, east Africa, west Africa, and southern Africa. Each of these regional subsystems has experienced some degree of internal evolution at varying paces. Each subsystem's evolutionary path has been influenced by processes emanating from other regions, adjacent and otherwise. In this fashion, each region may evolve but is also subject to some varying degree of coevolution.

Since the current question is centered on the transition of political-economic and military leadership from east Asia to western Europe, it should come as no surprise to find that most of our attention needs to be focused on the two extreme ends of Eurasia. This is not an outcome dictated by logic. It is perfectly conceivable that the transition needs to be explained in terms of events and processes located in places other than east Asia and western Europe. And, in fact, strong arguments can be made for the pivotal significance at times of activities in the Middle East and central Asia in this story.[3] Nevertheless, some shortcuts must be taken. One shortcut, therefore, amounts to telling less than the full story involving multiple regions. Another involves spending more time on the less familiar east Asian case than on the more familiar west European case. A third shortcut entails simplifying the discussion of the (co)evolutionary patterns to two processes: long-term economic growth and military-political rhythms.

THE EAST ASIAN REGION

The center of east Asian population density was initially associated with relatively insular, agrarian communities organized around major river systems in north China. Economic prosperity, population growth and the diminishment of insularity via expanded trade tended to be associated with periods of imperial centralization. This generalization applies particularly to the regimes imposed by the Han (206 BC–220 AD), Sui/T'ang (589–907), and Sung (960–1279) regimes. Periods of central unification brought peace, order, and attention to infrastructural developments. Population density increased as T'ang China led the rest of the world in urbanization.[4] The expansion of territorial control to the south increased as well but more gradually. After the fifth century, however, the southern and northern regions were increasingly integrated. Grain was replaced by rice as the principal agricultural commodity. An extensive network of canals were constructed by the early seventh century to better move southern products to the north. The circumstances promoting regional economic specialization and exchange were facilitated greatly. The monetization of the economy also proceeded apace. Trade with Persia (seventh century) and the Abbasids (eighth century) expanded China's external maritime contacts and trade volume beyond the earlier high levels established in the Han–Roman era, and unrivaled anywhere else in the world. Even so, T'ang trade retained an overland bias. Nor was the gradual expansion of trade without its interruptions. Trade declined in the ninth century as the T'ang rule, increasingly dependent on Uighur military coercion, decayed after having peaked in the eighth century (Adshead, 1988: 107).

After a period of marked decentralization in tenth-century China, the Sung dynasty forcibly reunited the northern and southern regions. Revolutionary economic growth in the eleventh century, building on the more gradual expansion of the preceding several centuries, characterized much of the Sung regimes.[5] The major agrarian innovation was the 1012 introduction of a strain of Champa rice that permitted a doubling of rice production.[6] Gains in industry were symbolized by levels of iron production that were not matched in Britain's industrial revolution until the late 1780s. Population and urbanization, especially in the south, responded to these new levels of prosperity despite increased conflict with northern Sung's neighbors. Another underlying factor was a marked change in Sung governmental attitudes toward and/or capability to restrain private entrepreneurship. The Sung period is viewed as an unusual interlude in Chinese history in which governmental regulation of, and intervention in, the economic market was indirect, relatively subtle, and highly supportive of commercial interests. Some of this novel approach no doubt reflects the shift in the economic center of gravity to the south and its more commercially oriented élites. Whatever the mix of factors, Lewis (1988: 161) highlights the outcome: "Never before or since in Chinese history were we to see a more maritime commercially oriented government than that of the southern Sung."

The eventual loss of control over northern China by the Sung (1195) actually worked in favor of increased economic modernization and a maritime orientation. Some of the military expenditures associated with the losing defensive effort in the north were no longer needed quite as badly (Adshead, 1988: 114). The significance of maritime commerce was enhanced by the need to compensate for the loss of northern revenues (Lewis, 1988: 130). It was in the increasingly prosperous era of the southern Sung dynasty that governmental revenues from commerce and trade first exceeded agrarian taxes. As described somewhat poetically by Gernet (1982: 328):

> Cut off from access to central Asia, blocked in its expansion towards the north and north-west by the great empires which had arisen on its frontiers, the Chinese world turned resolutely toward the sea. Its centre of gravity shifted toward the trading and maritime regions of the Yangtze and its tributaries. The sea routes starting from the Abbasid empire and connecting

the Persian gulf with India, southeast Asia, and the Chinese coast no doubt also played a part in this call of the sea.

Gernet's center-of-gravity shift had begun long before the loss of the north and even before the advent of the Sung. However, by 1195, geopolitical circumstances practically ensured that a commercial-maritime economic strategy would be pursued vigorously. At the very least, most of the alternatives were no longer available.

The Southern Sung dynasty fell in 1279. Its Mongol successor regime attempted to perpetuate the movement toward economic modernization that it had inherited by continuing some of the Sung practices, but with mixed success. The Mongol conquest resulted in economic and demographic losses. Mongol rule, in turn, altered some of the constituent components of Chinese economic growth. Iron production, for instance, never returned to anything resembling its peak output. Alternatively, the Mongols did encourage foreign trade. But unlike their Sung predecessors, Mongol rule extended throughout central Asia which encouraged an expansion in the volume of overland traffic on the Silk Roads. Coupled with the ongoing maritime commercial expansion, the economic significance of Chinese trade (at home and throughout Eurasia) attained record levels in the twelfth through early fourteenth centuries (Abu-Lughod, 1989). Yet, at the same time, a considerable amount of shipping was destroyed in failed attempts to conquer Japan. Mongol rulers also favored non-Chinese traders over their local competitors to the point that it is argued that Chinese merchants as a whole were impoverished (Elvin, 1973: 217; Eberhard, 1977: 242). Mongol economic management, moreover, led to increased inflation and a discredited paper currency.

The Ming successors to Mongol rule chose not to continue many Sung–Mongol practices. Whether due to an inherent distrust of merchants by the first Ming emperor, the economic devastation caused by Mongol–Ming warfare and the pressing need to reconstruct the agrarian food system, the equally intense need to establish political control and the related need to differentiate Ming from earlier regimes, the need to reduce the power of the southern elite, or, more likely, some combination, the Ming dynasty moved to suppress private trade. Elvin (1973: 216–217) notes that the Sung and Mongol regimes had also attempted to monopolize trade but that in both cases, governmental monopolies had given way to licensing systems. However, Mongol restrictions had been resumed at the expense of Chinese merchant participation in trade. The Ming took this process one step farther and through a chain of prohibitions between 1371 and 1452 managed to totally eliminate legal coastal shipping (while also increasing the volume of smuggling). In doing so, they may have managed to severely aggravate their domestic economic problems (Elvin, 1973: 221). The trade restrictions overlapped with, and could hardly help overcome, a liquidity crisis inherited from the inflation and devaluation of the preceding Mongol era.

Ironically, the Ming dynasty is remembered in particular for the dramatic expansion of Chinese naval power throughout the Indian Ocean in the first third of the fifteenth century. Between 1405 and 1433, seven large fleets were sent as far west as east Africa. But these were governmental fleets operating as part of an initial Ming strategy of military-political expansion. The fleets supported Ming military expansion in Indochina. They greatly expanded the number of tribute missions, an acknowledgement of politico-economic hierarchy and a form of governmental-controlled trade, sent to China from states in southeast and south Asia. They may also have been intended to assist the establishment of greater control over Chinese trading communities scattered throughout southeast Asia. Yet the Ming naval activity ended abruptly after military reversals in Annam and elsewhere as well as severe economic crisis at home. In effect, an expansion strategy was replaced by one of withdrawal and isolation. Any possibility of Chinese maritime hegemony throughout the Indian Ocean and perhaps beyond was ended.

The long-term pattern of economic growth in east Asia, both before and after the fifteenth century, interacted with political-military rhythms. Centralization in China has been characterized by irregular cycles – Han (206 BC–220) , Sui/T'ang (589–907), Northern/Southern Sung (960–1279), Mongol/Yuan (1280–1368), Ming (1368–1644), Manchu (1644–1911). But the point to be emphasized is that these were episodes in Chinese centralization and not necessarily the centralization of all east Asia. During most of these unification bouts, there were independent states to the north in Manchuria and Korea, to the east (Japan), the south (Champa, Annam), and, perhaps most importantly, various types of nomadic groups to the east and north with their own cycles of centralization.

While it is true that the degree of Chinese unification usually had implications for the degrees of freedom enjoyed by adjacent states, we need to be careful not to confuse China with the entire Eurasian eastern region. The degrees of concentration within the region varied just as it did within what became China. For example, the Sung periods and the period immediately preceding the two Sung regimes were notably eras of multistate competition; the Mongol/Yuan period much less so. Nevertheless, the fundamental regional dynamic was not what we tend to think of as one of interstate competition. Instead, the most basic rhythm in the region until the Europeans began to penetrate beyond the coastal fringes of the region in the nineteenth century hinged on relations between and among the nomadic tribes and successive Chinese dynasties.

Barfield has developed the best model of this dynamic, which he (1989: 302) refers to as one "of the oldest cycles of international relationships", lasting as it did from 800 BC through the nineteenth century. Focusing only on two groups in east Asia – the nomadic steppe tribes and the successive dynastic authorities in China – both groups moved in and out of periods of centralization more or less in tandem. The reasons for this interdependence were primarily a mixture of strategy and political economy. The two groups preferred entirely different approaches in both arenas. Nomads specialized in cavalry, mobility, and hit-and-run campaigns. Chinese dynasts defended sedentary agrarian and urban settlements with large armies of infantry expected to respond quickly to frontier attacks. Neither side found it easy to destroy their opponents. The nomads could always withdraw and retreat from infantry attacks. The nomads also had few incentives to conquer the sedentary Chinese. There were a very large number of Chinese to govern and not many nomads. More importantly, nomadic raids constituted a form of economic extraction that was essential to the health of the steppe economy and its inhabitants.

The basic problems were that pastoral resources were limited and could not be stored in reserve like grain or even as readily taxed as agrarian output. Steppe rulers, therefore, needed external sources of financing to fund their political ambitions, just as steppe inhabitants needed external sources of food and weapons. The Chinese could supply these commodities through normal trade and the payment of tribute and thereby minimize the probability of raiding from the steppes. Or, they could try to withhold these goods from the nomads and defeat the consequent raids. It was much less expensive to buy peace with the nomads through tribute than to maintain large numbers of troops engaged in constant warfare along the frontier.[7] Additionally, there was the risk that military commanders might not remain on the frontier and choose instead to overthrow the ruling dynasty or to create a separate kingdom in one of the outlying provinces. While the wisdom of appeasement versus militarized aggression against the nomads was frequently debated in Chinese policy circles, appeasement often prevailed as the more cost-effective strategic preference.[8]

When dynastic control in China disintegrated, the more pacific linkages between the steppe and Chinese political economies disintegrated as well. Conflict among the nomadic tribes, between nomads and the Chinese, and within China could all be expected to increase. When dynastic control in China was reasserted, conflict within China would be gradually suppressed. Conflict between the nomads and China might be minimized if appeasement strategies were pursued consistently. Greater unification of the steppe tribes also became more possible thanks to Chinese subsidization.

The general rule was that the Chinese did not have to fear conquest and subordination from alien steppe rulers. The one exception was the Mongol conquest which began in the usual way – frontier raids after the cessation of appeasement – but mushroomed into something else entirely. That highly significant exception aside, alien rulers were more likely to come from the Manchurian north when weak Chinese dynasts were preoccupied with internal revolts and frontier warfare with steppe tribes.

In retrospect, the Mongolian exception seems to have thrown this well-ingrained, regional dynamic out of kilter. Although the Ming successors to the Mongols were a native Chinese dynasty, successive Ming emperors refused to follow Han, T'ang, and Sung precedent in appeasing (at least intermittently) the steppe nomads. As a consequence, the Ming dynasty "suffered more years of frontier warfare than earlier dynasties" that drained the economic and military resources of the Chinese empire (Barfield, 1989: 231). Indeed, the Ming dynasty made its frontier problems even worse by moving its capital north to Beijing near the border to better symbolize its commitment to the destruction of the nomadic threat.[9] Unfortunately for the Ming, this move only increased their vulnerability to border raids and the expenses associated with attempting to counter the raiding.

Barfield rightly finds the Ming strategy puzzling. Why did they break with traditional common sense? Two answers are advanced by Barfield (1989: 248–249).

One, the Mongol conquest had been so unprecedented and dramatic that Chinese interpretations of the threat posed by nomadic raids had altered. The fear was that history might repeat itself with the reimposition of Mongol rule if the threat was not contained and deterred at the border. A second and related factor may have been an effort to avoid what had happened to the Sung dynasties. Despite considerable appeasement, first the Northern Sung and then the Southern Sung had eventually been overwhelmed by Jurchen and Mongol attacks. Thus, the likelihood of success associated with making extortion payments to the nomads had been significantly devalued.[10]

Another possibility, suggested by Waldron (1994), is that the Ming initially chose to pursue an expansionist policy not only against the Mongols but also in southeast Asia. The failures and draining expenses encountered in the attempts to expand territorial control, coupled with the inability to generate sufficient economic resources to pay for rising military costs, led eventually to a major policy reversal in the mid-fifteenth century. The 1449 Mongol capture of a Ming emperor probably helped to accelerate even further the rethinking of Chinese strategy. Activist attempts at expansion had already given way to a retreat from southeast Asia. In the north, a reversion to the defense of fixed points came to predominate. Later in the sixteenth century, the Ming even returned to a policy of full appeasement in their dealings with the steppe nomads.

In this context, the dramatic retreat from naval supremacy from Korea to east Africa is less curious. It was part of a more comprehensive effort to retrench in the face of external defeats and shocks and internal resource depletion and overextension. The naval expansion had been part of a concerted expansionist effort on the part of the Ming in a number of different theaters. It may also have been motivated initially, in part, by an attempt to outflank the land threat posed by Timur in the early fifteenth century. Not only could some sort of control be extended over the scattered Chinese trading communities outside of China, but there may have been a perceived possibility of an alliance with states in the Middle East who were also threatened by Timur's own expansionary efforts.[11] Moreover, the turmoil in central Asia wrought by Timur disrupted the overland Silk Routes and increased the appreciation for the more southerly maritime routes. Timur's death in 1405 ended both a major military threat and a source of overland trade disruption (Eberhard, 1977: 268). The relative value of naval supremacy in the Indian Ocean would have been depreciated accordingly, especially in the prevailing economic circumstances. State expenditures exceeded revenues, putting a premium on governmental spending that could be curtailed. Trade within China had returned to the routes established by the canal system that had been reopened around 1415, making the maritime routes along the eastern seaboard less important.

This same eastern coast was under attack by Chinese and Japanese pirates who were responding to Ming attempts to impose governmental control over Chinese trade, not unlike the raiding behavior inspired by cutting subsidies to the nomadic tribes along the land frontiers. The Ming response to these maritime raids was to impose further restrictions on Chinese participation in foreign trade, move some portion of the coastal population inland (some eight million between 1437 and 1491 according to Swanson, 1982: 41), and to essentially abandon the coastal areas as still another peg in the overall grand strategy of defensive withdrawal from zones of conflict. Under the circumstances, maintaining an expensive navy had few attractions and fewer adherents.

THE WESTERN EUROPEAN REGION

The evolution of the western European region was characterized by a combination of more and less distinctive processes. One thing very much shared by western Europe and eastern Asia was a dynamic of regional growth predicted on the synergistic exploitation of frontier land, population growth, agrarian productivity increases, urbanization, monetization, and regional and interregional trade. Whereas the northern Chinese moved toward the less-populated south and southeast, population density in western Europe was initially greatest in the southeastern Mediterranean (Greece and Italy) and much later in northwest Europe (McEvedy and Jones, 1978: 31). Between the heydays of Athens and Rome and the medieval emergence of places such as Bruges and Antwerp, there was considerable room for expansion within the region. Forests had to be leveled, marshes drained, and dikes and roads built.

After the instability of the "Dark Ages", due to imperial disintegration, plague, and nomadic invasions, had played itself out over several centuries, long-term economic growth resumed. The local "gears" were accelerating. Population growth could be sustained by incorporating new land and by the adoption of new crop rotation techniques (two crops to three crops) and agricultural technological innovation (for example, the development of plows more suitable to northwest European soil).[12] Urbanization could also be sustained by these agricultural improvements. Urbanization at scattered points throughout the region encouraged the growth of intraregional trade and specialization. Interregional trade and a revolution in maritime commerce was also encouraged by growing demand, technological change, and by taste changes influenced by the Crusades – another manifestation of western Europe's refound expansiveness. Monetization of the economy spread and with it came new incentives and opportunities for state-building as older, feudal arrangements became increasingly obsolete. Feudal levies gave way to standing armies and the need to expand state revenues.

Yet none of these developments were particularly distinctive to western Europe. As Crone (1989: 148) observes:

> To a historian specializing in the non-European world there is something puzzling about the excitement with which European historians hail the arrival of cities, trade, regular taxation, standing armies, legal codes, bureaucracies, absolutist kings and other commonplace appurtenances of civilized societies as if they were unique and self-evident stepping stones to modernity: to the non-European historian they simply indicate that Europe had finally joined the club.

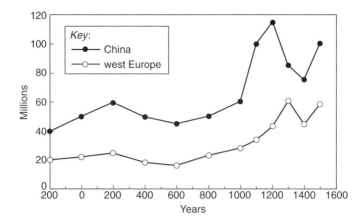

Figure 4.1 Chinese and west European population growth, 200 BC–1500 AD

Crone adopts the appropriate tone here. Rather than emphasize a unique constellation of factors, what is more important is that the typical factors involved in regional growth were accelerating in western Europe in the eleventh and twelfth centuries. The factors were similar to the processes that had facilitated revolutionized economic growth in Sung China. The European development lagged behond those of China but not by all that much. Figure 4.1 helps illustrate this observation by comparing population growth in China and western Europe between 200 BC and 1500 AD. To be sure, the relationship between population and economic growth surges is probably reciprocal and subject to changing signs over time (from positive to negative). All Figure 4.1 can do is suggest the relative timing of local expansion in the two regions. The more numerous Chinese (demonstrated in Figure 4.1 in addition) also enjoyed access to larger markets (at home and abroad) and better technology (paper/printing, junks with rudders, compasses, gunpowder). Yet first-mover advantages last only as long as the innovation momentum is maintained.

As we have seen, the Chinese momentum was not maintained. While it was not quite stopped dead in its tracks, the Mongols and Ming made a number of choices that hardly contributed to the maintenance of the innovation momentum, let alone its renewal. The European momentum also faltered in the fourteenth century but picked up speed again in the second half of the fifteenth century. The second half of the fourteenth and first half of the fifteenth centuries were characterized by the interaction of economic depression, disease, famine, and conflict. The effects of these problems more or less played themselves out by the second half of the fifteenth century which ushered in a new phase of reinvigorated European expansion (in population growth, urbanization, and commerce) that led directly to the dramatic events of the 1490s.

The political-military concentration process worked differently in western Europe than in eastern Asia. Ecology and disease may have made territorial unification less likely in western Europe. Jones (1981) argues that the European environment helps explain why such things as income equality, epidemic rates, fertility practices, and the inter-state system were different in Europe than in the rest of Eurasia. Adshead (1988: 61) suggests that the Chinese imperial reconcentration under the Sui and T'ang was more likely because eastern Asia experienced less plague after the decline of the Han than western Europe experienced after the decline of Rome. Some definite European reconcentration was accomplished in the Carolingian era (751–987), but it was noticeably short-lived. After Charlemagne and his grandsons, the usual interpretation is one of a region that gradually splintered into literally hundreds of independent jurisdictions. That is not say that efforts were not made to unify western Europe but the early efforts tended to be either unsuccessful or partial. An example is the consolidation of France from an initial Capetian control of territory around Paris to a set of boundaries in the mid-fifteenth century that approximated Charles the Bald's (one of Charlemagne's heirs) western Francia in the tenth century (Ladurie, 1987: 33–34). Reconcentration efforts were certainly at work. However, conditions (ecology, royal poverty, feudal levies) favored a smaller scale and a slower pace that was not to pick up until after the 1490s.

Aside from the Hapsburg exception of the mid-to-late sixteenth century, it was only much later that serious efforts to coercively reunite western Europe were attempted. Napoleon and Hitler, for brief periods of time, were able to replicate earlier Roman and Carolingian boundaries. Thus a high degree of multipolarity prevailed in European international relations with at least two consequences. One was an increasingly intensive dynamic of military competition among the units which led to the development of increasingly powerful states (Rasler and Thompson, 1989; Tilly, 1990) differentiated, in part, by evolving constitutions distributing internal political power in various ways depending on the circumstances of domestic political combat and the resources available to different types of actors. A second consequence had to do with a trend toward fewer independent actors as the winners of wars and clever royal marriages expanded the extent of their territorial control. The major qualification to this trend toward fewer actors was the survival of small sea powers and merchant republics that occupied niches on the Mediterranean, Atlantic, and Baltic coasts. If they had emerged in another region, the probability of their survival would have been much lower. In western Europe, they not only survived, they also thrived. Moreover, their survival/success had important implications for reversing Europe's longtime peripheral and dependent position within the Afro-Eurasia economy. Their survival/success also created a basic dualism (land versus sea powers) in European regional geopolitics that was to lead to a distinctive type of regional power balancing. The outcome of this balancing dynamic that began to emerge in 1494 (but especially after 1580), in turn, facilitated the perpetuation of European multipolarity for nearly 500 years.

Comparing the two regions and their coevolution

Four interrelated factors thus help explain why the Chinese lost their lead to the west Europeans and/or why the west Europeans gained the lead:

1   the Mongols;,
2   the development of a relatively unusual type of aggressive trading state in the Mediterranean;
3   the differences in the basic international dynamics of western Europe and eastern Asia;
4   the choices made by successive Ming rulers.

The Mongol conquests were spectacular in their scope. Their impacts were also different in various parts of Eurasia. The area around Baghdad, for instance, was devastated thereby ensuring the unlikelihood of a resurgence of relative capability in the eastern Fertile Crescent area. In east Asia and especially in China, the devastation and loss of life was severe but not so great that the losses could not be made up. But unlike other parts of Eurasia, the decline of the Mongol regime did not mean the end of the Mongol problem for Chinese rulers. Ming grand strategy was fixated on resolving the enduring Mongol threat. Appeasement, for a long time, was out of the question. So, too, was any latitude for independent power bases as represented by Chinese merchants participating in Afro-Eurasia trade networks. To a great degree, the fifteenth-century Ming retrenchment and isolationist tendencies revolved around the failure to solve the problems of reestablishing indigenous dynastic control after the Mongols had been forced out of China but not far enough to no longer pose a continuing threat. That initial Ming attempts at expanding their control over both territory and economic activities only made their position more difficult goes without saying. But while Ming preferences in grand strategy were not inevitable, they were made more probable by the distinctive nature of sedentary nomadic interactions in eastern Asia as well as by their need to overcome the trauma of Mongol rule. Ironically, just as the development of encircling, non-Chinese empires had earlier increased the probability of Sung China developing its maritime-commercial potential, the lingering impact of the dramatic successes of one of those nomadic groups increased the probability of China turning inward.

In the west, the Mongol impact was threefold. First, the Mongols failed to extend their rule farther west than Hungary. Most of Europe, therefore, was spared the direct impact of Mongol rule. It could remain considerably decentralized despite the earlier successes of the Romans and Carolingians. Decentralization would prove to be a mixed advantage but its most important feature is often underappreciated. Decentralization meant that it was possible for small trading states that were controlled by traders and not the usual landed warrior aristocracies to not only survive but also to flourish. States such as Venice, Genoa, and later, the United Provinces of the Netherlands were able to establish and maintain niches for a much longer period of time than was possible anywhere else in Afro-Eurasia. The normal pattern, as exemplified by the Phoenician experience, was for successful trading city states to be absorbed by adjacent empires. After absorption, trade might or might not be tolerated but merchants could no longer operate as autonomous entities. They were now subject to imperial preferences and fortunes, with trading interests subordinated to imperial interests.

Venice, Genoa, Portugal (an unusual hybrid involving landed aristocracies who heavily engaged in and were, therefore, favorable to trade) and the Netherlands were all overrun eventually by adjacent land powers.[13] But they were not overrun before they were able to provide a solid European link to the Afro-Eurasian long-distance trade network. In this process, they were aided initially by the Mongol conquests which, for about a century, enabled the overland Silk Roads to function unusually well. Venice and Genoa were able to tap into this development via the Black Sea and transport the commodities for distribution throughout the European region. In this fashion, western Europe was able to benefit almost directly by exposure to the impact of Chinese prosperity. Venice and, to a lesser extent, Genoa were also able to tap into the southern maritime routes to the Indian Ocean via the Crusader enclaves in Palestine and by arrangement with the Mamluks in Cairo. Not only long-distance trade commodities were brought into western Europe. Critical technological innovations were also borrowed although exactly how these adoptions took place is not entirely clear. But there is simply too much coincidence in the timing of Chinese innovations and their subsequent appearance in the Mediterranean to be entirely a matter of independent invention.[14]

Portugal imitated the Venetian–Genoese model of coercive trade monopolies that, in turn, had evolved in the polarized climate of Muslim–Christian hostility in the eastern Mediterranean (after the seventh century). The Portuguese were beneficiaries of Genoese investment and knowledge as a consequence of the Genoese turn towards the western Mediterranean, partially as an outcome of the Venetian victory over Genoa for trading hegemony in the eastern Mediterranean. The Portuguese also copied the strategies of the Genoese in attempting to cut the Egyptian middlemen out of east–west trade. When they eventually found a new route to the Indian Ocean, they introduced the coercive Venetian–Genoese model to the very heart of maritime commerce in the Afro-Eurasia economy at a propitious time. At the end of the fifteenth century, there was no real competition for maritime dominance in the Indian Ocean. There had been earlier and there would be later. The Portuguese found a window of opportunity and exploited it ruthlessly as long as they could until their own position in Asia was usurped by the Dutch.

The story of successive European maritime-commercial dominance in the Indian Ocean and Asia, and their growing power *vis-à-vis* the traditional land powers of Asia need not be retold here. Suffice it to say that the traditional Asian land powers declined and disintegrated at varying rates while the Europeans grew even more capable of penetrating beyond the coasts, thanks ultimately to continued technological innovation and asymmetrical exchange relations. Yet it is not the case that the traditional land powers missed out entirely on the new innovations available throughout Eurasia. Rather, they chose to apply them differently. For instance, Hodgson (1993: 26) notes that the Ottomans, the Safavids, and the Moghuls all built their gunpowder empires around a singular Chinese invention. But by applying gunpowder to territorial conquest purposes, they effectively turned their backs on the Indian Ocean and long-distance trade precisely at the time when some Europeans were employing Chinese inventions to expand into the Indian Ocean. Ottoman,

Safavid, and Moghul choices, in addition to those of the Mongols and the Ming, thereby made European maritime expansion easier. This is another story of regional subsystems that coevolve while evolving along different trajectories.

Nevertheless, the most critical significance of the development of the European trading states is that they were political units controlled by commercial interests and not simply places where commerce was tolerated intermittently. The intervention of government into economic affairs can be either beneficial or detrimental to economic prosperity. What happened in China was that non-commercial interests and considerations ultimately triumphed after the fall of the Southern Sung.[15] The Sung state, itself, was not a state in which merchant interests dictated state policy. But the explosive growth of the Sung era seems to have caught more conservative élites off guard. It was a runaway process that they could not control very well even though some efforts were made to do so. Once underway, Sung élites, especially in the south, became increasingly wedded to the idea of promoting commercial interests because their own prosperity depended upon it. Indeed, one of the reasons the Ming capital was moved north may have been partially motivated by the desire to distance the political center from the more commercially oriented élites that had survived the Mongol conquest (Adshead, 1988: 176). What might have happened in the absence of the Ming dynasty can only be speculated about; but all commentators are agreed that the Ming era was unusually successful at throttling economic growth. That was not the intent but it certainly was the outcome of efforts to centralize political and economic control.

Other parts of Afro-Eurasia were quite familiar with vigorous merchant activity and even with states that favored or at least tolerated merchant activity. Blaut (1992: 25) is correct in noting that "small mercantile-maritime cities and city-states dotted the coasts of the Indian Ocean and South China Seas like pearls on a string". But he is wrong to conclude that this string of pearls operated on western European principles.

Where Asian ports (for instance, Malacca) enjoyed some degree of autonomy, their rulers were comparatively passive (compared to their western European counterparts). By and large, they did not use force to improve their competitive position; nor did they have much naval capability to apply to such undertakings (Pearson, 1987: 81). A few Asian maritime empires were developed (the Cholas in southern India and Srivijaya in Indonesia) but the scope of their control was limited and they may have been too dependent on the absence of Chinese direct involvement to survive past the twelfth century (Das Gupta, 1987: 241–242).

The problem elsewhere was that governmental favoritism or tolerance was intermittent (see Kathirithamby-Wells, 1993; Thomaz, 1993). Merchants often were sets of foreigners (for example, Karamis, Gujeratis, Chinese) living in port-city enclaves and interacting with diasporas of co-"nationals" scattered throughout the trading networks. The attention of rulers could easily be diverted by political and military matters and crises that were given higher priority. Contrastingly, in trading states in which traders constituted the primary political élite, it was far more difficult to relegate trade to a secondary priority. It was also less probable that governmental intervention in the economic sphere would have negative effects for long without serious attempts being made to alter the harmful policies or to remove the policy-makers.

A prominent example of the problems encountered by merchants is the story of the Karamis, a society of Muslim merchants who dominated much of the trade in the western Indian Ocean. Despite the reputation of Islam as a culture unusually receptive to merchant interests thanks, in part, to Mohammed's commercial career, the Karami network was abruptly destroyed by a 1429 Mameluke decision to assert monopoly control of the pepper trade (Bouchon and Lombard, 1987: 61).

Another case in point was the Mughal Empire. Pearson (1991) argues convincingly that the Mughal Empire was too great in area, population, and resources for rulers to become much interested in matters of long-distance trade.

> The whole mind-set of the Mughal emperors and their nobles was land-based. Prestige was a matter of controlling vast areas on which were located fat, meek peasants. Glory was to be won by campaigns on land, leading one's contingent of cavalry, galloping over the plains. To courtiers, including the emperors, the sea was a marvel, a curiosity, a freak. This was not an arena where power and glory were to be won.
>
> (Pearson, 1991: 96)

Mughal emperors might not interfere in Indian merchant activities, but they were unlikely to help them much either because they could see few incentives to do so as long as their revenue base continued to be land-bound. One consequence was that Indian and other Asian port cities were often dominated by nonindigenous merchant networks who enjoyed considerable autonomy and low customs duties. What they lacked was access to the state's coercive capabilities. In contrast, as Pearson (1991: 77) notes, the rulers of states that are relatively poor in resources and small in size and population have little choice but to pay close attention to trade. This is all the more true if there was little difference in identity between rulers and merchants. These conditions prevailed initially only in the Italian and Hanseatic city states where "Europe's most distinctive social types [warrior-merchants] first appeared" (Brady, 1991: 123). Genoa and Venice constituted early exemplars. Their practices diffused slowly to the western maritime periphery of Europe (Portugal, the Netherlands, and England), although in each of these three cases, civil wars had to be fought and won before the adoption of the Italian practices could be implemented with state backing.

Table 4.1 summarizes the nature of this particular part of the argument. Maritime states with naval capability could be found throughout the southern littoral of Eurasia, but only intermittently. After 1000 AD they became a constant along the periphery of western Europe. While one maritime power usually led the others, the leader always had competition at sea so that if the leader declined, challengers were prepared to take the fallen leader's place. Indigenous merchants were also widely distributed, except in southeast Asia. It was pro-merchant governments and supportive policies that were particularly prevalent in western Europe, or, more

Table 4.1 The presence or absence of certain critical factors in the transition of economic growth leadership from east to west

Regions	Maritime states	Indigenous merchants	Pro-Merchant governments
Southeast Asia	Episodically (Srivijaya)	Few	Limited
India	Episodically (Cholas)	Some but likely to be identified with one part of Indian trading networks (for example, Gujerati)	Limited
China	Episodically (Sung, Yuan, Ming)	Present but with variable influence	Only in Southern Sung
Middle East	Episodically (Fatimid)	Present but with variable influence	Intermittent
Western Europe	Present (most noticeably in Genoa, Venice, Portugal, the Netherlands, and Britain)	Present with great influence in some states	Present in several states

precisely, in certain European locations. Examples could be found elsewhere on an intermittent basis at best. Only in Sung China, and especially Southern Sung China, and the merchant republics and pro-merchant kingdoms of western Europe could one find governments prepared to encourage a mixture of private and public participation in Afro-Eurasian trade, with force if necessary.

Therefore, it is not so much that western Europe was characterized by multiple political units. It was, but this had its advantages and liabilities. Since some of the units were relatively small and weak, it was more probable that some rulers would find themselves forced to exchange privileges for resources in order to survive (Pearson, 1991; Blockmans, 1994). But lesser degrees of autocracy in some corners of Europe were countered by the high degree of deadly competitiveness implicit to a multipolar system in which the trend was toward creating larger-scale and better-armed units to best survive and prosper in the intensely competitive environment. Other things being equal, the small and weak states should not have survived. Many did not. Nevertheless, what is particularly distinctive about western Europe is that it proved possible for a few small states strongly oriented toward trade to not only survive but also to prosper out of all proportion to their resource base.

Lest there be some misinterpretation, it is worth emphasizing that this is not a monocausal argument about trade-driven growth. On the contrary, trade requires supply and demand. It responds, therefore, to the expansion/decay of populations, urbanization, and prosperity. For local growth to be maximized, however, it needs to be linked to wider arenas through trade and exchange. Innovation also makes trade more probable and trade makes innovation more probable. Local growth chances are normally improved if they are exposed to external ideas and technological advances, especially if outside technology is more advanced than that which prevails within the local system or subsystem. In this respect, it is not trade *per se* that is critical. Rather, some types of trade functioned as innovating, leading sectors for economic growth in the period before the nineteenth century, and at least back to the tenth century.[16] The complete reverse situation is exemplified by systems that attempt to turn their backs on the outside world (Ming) or to withdraw temporarily to develop independently of the outside world (the late Soviet Union). Western Europe of the late fifteenth century needed to improve its linkage to the rest of Afro-Eurasia (and the Americas) if it was to maintain its regained momentum toward expansion. By improving those linkages, domestic growth trajectories were more likely to be optimized. And the states that led the way in improving those linkages found their growth prospects to be optimized best of all, albeit for finite periods of time.

Interestingly, this argument overlaps but also differs significantly from one attributed to Karl Marx. Palin (1992: 103–105) argues that Marx's perspective on the rise of Europe entailed a conjuncture between an emerging world market and the dynamics of the European periphery. Europe came out on top because it created a world market by discovering new sea routes. Without this world market, the capitalist mode of production dynamics found in the European periphery (Spain, Portugal, Holland, England, France) would have remained peripheral to other economic practices throughout the world. But the world market would have disappeared without the capitalistic practices and the fact that capital accumulation continued in different parts of Europe. When one center fell, another arose, with "each new center drawing upon an arsenal of innovating practices its predecessors had been developing, adding a distinct element of its own" (Palin, 1992: 105).

This last line can be endorsed fully with the caveat that Marx did not have the actor sequence quite right. The sequence began in Sung China and migrated to Genoa and Venice before moving to the far western periphery of Portugal, the Netherlands, and England. Spanish and French governmental orientations, on the other hand, often came closer to resembling the long-distance trade attitudes of the Asian land empires than they did those of some of their trading state neighbors. Marx was right to emphasize the significance of a periphery of Europe as opposed to Europe as a whole. He was wrong to think that European maritime expansion could be equated with the creation of a world market. The Afro-Eurasian world market long preexisted the development of the European periphery. So, too, did capitalistic practices. Nonetheless, their linkage has been fateful for political-economic developments of the past 500 years.

Equally critical to the argument being constructed here is that the development of independent trading states oriented primarily toward profiting in long-distance trade and avoiding entanglements in Europe whenever possible led to the development of a basic dualism in the European region. On the one hand, there were a few, small, externally oriented, sea powers that tended toward republican political principles. There were also a number of the more familiar large, land powers attempting to expand their territorial control within the region and favoring autocratic political constitutions when circumstances permitted. The onset of this dualism established a basic regional international relations dynamic that characterized western Europe international relations for much of the post-sixteenth-century era. Pitting sea powers specializing in long-distance trade against land powers specializing in territorial expansion, this fairly distinctive regional dynamic evolved into a fundamental dynamic of world politics. As a dynamic, it shares a great deal in common with the east Asian sedentary nomadic dynamic.[17] But the sea versus land power dynamic was gaining momentum as the sedentary nomad interaction was evolving into secondary importance. Not coincidentally, the ascendancy of western Europe was also gaining momentum while the salience of eastern Asia was declining.

"Balance of power" politics were not distinctive to western Europe. But the specific nature of the balancing process, dependent as it was on the ability by sea powers to introduce extraregional resources in order to thwart regional hegemonies by conventional, centralizing land powers may well have been distinctive to a particular time and place.[18] The "western question" (Black, 1994b), whether a single state would be permitted to control all of western Europe, was contested repeatedly. The 1494 French assault on Italy inaugurated the process.[19] The blocking efforts of a coalition of powers, but especially Castile and Aragon, also became a regular component, just as the French–Spanish (or Valois–Hapsburg) duel illustrated the struggle over regional dominance. Between 1494 and 1945, Habsburg Spain, France, and Germany were the primary challengers for regional hegemony. By the end of the sixteenth century, the nature of maritime-led opposition (the Netherlands and Britain) to these periodic attempts to concentrate resources in Europe had become equally clear.

The global war conflicts of 1494–1517, 1580–1609, 1688–1713, 1792–1815, and 1914–1945 were initially about control of western Europe. Over time and in accord with the gradual ascendance of the western European region to the position of the principal region of significance, these regional contests increasingly became struggles for control not only for European territory, but also for control of the old world economy. The rise of western Europe and the development of its fundamental conflict axis (maritime powers opposing regional unification by land powers) are thus very much interrelated. The development of the maritime powers provided the essential linkage of a peripheral but expansive Europe to the center of the Afro-Eurasian world economy. That same linkage enabled western Europe, or leading parts of it, to first benefit from the growth revolution pioneered in Sung China and, later, to seize the leadership in long-term economic growth when successors to the Sung "miracle" made the wrong choices. Moreover, the linkages connecting Europe to the rest of the world also strongly influenced the primary regional pattern of conflict that emerged subsequently.

What we have come to think of as "normal" patterns of competitive international relations, as well as the long cycle of global politics thus are very much tied to complicated and coevolving processes of long-term economic growth and dynamics of regional international relations that encompass two millennia. These processes thrust Sung China into the lead toward the end of the tenth century. Some of these same processes facilitated the Ming capitulation of that lead in the fifteenth century and the earlier transition of the principal source of long-term economic growth in a westward direction where circumstances were comparatively more favorable. But it is an error to think that conditions were more favorable throughout western Europe. They were not. Rather, they were most favorable in places that were able to continue the growth strategy discovered in Sung China 1000 years ago: the harnessing of local growth spirals with external trade networks and the wider resource base made available by that medium.

As the Italian city states and Portugal demonstrated, it was not necessary to control the domestic growth spiral within one's own boundaries as long as it was possible to become the main conduit to the external trade network. More recently, domestic growth spirals in industrial goods have become even more critical than they once were. The basic long-term growth process may have experienced another discontinuity of sorts in the late eighteenth century but it is not one that drastically alters the overall or long run nature of the process. It continues to be a matter of harnessing internal sources of growth to external ones. What has changed is that it is no longer possible to be the leader of the world political economy if the basis for economic leadership is restricted to carrying goods throughout the long-distance network. The Genoese, the Venetians, the Portuguese, and the Dutch enjoyed a transitional interlude in long-term growth processes that has returned in some ways to the time when China produced more silk than the rest of the world. But that transitional interlude was critical to the realignment of economic power in Afro-Eurasia that we have come to associate too narrowly with the dramatic decade of the 1490s.

CONCLUSION

There is no need to depict the 1490s as if it were a decade like any other. Too many dramatic things happened. But the question is whether the 1490s should be seen as the beginning of the ascent of Europe and the advent of capitalism on a world-wide scale. The answer is probably not. What happened in the 1490s was that some west Europeans found a more direct way to participate in the Afro-Eurasian world economy. In the process of doing so, they introduced a greater degree of coercion to maritime, long-distance trade than had been customary. But the capitalistic practices were not novel to the long-distance trade networks. On the contrary, the Europeans acquired their capitalistic techniques from the long-distance network, not the other way around. They did extend the reach of the old world economy to encompass resources from the Americas. They also made it much more likely, thanks to their

THE ASCENDANCE OF WESTERN EUROPE

aggressive coercion, timing, and sustained momentum, that the west European region
would become wealthier and more technologically advanced than other regions.
These are all important changes. Yet their development and impact was more gradual
than an emphasis on the discontinuities of the 1490s suggests.

The system of interregional political economy did not change so much as it began
to realign around a new center. But, with the advantage of hindsight, this realignment
process could be said to have begun with the fall of the Southern Sung and the shift
westward in innovation-driven, long-term economic growth. Once initiated by the
Sung dynasty, realignment became a fairly regular occurrence with the "torch"
passing from Northern Sung to Southern Sung, and then on to Genoa, Venice,
Portugal, the Netherlands, Britain, and, most recently, the United States. The torch
was passed not due to some mystical east–west predestination. Growth leadership
moved from one place where circumstances worked against maintaining the leadership in economic growth to places that were more receptive to the development of
radical innovations.

In the thirteenth century that meant that the growth leadership would move from
southern China to the Mediterranean receptivity of the merchant republics (Genoa
and Venice) and then on to the Atlantic, focusing first on one side (Portugal, the
Netherlands, and Britain) before crossing the ocean to the United States. Whether the
migration of the leadership in economic growth continues to migrate across the
Pacific will depend on the same fundamental conditions that governed the earlier
transitions: the gradual development of less receptivity to innovation in the incumbent center combined with the development of greater receptivity, in conjunction
with other appropriate preconditions, somewhere else in the global network.

The range of factors that can influence the timing and direction of these shifts in
growth leadership is great. They are a mix of endogenous and exogenous variables and
circumstances. Yet, in some respects, they can be reduced to how societies respond to
the opportunities implicit to this process of transitory leadership. Adams (1974: 249)
has observed that "the need to adapt to shifts [in patterns of symbiosis, predation, and
domination] probably constitutes the most overwhelming selective pressure to which
societies are exposed". As we have seen, some groups made the wrong choices if they
were to retain leadership. Other groups made equally wrong choices if they were to
seize the lead. Still other groups made the right choices in this 1000-year-old process
that continues to determine the structure of the world's political economy. In every
case, the choices were heavily conditioned by contexts that made some choices
more probable than others. The outcome of these serial choices, in turn, has created
a political-economic context that influences behavior on an increasingly planetary-
wide scale.

Where one sees breakpoints in these processes depends, in part, on when one sees
the processes beginning. While long-distance trade, episodic economic growth
leaderships, and even sea/land power dualisms can be traced back in time over 5000
years (Gills and Frank, 1993), it is less clear that a case for process continuity over the
very long haul can be sustained. On the other hand, it is possible to demonstrate
empirically a consistent pattern emerging around 1000 AD that has been maintained

for 18–19 waves of innovation-driven, economic growth. Closely related to the long wave pattern is the consequent leads in not only economic but also in political and military spheres that some states capture for periods of time. Another hallmark of the process is the periodic systemic crises and wars that are brought about by the destabilizing consequences of economic and political-military realignments. From this viewpoint, the real watershed took place nearly 1000 years ago. What has happened since has come to resemble essentially more of the same, albeit subject to important trends in technological sophistication, violence, commercialization, and complexity.

5

THE MILITARY
SUPERIORITY THESIS

One of the more intriguing historical and theoretical questions is how was it possible for an area often considered to be a peripheral backwater, rightly or wrongly, such as western Eurasia, to ascend to a predominant position over the rest of the world between around 1500 and 1900? One succinct answer is suggested by Geoffrey Parker (1988/1996: 154):

> [The] . . . sustained preoccupation of European states with fighting each other by land and sea had at length paid handsome dividends. Thanks above all to their military superiority, founded upon the military revolution of the sixteenth and seventeenth centuries, the Western nations had managed to create the first global hegemony in History.

The answer is extremely parsimonious. The West was able to conquer the rest of the world thanks primarily to its edge in military technology. This edge had begun to emerge as early as the sixteenth century due, in turn, to the intensive warring propensities of the region. The appeal of such an apparently simple explanation is undeniable, even though Parker's explanation is actually less simple than it appears at first blush. Moreover, the evident appeal is bolstered by the fact that western actors often did enjoy, and sometimes did so in ways that were demonstrated quite dramatically, various forms of military superiority over non-European opponents. The problem lies not so much in determining whether one side had military superiority or not. Rather, the real question is how much credit should be given to military technological advantages in accounting for the rise of the West. The military superiority thesis bestows explanatory primacy on one side's coercive advantage. While we need to be careful to avoid dismissing altogether the relevancy of coercive advantages, it is doubtful that European military might explains quite as much as the proponents of the thesis would have us believe. At best, military superiority was only one of several important factors. But it can also be argued that some of these other factors actually were more critical to the ascendancy of western Eurasia.

Other factors include most prominently the relative vulnerability of the targets of expansion, the interrelated need for local allies to make military victories on land possible, and the evolution of a global political economy structured increasingly to favor European interests. In the absence of local political vulnerabilities and allies, it is most improbable that European military advantages would have sufficed in the 1500–1800 period. If both of these factors were essential to establishing facilitative contexts for the exercise of coercive advantages, target vulnerability and local allies are at least as important, if not more so, than military superiority. If it can also be demonstrated that in some cases the military superiority exhibited by the Europeans was not due to early modern revolutions in military technology, the military superiority interpretation will have been shown to require even further discounting. Finally, an emphasis on one side's coercive edge in acquiring territorial control tends to overlook the macroevolution of a global political economy increasingly dominated by some western Europeans. Ultimately, this macroevolution is a more pivotal key to the finite ascendancy of the European region within the world economy than is military superiority.

After clarifying the nature of the military superiority thesis, and, in particular, Geoffrey Parker's (1988/1996) version, five important cases (Portuguese imperial expansion in the fourteenth–seventeenth centuries, the Spanish conquests of the Aztecs and the Incas, the Dutch involvement in Indonesia, and the British involvement in India) are reviewed with an eye toward assessing the comparative roles and significance of European military superiority, target vulnerability, local alliances, and global political economy evolution. The general impression that emerges from these quick case reviews is that European military superiority was clearly not the key variable in accounting for the emergence of the European region to military, political, economic and cultural predominance in the world system. Military superiority, at best, was only one of several interactive factors and, by itself, has quite limited explanatory powers. Moreover, too much emphasis on military superiority detracts from our ability to juggle systematically the multiple factors at play in the ascendance of western Europe and, potentially, other regions in the world system.

PARKER'S MILITARY SUPERIORITY THESIS

A large number of people have written about early modern European military revolutions. This is not the place to either review this material, question the utility of its revolutionary conceptualization, or challenge its various periodizations and claims about specific weapons systems. Suffice it to say that analysts continue to debate whether and how changes in military technology impacted upon early modern Europe.[1] However, the extension of some of these arguments to the ascendancy of Europeans over non-Europeans has been subject to considerably less dispute. One reason is that a strong articulation of the thesis appeared only fairly recently in the form of Geoffrey Parker's (1988/1996) *The Military Revolution: Military Innovation and the Rise of the West, 1500–1800*. Most of Parker's critics so far seem to be more comfortable focusing on European materials. Another reason for less resistance is that the military superiority idea seems anything but counterintuitive. How else can we explain small numbers of Europeans defeating large numbers of non-Europeans?

They must have been militarily superior to win or else they would have been over-whelmed by their numerically superior opponents. The Europeans must have had better weapons or, as it was described (erroneously) in a recent *Newsweek* article: "168 Spaniards under Francisco Pizarro could, in 1532, massacre an army of 80,000 Incas . . . [because] the Europeans had steel swords, horses, ships, and writing, and they carried germs like smallpox." (Begley, 1997:47).

The above passage caricatures unintentionally the extreme version of the military superiority thesis (even though acknowledging certain nonmilitary advantages). Eighty thousand Incas were not massacred in 1532. It is inconceivable that 168 Spaniards could have massacred so many Incas at one time with the weaponry then at their disposal. They were able to massacre several thousand unarmed Incas while the rest of the Inca army watched, and therein lies an interesting analytical problem. There is no puzzle in how a few heavily armed people could surprise and kill a large number of unarmed people in a confined space. The real question is how did they get away with it in the presence of a large and hostile armed force. The answer, it will be argued, has less to do with the coercive advantages of the sixteenth-century Spanish conquistador and more to do with Inca political vulnerabilities.

Nonetheless, Parker does not argue that 168 Spaniards massacred 80,000 Incas. We need to first outline just what it is that he does argue before proceeding to the development of a counterargument. The following four statements may be said to summarize economically the portion of the Parker thesis which is most at stake in advancing a military superiority explanation of European ascendancy.

1   In the sixteenth century, western Europeans revolutionized the way they conducted their warfare. On land, gunpowder-based weaponry and one of its consequences, the *trace italienne* artillery fortress, increasingly determined how battles and sieges were fought and who won them. Another consequence, large standing armies characterized by organizational and tactical discipline, also evolved in the Europeans' military favor. At sea, sailing ships with the increasing ability to fire on opponents at some distance assumed the ability to control strategic sea lanes.

2   Western Europeans utilized these military advantages against non-Europeans to compensate for their inferiority in relative population size and natural resources. Ottoman expansion was resisted successfully (sixteenth and seventeenth cen-turies). European control was extended gradually over the Americas (sixteenth through eighteenth centuries), Siberia and most of Indonesia (seventeenth century), and much of India and parts of coastal Africa (eighteenth century). Whereas small groups of Europeans were able to bring about the abrupt collapse of two powerful empires in the first half of the sixteenth century, western Europeans had little impact in India until after the 1740s' rapid improvement in military methods.

3   Nineteenth-century improvements in weaponry (rapid-firing guns and armored steamships), facilitated by the Industrial Revolution, and the acquisition of Indian population resources enabled the Europeans to overcome the last

effective resistance in east Asia. While China and Japan, unlike much of the rest of the non-European world, had been especially attentive and receptive to European military innovations when the Europeans had first arrived, the receptivity had been due to concurrent domestic instability and the premium placed on improving military capabilities. Once domestic stability was restored, the military innovations were marginalized handicapping China and Japan's ability to resist European incursions in the nineteenth century.

4   European dominance then was primarily a function of western innovations in military technology and the failure of non-westerners to adopt that technology quickly enough to offset the resulting military imbalance.

Obviously, Parker's military superiority argument is not without major caveats. He does not argue that western Europeans invented new weapons around 1500 and after and then proceeded to sally forth and conquer the rest of the world. For that matter, Parker (1988/1996: 132) does not even argue that the Europeans were particularly interested in conquest and describes it as anachronistic to think otherwise.[2] He recognizes that the Europeans had considerable trouble in their own Mediterranean backyard with the Ottomans. In the fifteenth through seventeenth centuries, the European–Ottoman confrontation might be called something of a draw. Parker is also well aware that the European expansion was a gradual affair, with the Europeans, by and large, restricted to small fortress-protected enclaves on the coasts of Afro-Eurasia for several hundred years. Stunningly quick victories in Mexico and Peru were not repeated elsewhere, even in the Americas where European-induced diseases played so prominent a role in decimating the Amerindian population. European territorial control in Africa, India, and Indonesia took several hundred years to happen. East Asia proved to be the hardest nut to crack militarily and that effort depended on an intervening industrial revolution.

Given these many and careful qualifications, it might well be asked how could such a nuanced argument possibly be challenged? The answer is that the crux of the problem with the military superiority thesis is not concerned with: (1) the West's possession of some forms of military superiority or; (2) the timing of western expansion. Rather, it rests with the weight of military superiority in the explanatory balance. Most, if not all, analysts would certainly accept that other factors had significance as well. The main problem with the military superiority thesis is that its proponents argue that an edge in coercive technology and organization was the most important factor.[3] That is a far more debatable proposition than whether the Europeans enjoyed some military advantages and sometimes exploited the advantage in conjunction with other factors.

There is a standard methodology in the social sciences for such questions about the relative weighting of multiple explanatory factors. Ideally, the analyst collects information on cases that vary in outcome and that also vary in terms of the mix of explanatory factors that are relatively present or absent in each case. Then it becomes a reasonably straightforward matter of determining relative weights for each explanatory factor through some form of statistical analysis assuming, of course, a sufficient number of cases and an adequate ability to measure the factors that are thought to be important.

The problem in explaining the gradual expansion of western Eurasia's predominance is that there is little variance on the y-variable (the outcome that is to be explained) and not much variance on the military superiority variable. European encounters with non-European groups did not always lead immediately to a European victory, but eventually the outcome did tend overwhelmingly to favor the Europeans. The question then becomes what is the appropriate unit of analysis? Do we examine every battle and attempt to control such factors as terrain, specific weapons involved, tactical errors, overconfidence/timidity, luck and so forth? Or do we take specific areas or zones such as, say, south Asia for X number of years and code the outcome at the end of said X number of years?

The answers to these methodological questions are not self-evident and, even if they were, we might still have reason to pause before undertaking a highly rigorous analysis. Assuming we could take care of the lack of variance in the outcome variable, there remains the question of how to code military superiority. Does any military superiority count? If the Europeans frequently had uncontested naval superiority does that suffice to explain how they were able to defeat larger armies on land? If European steel swords beat non-European wooden clubs in combat, does that support a thesis that early modern European military revolutions were responsible for the rise of the West? Or do we need to find very specific links between the early modern military revolutions and the victories in the non-European theaters?

Finally, even if we could resolve the X and Y variable coding problems, there remains the problem of theory. The military superiority argument is really a hypothesis that a certain factor deserves primacy in the explanatory equation. One thing the military superiority thesis does not do is specify exactly which rival explanatory factors may be significant but of lesser importance. Another way of describing this problem is that the military superiority thesis is not a comprehensive theory about the rise and fall of regions to positions of political, economic, cultural, or military dominance over other regions. Rather, the thesis says that whatever else might be involved, it is military superiority that counts most or, at least, counted most in the period between 1500 and 1800.

All these methodological considerations suggest that a definitive answer to how much weight we should give to military superiority must wait for better theory and more appropriate data than we currently possess. In the interim, however, it is conceivable to explore further the substantive problem of the role of military superiority with the assistance of a purposive sample of cases falling between 1500 and 1800. If we examine more closely some of the most important cases (utilizing a fairly loose definition of what constitutes a case), the questions to raise preliminarily is whether we find: (1) unambiguous evidence that European military superiority linked to early modern military revolutions was involved in the European victory and; (2) whether it is equally clear that military superiority seemed to have been the most important factor in each case?

We might propose to carry out this task as a completely open-ended search.

However, instead, a rival interpretation will be advanced. Equally, if not more so, to the temporary rise of western Eurasia – or, more accurately, some peripheral parts of western Eurasia – over the rest of the world were two additional factors that interacted with each other and with military superiority. In their absence, military superiority would not have sufficed to bring about the regional primacy of western Europe. The two additional factors were the ability to cultivate local allies and the ability to manipulate the weaknesses and vulnerabilities of indigenous political structures against their non-European opponents. Without local allies, especially in the 1500–1800 period, European military superiority would have been unlikely to have been able to compensate for European numerical inferiority. Without the possibility of manipulating the vulnerability of opposing political organizations, the Europeans would have been more likely to have faced something approximating the full mobilization of the resources available to their opponents. To their good fortune, the Europeans hardly ever had to deal with opponents functioning at full strength. Instead, they either capitalized on classical *divide et impere* tactics or they avoided showdowns with patently stronger opponents. It is within this twin context of local allies and the strategic manipulation of political structure weaknesses that Europeans were able to make most use of whatever variable military advantages they possessed. The avoidance of stronger opponents is also the principal reason it took so long for the European ascendancy to be manifested.

Local allies and political structure weaknesses hardly exhaust the possible factors involved in the European ascendancy around the world. But, it is argued, they were as uniformly involved as was military "superiority" and, in some respects, even more so. Still, rather than quibble about whether one factor was more key than another, perhaps the most reasonable approach is to suggest that it was the interaction among local allies, political structure weaknesses, and military superiority that best explains European territorial expansion between 1500 and 1800, and later, in the "Columbian era" of world history. None of the three taken in isolation are capable of providing a satisfactory explanation. Viewed as an interactive trinity, however, a more powerful explanation emerges.

For instance, the strongest element in the military superiority thesis (for the sixteenth and seventeenth centuries) is the emphasis on the development of naval superiority. Without this advantage, some western Europeans would not have been able to reach the Americas, and southern and eastern Eurasia. Nor could they have survived, once they had reached these regions, without maritime predominance. Yet maritime predominance was only necessary. It was not sufficient for European ascendancy. Predominance afloat facilitated survival prior to the nineteenth century. A lifeline to distant European resources was established just as European growth was reinforced by non-European resources (McNeill, 1982: 143). It is, no doubt, also fair to say that naval superiority facilitated the development of local allies. Some enclaves in Afro-Eurasia that formed links in European maritime networks were also defended by *trace italienne* fortifications.

European territorial conquest came early in the Americas thanks primarily to less resistance (compared to Afro-Eurasia) in the form of geography, population density, primitive technology, indigenous disease susceptibilities, and the vulnerability of local empires to defection (Cipolla, 1965). Local allies and the clever manipulation of their oppositions' vulnerabilities complete the picture. Military technological superiority was evident but its significance should not be exaggerated.

European territorial conquest came much later to Africa, and southern and eastern Eurasia. There, the potential for resistance was greater, although not identical in all parts of Afro-Eurasia. Some places were more difficult to penetrate, more densely populated, and less behind in technology. In Afro-Eurasia, disease susceptibility was more of a problem for Europeans than the other way around. Military technological superiority in the form of organized firepower did become increasingly important in the eighteenth century, in conjunction somewhat later with Headrick's (1980) emphasis on nineteenth century technological innovations (gunboats, medicine, rapid firing weapons, transportation and communication systems). But once again, local allies and the variable vulnerability of their opponents were also important, albeit not necessarily as completely independent processes. Various forms of military superiority made local allies more probable and, no doubt, contributed to the vulnerability of Afro-Eurasian land powers.[4]

Even so, there is still something quite important that is missing. A focus on European territorial expansion outside Europe cannot fully account for the European ascendancy because it was not territorial expansion *per se* that explains the rise of the West. On the contrary, territorial expansion frequently was an undesirable and unplanned byproduct of European attempts to control east–west, maritime trade routes (Thompson and Zuk, 1986). It is the attempt to control the Eurasian maritime trade routes, the subsequent elevation of the maritime routes over ones on land, and the consequent accelerated globalization of the Eurasian political economy that is more important than one of its unintended consequences to explaining European ascendance. The ascendance of western Eurasia from periphery to primacy did not hinge on the control of long-distance trade alone, but in its absence, it is hard to imagine the development sequence which we associate with European "moderniz-ation" and regional predominance.

To explore these ideas further, five cases are worth reviewing.[5] As cases, they are not equal in the types of structural focus they offer. Two (the Aztec and Inca cases) concentrate on events that occurred quite suddenly while the other three (Portuguese, Dutch, and British expansion) highlight slower moving processes. The Portuguese case encompasses a wide focus between west Africa and Malacca while the other four are limited to more specific area foci (what is now Mexico, Peru, Indonesia, and India). In all five cases, the information discussed is highly selective and, therefore, can at best only support the arguments at risk. On the other hand, the five cases do tackle, and not coincidentally so, most of the main theaters of European expansion in Parker's 1500–1800 period.[6] One element to watch for is the degree to which military superiority appears necessary, sufficient, or merely facilitative. Other elements that need assessment for relative significance purposes are the role of local allies, the political vulnerabilities of the European opponents, and the strategic motivations underlying the expansion of European influence.

The reader should also keep in mind that these cases of expansion do not constitute the expansion of European influence as a regional whole. Rather, they are cases of iterative waves of expansion in which only some Europeans participated. Almost exclusively, they came from Europe's western maritime fringe. The selective identity of the agents of expansion also tells us something about the role of military superiority in the expansion process. Aside from the indisputable naval advantages of the people engaged in "European" expansion, the agents of expansion were not necessarily the principal sources and primary beneficiaries of European military innovation, at least in Europe. If they had been, they might also have been less inclined to forge new links to the Americas and eastern Afro-Eurasia.

THE PORTUGUESE CASE

This first case is admittedly different than the other four. It does not involve a specific confrontation or serial confrontations in one corner of the world between one set of Europeans and another set of non-Europeans. Rather, it focuses on Portuguese expansion throughout the world, with special emphasis on the fifteenth through seventeenth centuries. It can be justifiably treated as a case because what the Portuguese did in that time period did not vary all that much and that in itself is most informative. The limitations experienced by the Portuguese also were not all that different from much the same limitations experienced by their Dutch and British successors. Most significantly, the Portuguese, Dutch and British aims were similar even if their strategies were not always identical. Beginning with the Portuguese case, therefore, helps set the stage for subsequent efforts on the part of some Europeans to break out of western Eurasia. It also affords a good opportunity to introduce the Venetian model which, it is argued, served as a common foundation for European expansion in Afro-Eurasia (but not the Americas).

Another interesting dimension of the Portuguese expansion is that while it certainly capitalized on, and was partly responsible for, the improvements in European ships and navigation skills, the Portuguese expansion began before the full advent of the early modern military revolutions in gunpowder, *traces italienne*, and infantry tactical training and discipline, or at least the ones with which Parker is most concerned. The 1415 attack on Morocco was a more traditional military invasion, conducted, in part, to allow aristocratic offspring to win their spurs in battle. Nevertheless, the initial outcome characterized Portuguese and other European encroachments in Afro-Eurasia for the next 300 years or more. The Portuguese could capture cities, and sometimes could hold them, but they were not usually very successful in moving into the interiors of the areas in which they were interested. In short, they lacked the military capability to do so.

More generically, the Portuguese came to rely primarily on what might be called the "Venetian model" to create a string of fortified enclaves focusing on the area between the East African (Sofala), the Persian (Ormuz), Indian (Goa) and Malay coasts (Malacca).[7] The leading historian of Venice, Frederic Lane (1987: 27), summarized what he perceived to be the essence of the Venetian model in the following passage:

> The Venetians sought sea power, not territorial possessions from which to draw tribute. Their wars were fought to effect political arrangements which would be disadvantageous to rival sea powers, which would make Venice's established trades more secure in Levantine waters, and which would gain them trading privileges permitting commercial expansion into new areas.

By disadvantageous political arrangements, greater security and trading privileges, Lane was suggesting politely that Venice, operating as a political-economic unit specializing in maritime commerce, sought to exclude all rivals whenever possible in order to minimize the uncertainties associated with commerce conducted far away from the home base. Maximizing the profits to be generated from long-distance trade was equally, if not more, important. Some application of coercive force usually was required to obtain trading privileges/monopolies from some foreign political authority. It could also more directly reduce the number of competitors operating in a specific market or area. Given the nature of the long-distance and maritime operations that were involved, naval power was indispensable in projecting coercive force.

Two other features of the Venetian model included a domestic variation on the monopoly principle and the development of a trading enclave network. The absence of foreign competitors greatly facilitated ready access to desired commodities at predictable and attractive prices. The same principle was applied within the Venetian trading community as well by governmental encouragement of the formation of purchasing cartels so that Venetian buyers would be less likely to compete with other Venetians. Governmental regulation was enhanced in the fourteenth century by the practice of official convoys. Certain high profit goods, purchased in the Middle East, particularly spices, could only reach Venice by traveling on leased galleys owned by the state. The galleys proceeded to Venice in escorted groups on scheduled dates. In this fashion, Venetian merchants received state protection in return for surrendering their autonomy to compete in the realm of transportation costs, routes and timing. The power to deny access to transportation must also have proved useful in policing entrepreneurial behavior.

The trading enclave network was a combination of maritime linkages between the home port and the most important trade centers and selective militarization of some of the nodes in the trade network. Where local political authorities were fairly powerful, merchants had little choice but to accept whatever arrangements were offered. This usually amounted to operating out of an enclave designated for foreigners but subject to the laws, taxes, and whims of local rulers. The risks and uncertainties associated with these foreign endeavors, however, could be reduced if the commercial enclaves could be made autonomous, fortified and/or made to double as naval bases.

By making some of the nodes in the trade network more dependable, commercial activities would function more predictably and more safely. A string of well-placed naval bases also served to protect trade against piracy and other types of competition. The same bases could also be used to expand commercial opportunities into areas where resistance to trade was encountered. Invariably, some naval bases were particularly likely to become full-fledged colonial possessions with the gradual expansion of territorial control from an initial coastal fort into the surrounding countryside.

Hence, the Venetian model combined elements of long-distance trade specialization, sea power, coercive force, regulated competition among one's own nationals, and a trading enclave/base network. Too much resistance meant that the network node would be moved somewhere less difficult. Little resistance but a strong local power meant that at best one had to accept a trading enclave situation that was at the mercy of the local ruler's whims. The combination of little or moderate resistance and local weaknesses led to a higher probability of initial bases that evolved into colonies.

The Portuguese did not begin with this Venetian conceptualization in mind.[8] Their fifteenth-century Moroccan campaigns initially resembled old-fashioned land conquests in the Iberian Peninsula. The inability to penetrate beyond a few coastal cities led to a trial-and-error search for other strategies and, ultimately, the pioneering export of the Venetian model to the Indian Ocean. Muslim resistance to this intrusion ensured the need for coercion. But the development of a string of Portuguese bases around the Indian Ocean littoral and beyond depended as much on finding weak links to exploit as it did on the offensive firepower of Portuguese ships. Richards (1993: 239) captures this aspect of European expansion particularly well when he notes that, in general: "Along the coasts, whenever gaps in strong indigenous state power occurred, the European trading companies built autonomous city-states similar to Portuguese Goa."

Another perspective, then, is that the Portuguese, and their successors, were reproducing small-scale versions of what they themselves constituted in western Eurasia (small enclaves oriented to long-distance trade and adjacent to large and more powerful land powers). The main objective was to better control the east–west maritime trade routes and the long-distance trade that utilized these routes. A strong interest in long-distance commerce was not unique to Europe but it was only in coastal Europe (the Mediterranean, Baltic, and Atlantic fringes) that a few small states emerged with the advancement and protection of commerce as their principal *raison d'être* and survived long enough to have considerable, long-term impact.

Ultimately, most of these European exceptions to the rule suffered the conventional fate of commercially/maritime-oriented city states throughout Eurasia – absorption by neighboring land empires. But, in Europe, the strategies of the small city state with maritime–commercial orientations and the Venetian model were adopted by successively larger nation states (first Portugal, then the Netherlands, and then England) all located on the seaward periphery of western Eurasia. These states, in turn, constituted the leading edge of the rise of western Eurasia as the predominant region in the world system.

Leading edge they may have been but they still operated under conditions of severe limitations on military capability. They experienced little in the way of genuine, non-western competition at sea because their ships were blue water (as opposed to galleys) vessels that were strong enough to carry and employ increasingly large amounts of artillery. This naval superiority enabled its possessors to capture specific coastal cities ("wherever gaps in strong indigenous state power occurred") and to hold onto them as long as they could prevent simultaneous attacks from the sea and from the land. For a small state such as Portugal, just such a mobile maritime network strategy was critical, for it lacked the manpower resources to do much more than hold on to a string of coastal bases. An attack on one node in the network could be met, albeit sometimes only barely, by moving resources from the rest of the network to the point under attack.

Yet the defense of the Sofala–Ormuz–Goa–Malacca core of this network was facilitated greatly by the fact that some of the most powerful land powers in the area were usually relatively indifferent to Portuguese and later European coastal encroachments. Of course, this generalization applies less to the Ottomans and more to the Mughal Empire and other large land powers in India. Indian rulers, as Pearson (1991) argues, were more likely to become concerned about trade only when it was interrupted or when tax revenues seemed to be eroding or clearly threatened. The identity of who conducted trade, as long as they more or less behaved themselves, was not the most important issue to rulers who were more interested in expanding agrarian revenues and engaging in traditional land warfare. These same rulers often never went anywhere near the oceans that bounded some of their domains. Hence, the Portuguese (and other later European) trading enclaves were attacked from time to time by local and European rivals but they were not constantly besieged by the most powerful land forces in the general south Asian vicinity. If they had been, it seems likely that the Europeans would not have been able to hang on to their trading enclaves in India.

Outside of the Sofala–Malacca core, the Portuguese employed different strategies. East of Malacca, they competed to some extent in the sixteenth century with the Spanish based in the Philippines but they were not in a position to compete with the Chinese or the Japanese who restricted and regulated trading contacts with the Portuguese. They are not considered to have had much impact on the Spice Islands or the Malay–Indonesian Archipelago.

To the west of Ormuz, the Portuguese failed, despite repeated attempts, to capture Aden which would have closed the Red Sea route to the Indian Ocean. They had access to several bases along the east African coast which did not require as much military protection as in Eurasia but made little headway into the interior of east Africa for some time. One index of the difficulties they faced was manifested in the 1541–1543 intervention in defense of Christian rule in Ethiopia. The Portuguese defenders fared poorly against a Somali invading force accompanied by 1000 Turkish musketeers. Only when most of the Turkish musketeers had left the area thinking their task had been completed were the Portuguese, in conjunction with an Ethiopian army, able to enjoy some success in the field.[9]

The Portuguese also had bases in west Africa and did attempt to move inland in the Congo–Angola region. After 100 years of military campaigns relying heavily on African troops using traditional weapons in the sixteenth and seventeenth centuries

(1579–1675), the Portuguese had penetrated about 150 miles east of Luanda. Another indicator of the limitations to Portuguese military superiority in west Africa is that Portuguese troops were engaged in war in that region almost every year between 1579 and 1921 (Wheeler and Pelissier, 1971: 40).

The Portuguese thus established an Afro-Eurasian pattern of European incursions that was to be maintained until at least the second half of the eighteenth century, and, in some respects, even longer.[10] The Europeans usually possessed military superiority at sea and could capture and hold on to small coastal enclaves in Africa and the area between southwest and southeast Asia, if necessary. However, their ability to do so depended on avoiding the wrath of large land powers and taking over small niches that already enjoyed some autonomy from adjacent empires. It also helped if the target was characterized by some type of internal disaffection. For example, when the Portuguese ran into resistance at Calicut, they were able to move down the coast to Cochin whose ruler was seeking greater independence from Calicut. Malacca's sultan, another good example, had just executed his chief minister over a harem dispute. This seemingly trivial incident (although not so from the minister's perspective) antagonized further local Malay–Tamil tensions and had also managed to alienate Chinese and Javanese merchants. In this context, the Portuguese attack, with a force that was about 40 percent Indian in composition, received some support from resident Chinese traders (Cady, 1964: 175).

In eastern Eurasia, the Portuguese had to be content with whatever was offered. For there, powerful rulers were less indifferent to the presence of foreign traders and the Chinese had, in fact, defeated two Portuguese naval squadrons in the early 1520s.[11] Survival on land was greatly facilitated by local allies and relative indifference to what groups performed external trading functions as long as it did not pose a threat to internal stability.[12] What inland expansion was possible required not only local allies but also their soldiers, often as not employing traditional weaponry. The Portuguese clearly benefitted from European technological changes in maritime capabilities and were, in fact, leading innovators in this sphere. Without this type of superiority, the Portuguese could not have penetrated the Indian Ocean and beyond. Nor could they have survived once they had penetrated – something also facilitated by the construction of European-style fortresses. Otherwise, historians find nothing much remarkable about Portuguese military operations on land in terms of organization, tactics, or even weaponry.[13]

THE AZTEC CASE

Hernando Cortes landed on the Mexican coast in 1519 with approximately 500 men, one-fourth of whom were stranded sailors.[14] The Spanish group fairly quickly proceeded to defeat the Tlaxcaltec tribe in two battles. However, this early Spanish victory may have benefitted from the Tlaxcaltec incentives for finding new and strong allies in their own struggle with the Aztecs. Shortly after, the Spaniards, accompanied by a large force of Tlaxcaltec allies, were invited to visit the Aztec capital of

Tenochtitlan. Once inside the capital, the Spaniards were more impressed with the potential capability of the Aztecs than they had been previously, and that, presumably, was the main reason for the invitation in the first place. Impressed or not, it did not stop the Spanish capture of Moteuczomah Xocoyotl within the first week of their arrival. This action at the least bought them some time for the Aztec ruler was prepared to cooperate in order to survive. He was also useful in suppressing initial dissent within the Aztec community against a cooperative policy. The timing of the visit worked in the Spanish favor as well. A respectable proportion of the population from which the Aztec army was recruited when needed, aside from the warrior élite, was committed to harvesting activities.

Eventually the Aztecs chose a new ruler and forced the Spanish to fight their way out of Tenochtitlan with considerable casualties. Once evicted from the capital, Cortes' strategy shifted from a direct assault on the Aztec center to attacks on the surrounding region and a gradually tightening siege of the Aztec capital.

Moteuczomah Xocoyotl died in the retreat from the Aztec capital. His successor died within three months of smallpox – something the Spanish had introduced to Mexico with their arrival. The rapid turnover in Aztec rulers created a significant political problem. The Aztec empire, for the most part, was a loosely knit empire over which the Aztecs presided. Their ability to rule depended less on bureaucratic monitoring than it did on the perception by the various groups within the empire that the Aztecs had more military power than anyone else and the inclination to employ it against dissidents. New Aztec rulers, therefore, were required to demonstrate their capability early on to keep the empire from unraveling. This expectation proved difficult to realize with three rulers in a very short period of time and the third ruler (Cauhtemoc) in the quick succession made matters worse by eschewing any power displays at all. As a consequence, Cauhtemoc was perceived to be weak, thereby inviting rebellion. Imperial defections were likely in any event. Demonstrations of power could suffice only as long as the central Mexican system remained unipolar. The Spanish–Tlaxcaltec alliance constituted a second pole and in a bipolar system, something more than a demonstration of power would be required to hold the empire together.

That "something more" proved difficult to achieve in the circumstances. The Spanish strategy kept Tenochtitlan besieged and gradually cut off its supplies of food and water. Aztec numerical superiority declined as various subject groups defected to the other side. Attempts by supporters to come to the aid of the Aztec capital were defeated militarily as they arose on a piecemeal basis. Eventually, starvation and disease reduced the power of the Aztecs to hold out any longer, leading directly to their final military defeat in 1521.

The Spanish did have better arms and armor but, as one anonymous reviewer noted in response to an earlier version of this analysis, any Eurasian invading force would have had better arms and armor than the Aztecs. European steel, for that matter, was derived primarily from Indian and Middle Eastern technological advances. The Spanish also had a few horses, firearms and cannon. Yet the Aztecs seemed unusually quick in developing countertactics to deal with these advantages.

The principal key to the Spanish allied victory over the Aztecs was the development of a strategy that used the nature of the political organization of the Aztec empire to undermine its ability to compete and, ultimately, to function. As Hassig (1988: 267) states: "The Spanish conquest was not one of superior arms and wills but one that took advantage of existing cleavages within the system to split the empire, turn its members on the Aztecs, and rend it asunder."

THE INCA CASE

In 1531, Francisco Pizzaro invaded the Inca empire with less than 200 men and a small number of horses (27 initially and reinforced to 62).[15] The timing of the Europeans was propitious. The empire, which may have reached its maximum size only a generation before, was in the ending phase of a vicious civil war over succession rights, essentially pitting the north against the south. The Spanish exploited this situation by offering assistance to both sides at different times, as well as to various tribes that wished to remove themselves from imperial control. Some amount of the devastation wrought by European-induced smallpox had also preceded the arrival of the conquistadors.

After several months of meandering through Inca territory without being attacked by a large force, Pizzaro's group was invited to a meeting with the Inca at a camp at Cajamarca. To their documented horror, the Spanish found the Inca ruler guarded by an army at least 80,000 strong. Spanish chroniclers of the encounter understandably emphasized their own initial fears and apprehension.[16] However, Pizzaro quickly managed to trick the Inca ruler, accompanied by 7000 unarmed soldiers, into visiting their own encampment wherein the Spanish proceeded to massacre the guards, with the assistance of a few cannon but principally with cavalry attacks and hand-to-hand combat between armed versus unarmed soldiers caught within walled confines. The Inca was captured and he then ordered the considerable remainder of his army not to attack or to resist further.

Pizzaro thus controlled the absolute Inca ruler in a highly authoritarian political system. But the massacre had also worked to his structural advantage in that Inca armies tended to be constructed around a small hard core of Inca troops. Conceivably, most of the massacred troops were likely to have been Inca. The rest of the army in place is presumed to have been tribal levies, representing groups conquered by the Incas not that long before, and perhaps with mixed incentives as to whether it was in their interest to respond to the crisis.[17] Another large Inca army was still engaged in civil war operations some distance to the south. Subsequent battles involving relatively large and small numbers of Inca troops and equally variable numbers of Spanish appear to have been won largely by the advantages of surprise, better armor and, most importantly, the steel swords and lances of the Spanish cavalry. The Amerindian opposition to Spain in the Peruvian–Chilean area eventually did develop weapons and tactics to deal with cavalry but not soon enough to expel the Spanish.

What stands out in both the Aztec and Inca cases is the very good luck and timing of the Spanish efforts, as well as the inability of the Spanish conquistadors to perceive accurately their own comparative weaknesses. Both the Aztec and Inca empires functioned best when they could intimidate their opponents.[18] With hindsight, it is easy to say that both Amerindian rulers erred tremendously in inviting the Spaniards to Tenochtitlan and Cajamarca. They should have engaged in hit-and-run tactics almost immediately which probably would have worn down the invaders by attrition if nothing else. But it is also easy to see what their strategies were about and that they had worked on previous occasions. The Spanish adventurers should have been more intimidated than they were when they were exposed to the respective strengths of the Aztecs and Incas. The inability to intimidate sufficiently the Spanish invaders and their allies greatly facilitated the Spanish abilities to overthrow the two most powerful empires in the Americas.

In like fashion, the Spanish were successful in exploiting the structures of the imperial polities to their own advantage. In the Aztec case, Spanish successes in the field, siege tactics, and avoidance of combat with the Aztecs at full strength encouraged additional defections to add to their initial and considerably important alliance with the Tlaxcaltecs. In the Inca case, an intensive civil war preceded the arrival of the Spanish which made it easier for the new arrivals to make allies and to avoid fighting the Inca army at full strength. In both cases, arms and armor no doubt facilitated the Spanish military victories. But the arms that mattered most were not based on gunpowder or fortifications. Steel swords and cavalry had long preceded the military technological revolutions in Europe of the late fifteenth and sixteenth centuries. Another non-technological element, European-induced diseases, definitely contributed something to the Spanish victories as well, although probably not as much as the weaponry advantage. Ironically, the fact that the populations of the Aztec and Inca empires had some experience in centralized rule may also have helped the Spanish conquests. The Spanish had much more trouble dominating Amerindian groups who remained outside the two, in some respects at least, highly centralized empires.

THE DUTCH–INDONESIAN CASE

The Portuguese had attempted to supplant Malacca's fifteenth-century commercial dominance in maritime southeast Asia. They were able to seize Malacca in 1511 but they were never quite able to replicate the extent of commercial influence Malacca had attained prior to their arrival. Alternative entrepôts controlled by Aceh and Johor continued to offer respectable competition throughout the sixteenth century. The Dutch movement into this market was (or came to be) predicated on an early sixteenth century plan that envisaged achieving a commercial hegemony on all trade in Asian waters. For the most part, territorial control was to be avoided as an unnecessary diversion of resources. A network of bases with, at most, control of a few key small islands should suffice as the infrastructure for the commercial empire.[19]

This Venetian network strategy was sabotaged early on and unwittingly by developing the central base of the network at Batavia (Jakarta) on the large island of Java and near a major source of spices. The Dutch required resources from the local population and some minimal level of security in which to create their spice monopoly. If the Dutch East India Company (VOC) had confined itself to the small islands originally contemplated or if the Indonesian archipelago had resembled the Philippines more, things might have worked out differently.[20] But the rise, fall, and violent competition of major indigenous land and sea powers in Java and elsewhere in the archipelago forced the Dutch to select allies among the competitors. They had little choice because, while they had access to superior arms and better trained military forces, they never had enough military force to overcome the numerical superiority of their opponents. They could not hope to defeat or defend themselves against a major Javanese military power without local allies. Since part of the Dutch plan involved seizing a monopoly position in the transportation of Indonesian spices, that objective required selective uses of force to suppress uncontrolled sources and punish interlopers. If they had abstained completely from intervening in local politics, the monopoly position could not be achieved peacefully; nor could they anticipate the food, shipbuilding materials, and security from attack that they desired. For that matter, the Dutch required considerable military capability to hold off their European competitors.

The basic pattern that emerged entailed Dutch intervention in local succession struggles or rivalries. The Dutch would exchange their military capability in return for political subordination, trade concessions, and outright payments. But then the Dutch would be faced with the prospect of forever defending weak rulers. These same weak rulers sometimes lacked the capability to obtain their kingdoms on the basis of their own capability in a system that demanded repeated demonstrations of military power to stay in power. There were three implications. The VOC found itself constantly embroiled in military conflict and, therefore, needed to develop its own military capability at high expense for what was supposed to be a commercial endeavor. At the same time, there were always limits to the extent to which Dutch military forces could penetrate into the interior of Java. Opponents could retreat into the mountains and return when their own capability had been renewed. Intervention gave rise to more interventions with local rulers becoming increasingly tied to the Dutch for protection. By the mid-1700s, Dutch decision-makers had come to the realization that they might just as well rule directly over Indonesian territory as indirectly. In this manner, the initial idea of a commercial network (d)evolved into an older-fashion, territorial empire after 150 years of official resistance to the idea.

One of the fundamental ironies of the Dutch strategy was that the VOC virtually bankrupted itself in the eighteenth century pursuing the focus on monopolizing spices because of the associated military expenses with the way they did business. Moreover, by the time the Dutch had achieved something approaching a monopoly position in the Indonesian archipelago, the emphasis of European consumer demand for spices had switched to textiles and tea which were predominately being produced elsewhere. It took the Napoleonic Wars and British troops to restore Dutch control in Java and the restoration was accompanied by the assumption of full sovereignty of territories in the "Spice Islands" now devoted primarily to coffee and tea production.

THE BRITISH–SOUTH ASIAN CASE

The initial European movement into south Asia in the 1490s immediately preceded the expansion of the Mughal empire from 1526 on. By and large, south Asian rulers were either indifferent or ambivalent to commercial transactions as long as goods continued to move in and out of the subcontinent and as long as they received some share of the profits. Partially, as a consequence, long-distance trade in India was conducted primarily by non-Indians. The Portuguese arrival encountered the resistance of Moslem traders which could sometimes be translated into conflict between the Portuguese and local Indian rulers. But if one ruler objected to the presence of the Portuguese, it was always possible to sail down the coast and find another ruler who was more obliging and possibly in a conflictual relationship with the first ruler. Portuguese naval power was utilized to make selected friends and to support fortified enclaves on Indian territory. The Portuguese might have aspired to greater territorial control but completely lacked the resources to attempt such an undertaking. Nor could they do much to prevent the creation of Dutch, English, and French enclaves in the seventeenth century, all of whom made their own arrangements with local rulers.

How this process functioned in the seventeenth century is well-illustrated by what almost happened to the English East India Company.[21] Friction in Bengal with a provincial Mughal ruler in 1686 inspired the company decision-makers to attempt the seizure of Chittagong and Dacca with several companies of imported infantry. The English possessed local naval superiority but lacked any allies on land and were forced to retreat by a large Mughal army. Since the Mughal Empire was also busy militarily elsewhere, the Bengal operation was viewed by them as an unneeded distraction. A series of protracted negotiations ensued but while these continued, the English tried a second attack with more troops accompanied by naval bombardments. The Mughal reaction was one of irritation and in 1688, the emperor ordered the elimination of all English from throughout India. There was little the English could do to prevent this as long as the issue remained a priority Mughal policy, but it did not remain one for long. The Mughals were still preoccupied with fighting their long-time rivals, the Mahrattas. By 1690, the English had talked their way back into the good graces of the Mughal Empire. Their trading privileges were restored in exchange for the payment of a fine. For the next 50 years, the English East India Company avoided irritating the Mughal Empire.

Circumstances changed in the eighteenth century in two important respects. After 1707, the Mughal Empire had peaked and was in decline. The last vigorous emperor, Aurangzeb, died in that year and was followed by as many as eight successors in nearly as many years. As the empire disintegrated, provincial governors became the rulers of nominally independent states even though they maintained the fiction of Mughal overlordship. Disintegration invited successful outside attacks from the northwest by Persians and Afghans, and from the inside by the Mahrattas and ambitious nobles seeking to expand their localized empires.

When war between the British and the French broke out in Europe in the 1740s, their commercial company agents in India at first attempted to coexist peacefully but in 1747 a French force attacked British holdings in Madras. The force included Indian peons armed with flintlock muskets (as opposed to clumsier firing matchlocks) and drilled in the European line of advance style. These innovations had been developed in Europe 50 years earlier but were only appearing in India at the end of the War of the Austrian Succession as a manifestation of European rivalries. The British responded in kind by bringing in more European troops and by training their own peons.

The Nawab of Arcot felt that the French should surrender the captured Madras to its rightful owner, namely himself. However, his army, consisting largely of traditional cavalry, was defeated easily by the combination of French infantry and artillery. This marked the first time that a European force had been able to defeat a larger Indian force so dramatically. Whether accurately or not, the impression became widespread that the new European-style fighting could prove to be the decisive factor in intra-Indian combat.[22]

After the conclusion of the Anglo-French conflict in 1748, the now enlarged, European company forces were essentially rented as mercenaries to local Indian rulers in return for fees and concessions. With the resumption of Anglo-French fighting in the Seven Years War, the European forces in India were expanded further. At Plassey in 1757, a 3000-man British force defeated a 50,000-man Bengali army in another infantry-artillery versus cavalry situation. This time, however, the British victory had been facilitated by an arrangement with one of the Bengal Nawab's lieutenants to defect with some three-fourths of the army in return for promoting the underling to be the new Nawab. Subsequently installed, the new Nawab bestowed revenue collection rights in the Calcutta area on his British allies, thereby giving them their first substantial territorial holding. Not unlike the earlier Dutch pattern in the Indonesian archipelago, the Nawab came under Maratha and Mughal military attack. Additional British military protection was purchased at the cost of surrendering more tax collection revenue rights until the working arrangement fell apart. In 1763 a British force of approximately 8000 men faced another 50,000-man Indian force combining the forces of the Marathas, the Mughals, and the recently deposed Nawab of Bengal. The British victory at Buxar led to the Mughal surrender of tax revenue collection rights in Bengal, Bihar and Orissa.

This basic process continued through the rest of the eighteenth century, the Napoleonic Wars, and into the first half of the nineteenth century. The British, at first one of the strong independent powers within the south Asian region, would either intervene in succession struggles threatening its interest or else would ally with other Indian powers to suppress a mutual threat from another expanding Indian state. The outcome would be an enlarged British territorial domain. Continued conflict with the French and their allies also fueled the gradual expansion of the British, and the escalation of their military capabilities, as the ultimate successor to the Mughal Empire.

In both the Indonesian and south Asian cases, European strategies and capabilities roughly coevolved with changing Asian political circumstances. Naval power and fortified enclaves proved barely sufficient to maintain entry into Asian markets. They were insufficient to achieve the commercial wealth and degree of market control sought. Hall (1964: 301), writing about the VOC strategy, also captures an element of what happened in south Asia:

> There was no conscious change of programme, no ambition on the part of the directors to transform their commercial empire into a territorial one. Yet such a transformation was inevitable . . . if they were to maintain and consolidate the position they had won for themselves in defeating their European rivals. The alternative was decline and in all probability extinction.

European rivalry certainly was an important element, and no sooner would one European winner begin to lose steam when other European rivals would emerge to keep the competition going. The Portuguese bested the Castilians initially in the Old World only to be absorbed by the Spanish empire for some 60 years. The Dutch defeated the Portuguese, Spanish, and English competition only to succumb to the gains made by its British ally. Yet the "inevitability" of the process depended greatly on what took place within the environment in which the European companies operated. It was not inevitable that no central Javanese land power would emerge triumphantly in complete (as opposed to partial) control of Java, although Dutch military superiority made an indigenous Javanese hegemony less likely. It was not inevitable that the Mughal empire would begin to disintegrate after 1707. British military superiority had little, if anything, to do with the demise of the Mughal Empire. British military forces remained small in number, weak in capability, and largely employed in police, garrison, and warehouse guard capacities some 40 years after the death of Aurangzeb. European rivalry altered that situation and the subsequent changes in military capability then interacted with the decentralized character of opposition forces to lead eventually – but not inevitably – to the incremental British assumption of widespread territorial control in much of South Asia.

Assessment

Various sorts of military superiority were manifested in each of the five cases. Throughout all five, naval superiority was essential for the Europeans to reach the other parts of the world and, once there, to hang on in the face of potentially overwhelming odds. Naval superiority was especially important in the Portuguese, Dutch–Indonesian, and British–south Asian cases and somewhat less critical in the Aztec and Inca cases. Much the same can be said about *trace italienne* fortresses. They were most important in holding on to some of the Afro-Eurasian beachheads until naval relief could arrive to fend off local attackers. The ability to deploy steel swords from horseback against Amerindian warriors on foot seems to have been particularly critical, as far as military superiority goes, in the two American cases. On land, cannon, matchlocks/muskets, and highly disciplined infantry tactics may have been of some use but do not appear to have been either all that prevalent or critical until the late 1740s in India. They only became critical initially as a consequence of European infighting and the belated transferal of European tactics to Indian battle-fields. The introduction of the novel tactics led to changes in the training, permanence, firepower, and expense of Indian infantry just as it had earlier in western Europe.

Certainly some type of military superiority can be said to have been necessary in all five cases. In none of the five, however, can it be said to have been either sufficient or most important to the abrupt or gradual ascendancy of the Europeans. Local allies were essential in all five cases. Without them, European military superiorities could not have prevented defeat at the hands of large armies that had also been developed as tools of military expansion and conquest. Especially critical in every case, more-over, was the ability of the Europeans to find and exploit vulnerabilities in the way in which their opponents were organized politically. In the two Amerindian cases, the Spanish conquistadors took advantage of highly centralized but loosely organized empires that depended on displays of strength as much as outright military victory to expand their territorial domains. The Spanish were not immune to the displays of strength. They were less impressed than perhaps they should have been and they were able to manipulate that psychological edge to capture quickly the imperial heads. The Spanish victories in Mexico and Peru were not unlike judo throws in which a smaller player topples a much larger opponent through subterfuge and technique, as opposed to brute strength. They did not play out exactly the same way but Cortes' and Pizarro's strategies were similar and had similar effects in decapitating and disrupting their opponents' chains of command.[23]

The Dutch VOC bankrupted itself attempting to corner the European spice market by controlling the sources of the spices. Naval power and local allies enabled the Dutch to defeat its local competitors and to prevent hegemonic aspirants on land in Java. Yet the Dutch lacked the military capability to pacify the Javanese interior. In the process, the Dutch became increasingly committed to propping up dependent but weak indigenous rulers and ended up with territorial responsibilities that had not initially been thought desirable or profitable.

The Portuguese, Dutch, English, and French survived in India through the mid-eighteenth century as long as they avoided irritating the Mughal Empire. After the Mughal Empire declined, the European actors became part of the post-imperial mêlée over who was to control which pieces of territory. Not entirely intentionally, the British emerged from a position of acute weakness and one totally dependent on Mughal goodwill to become one of the stronger local powers and then, eventually, succeeded to the position of imperial center. The British Raj replaced the Mughal Raj after several decades of complicated succession struggles. Infantry tactics and artillery imported from Europe were crucial to this positional change but they would not have mattered as much without Indian infantry and allies and, in the absence of Anglo-French rivalry within the context of Mughal disintegration, it is debatable whether or when they would have been introduced in the first place.

European technological and military superiority became even greater after the late eighteenth-century industrial revolution. Yet it remains difficult to disentangle the offensive advantages of the Europeans versus the defensive vulnerabilities of the Chinese and the Japanese in the nineteenth century. Both the Ch'ing and Tokugawa regimes had been in decline for some time when they were "opened up" by European and US coercion.[24] Table 5.1 provides some limited objective information on this dimension. One indicator of the organizational health or viability of regimes based on military conquest is continued territorial expansion. Territorial contraction indicates that the military conquest machine is losing its effectiveness and/or that the political economy based on continued expansion is deteriorating.[25]

Table 5.1 suggests that the Inca and Aztec empires were not evidently in decline at the time of the Spanish arrival but that their imperial successes were not of very long duration. The Moghul and Ottoman empires peaked sometime in the seventeenth century thereby facilitating the scramble for south Asian territorial control in the second half of the eighteenth century and various "eastern questions" in the nineteenth century involving the Ottoman "sick man of Europe". In the Chinese case, Table 5.1 shows more or less continued territorial expansion from the seventeenth almost to the end of the eighteenth century which correlates with Chinese feelings of decline first enunciated in the last quarter of that century. The indicator does not apply very well to the Japanese once they were repelled in Korea at the end of the sixteenth and beginning of the seventeenth centuries but Totman (1993) argues for a periodization of Tokugawa decline beginning around 1710 and also supports this claim with data on increasing peasant unrest, another useful indicator of the decline phenomena.

Going beyond the limitations of the data in Table 5.1, there does not seem to be much disagreement about the decline, and the reasons for the decline, of the Chinese and Japanese regimes.[26] Both societies were, in part, victims of earlier imperial success in coercively imposing order and peace. The consequent doubling of the Japanese population (seventeenth century) and Chinese population (eighteenth century) outstripped the ability of the local political economies to meet the new demographic demands. In the Chinese case, population growth led to major internal migrations and group conflicts, exacerbated by an inflation in real tax rates (due, in part, to the silver outflow to pay for opium), an inability of peasants to pay their taxes, and an overextended and inefficient bureaucracy. Dealing with rebellions by Miao, Triads, White Lotus, Taipings, and Muslims often beginning in the areas in which in-migration pressures had been greatest became the primary priority of the Ch'ing regime. The British and later the French demonstrated their mid-nineteenth-century military superiority against relatively small numbers of Chinese troops who were poorly led, underfed, reluctant to fight, and organized in an anachronistic and deteriorating Manchu banner system that had to be abandoned by mid-century. At the same time, their political leaders had problems in taking the European threat

Table 5.1 The timing of imperial expansion and contraction (measured in squared megameters)

Year	Inca	Aztec	Moghul	Ottoman	Ming/Ch'ing
1250	0.005				
1307				0.025	
1359				0.07	
1368					3.1
1382				0.3	
1400					3.9
1438	0.05				
1440		0.015			
1450					6.5
1451				0.69	
1463	0.2				
1468		0.08			
1471	0.45				
1481		0.10		1.22	
1493	1.9				
1502		0.17			
1513					3.9
1519			0.03		
1520		0.22			
1521				3.4	
1525			0.8		
1527	2.0				
1560			0.8		
1571				4.7	
1580			1.7		
1600			4.0		
1635					3.9
1645					4.9
1650					6.5
1660					7.2
1683				5.2	
1690			4.0		
1700					8.8
1710			2.5		
1725					10.6
1730				4.5	
1760					13.2
1770			0.2		13.7
1790					14.7
1817				4.25	
1840					14.2

Source: Extracted from information in Taagepera (1997)

completely seriously as long as the implications of internal revolt and turbulence seemed more threatening to the survival of the Ch'ing dynasty.[27]

In comparison, the internal and external pressures experienced by the Tokugawa regime were not as great as those felt by the Chinese. But the Tokugawa regime had been in decline for some time, its economy was no more able to cope with demographic pressures than its Ch'ing counterpart, and, also like the Ch'ings, the Japanese political élite underperceived the degree of external threat. When the black ships finally came to Japan, the Tokugawa regime did not survive the shock to the political system. Civil war that had been held off broke out leading ultimately to the Meiji Restoration. Yet the general point remains that while there is no denying western military superiority in the nineteenth century, it was applied in rather limited ways against Asian regimes that were well into decline and less capable of effective resistance than they might have been a century before. Western forces did not have to be all that superior to defeat Asian opponents that were ripe for being vanquished by somebody as they struggled to cope with the conjunction of internal and external societal crises.

Obviously, we cannot claim that imperial decline, decay, and crises were solely responsible for the inability of the Chinese and Japanese governments to continue insulating their territories from the destabilizing intrusions of the world economy and various non-Asian agents. The claim is only that both pronounced Chinese and Japanese decline and European military superiority were present in the nineteenth century and that the two sets of internal and external phenomena interacted to bring about little in the way of effective Chinese and Japanese resistance to Western coercion. By this time (mid-nineteenth century) local allies were no longer as necessary as they once had been for European success.[28] But then territorial conquest was not as much in evidence as a primary goal in east Asia as it had been in the Americas, or as it became in the Indonesian islands or south Asia given the local circumstances of those theaters of operation.[29] Otherwise, the European encroachments and expansion efforts continued apace between the late fifteenth through the early twentieth centuries largely as a consequence of an interaction effect between varying external strengths and internal weaknesses. European coercive advantages played roles throughout this process. But they were not sufficient, sufficiently important, or even the same types of superiority in different parts of the world to qualify as the key to the rise of European primacy.

The military superiority thesis thus exaggerates the role of European military superiority and its origins in a competitive, multipolar region's sequential military revolutions. It is appealing, partly because it taps into an ancient process whereby lean, mean, and better-armed warriors from the periphery successfully attack and defeat the center in combat.[30] The annals of world history are replete with images of peripheral barbarians attacking with the material assistance of iron swords, chariots, phalanxes, composite bows, and light cavalry. The European hordes after 1500 seem to fit in as another wave in a very old process. Two items are omitted from the analysis, however. One, the emphasis is placed almost entirely on the advantages of the external attacker when, and in the older pre-1500 cases as well, the external attacks were invariably preceded by internal disintegration, decline, or disorganization. Strong centers were subjected normally to frontier raids but not full-fledged attacks, unless, of course, the raiding exposed greater vulnerabilities than the raiders had thought to have been the case.[31] Indeed, in some of the older cases, it is not clear from the archaeological evidence whether the attackers "triumphed" only after the target had already disappeared as an organized entity.[32] In this respect, the sixteenth-century conquistadors were exceptional only in that they had to work harder to amplify the vulnerabilities that were already there than has often been the case in the past. Yet the point remains that an exaggeration of the external advantages manifestly distorts the role of equally important internal disadvantages.[33] One dimension does not make as much sense as it might in the absence of the other.

The second omission is that an emphasis on military conquest masks the underlying political economy motivations and strategies. Just as it can be argued that many of the attacks of the peripheral warriors of yore were really contests over the control of trade routes, as opposed to simply the brutish demonstration of military prowess or an acquisitive lust for urban loot, the European (maritime) ascendancy was predicated not so much on violence alone but was especially focused on the control of trade routes connecting eastern and western Eurasia. Lacking the military superiority to accomplish this feat the way Alexander the Great may have tried to do it, that is, on land, the most western of the Europeans sought control of the maritime routes and as much of the commercial flow on those routes as could be acquired. They were not inventing new forms of exchange as much as they were attempting to eliminate the fifteenth century Venetian–Mamluk monopoly on east–west trade by circumventing the Red Sea–Egyptian route. This motivation, among others, led the Portuguese to move gradually down and around the African coastline into the Indian Ocean and the Spanish to stumble into the New World land mass thinking it was a shortcut to Asia.

Spanish silver from American mines turned out (after the 1550s) to be immensely facilitative of European trade with the rest of Eurasia, either through the Acapulco–Philippines connection or via the more indirect sieve of Hapsburg political-military ambitions in Europe. But the military conquest of South and Central America was not the leitmotif of European ascendancy. It was only one early unintended consequence. The main action, after the 1490s, was always focused on establishing a competitive position in Eurasian maritime trade. Gradual military conquests in the Indonesian archipelago and south Asia were more, largely unintended, consequences of engaging in coercive, long-distance commerce in an uncertain environment. In some respects, then, the European ascendancy occurred despite some forms of military superiority that tended to sidetrack strategies for commercial predominance. That is, some Europeans had just enough military superiority to stay around long enough to become bogged down in Afro-Eurasian territorial conquests in order to protect their coastal enclaves and commercial position but not enough to avoid the need to acquire extensive territorial responsibilities altogether.

European ascendancy in the world system was not predicated exclusively on gradually assuming control of east–west maritime trade. But the attempt to acquire that control was an important catalyst in fueling and contributing to economic growth in Europe. If for no other reason, within the European region it fueled the economic ascendancy of the maritime states over the larger, more traditional, agrarian states of Europe. It also greatly assisted the survival of those maritime states when they were faced with attempts at their absorption by adjacent land powers. The Portuguese were transitional in this evolutionary track and failed to prevent absorption by the more traditional and inherently agrarian-based Spanish empire. The Dutch and English fared better in their confrontations with the French, with the English managing to outlast even their twentieth century German confrontations. Part of the same evolutionary track, however, was the gradual supplantment of the maritime leader by new, more capable, more innovative maritime powers with successively larger populations. The Portuguese gave way to the Dutch who, in turn, were replaced by the British. The British were forced to give way to the United States.

The ascendancy of the European region thus involves at least three different structural dynamics. One dynamic involves the rise and fall of leading sea powers that tended to center on European actors until the late nineteenth century. Another involves the interaction between sea powers and land powers within the European region. One of the ironies embedded within this story is that early modern European military revolutions enhanced the coercive capabilities of both land and maritime powers. It is conceivable that if the European land powers had been able to defeat conclusively the maritime powers in their iterative clashes early on, the ascendancy of Europe as the predominant region for a time might never have taken place. The third dynamic concerns the commercial and territorial encroachments of Europeans primarily against other Afro-Eurasians located outside the European region. Within each dynamic, there are tendencies toward the rise and relative decline of leaders and the supplantment of incumbent powers by former non-leaders. To explain why Europe became predominant, ultimately, we need to explain how these separate and overlapping dynamics worked and why some places become more innovative and capable than others for usually finite periods of time.

CONCLUSION

To account for the evolution of differential regional success in the past half-millennium, it is unlikely to suffice to say that one region became militarily superior to other regions and then proceeded to demonstrate that superiority over a 300–400-year period. That did happen in a less than straightforward fashion, yet military superiority as the explanatory key simply leaves too much of the variance in what else happened, and how it happened, unexplained. The situation was too complex to rely so heavily on a single-factor explanation that focuses on one of the advantages exploited overtly by the winners without also at least examining the context in which various forms of military superiority could be exploited successfully. Finally, battlefield success is one thing. Just how eventual battlefield success throughout Afro-Eurasia and the Americas fed into technological and economic growth in Europe is another complicated problem that tends to be assumed away or ignored. At the very least, it is debatable whether, to what extent, and in what fashion territorial conquests outside Europe led directly to economic and technological innovation within Europe. The argument here is not that non-European conquests had nothing to do with the

European ascent but that we have yet to work out the theoretical ramifications and empirical specifics of the various types of connections. Some aspects are obvious; others are much more subtle. This is an analytical problem much in need of further research in tracing the interconnections among the multiple and coevolving structural dynamics at work in an increasingly complex and interdependent world system.

Part III

THE LEADERSHIP
CHALLENGE SEQUENCE

6

THE EMERGENCE OF A
CHALLENGE PROCESS

When we think of intense competition between the leading economies over the production of commodities utilizing cutting edge technology, the control of export markets, the activities of transnational firms, and investment/loan ventures, the first mental reference point is likely to be focused on current events. We might easily summon up images of competition among the United States, western Europe, either as an integrated ensemble of economies or in the German manifestation, and Japan. Both Germany and Japan have had different types of economic problems in the 1990s and an integrated Europe is not yet a reality. Thus, this image may not seem all that sharp at the moment but it still remains a very likely scenario over the next few decades.

In the short term, frictions between major trading states come and go. Yet some are more important than others because they represent ongoing or potential changes in long-term, systemic economic leadership. The end of the twentieth and the early part of the next century may be a case in point. The possibility of a shift in economic leadership from the United States to Japan remains conceivable, although certainly not inevitable. The question is how best to go about interpreting the possibilities and their implications. Short-term perspectives emphasize year-to-year fluctuations in the seesawing outcomes of trade negotiations and the relative health of the US and Japanese economies at given points in time. Longer-term perspectives are necessary to rise above the flux and noise of current events. The history of challenges for systemic economic leadership over the past millennia, 10 of which are featured in Chapter 8, provides one fairly unique vantage point. In conjunction with a systematization of these past transitional iterations, it is also possible to construct a testable model encompassing five variables that facilitates the differentiation of intense, militarized challenges from those that do not pursue such a route. The long-term generalizations that emerge from such an analysis can then be applied to the hypothetical course of more contemporary transitions in the near future. In brief, a long-term perspective suggests that while conflict over economic leadership in the next century might be anticipated, a war between Japan and the United States over this issue is not one of the more likely scenarios.

To arrive at this conclusion, however, some initial foundation must be established. After very brief discussions of late twentieth and late nineteenth century challenges, this chapter and the one that follows will focus on describing some of the activities of earlier leaders and challengers. The goal is to provide sufficient information to facilitate the reader following the more systematic evaluation of the challenge process undertaken in Chapter 8.

JAPANESE–AMERICAN FRICTIONS IN THE SHORT TERM

Since the end of World War II, Japan has moved away from a position of subordination to US technological preeminence in the era of automobiles and aerospace to a position of full-fledged competition over who will dominate innovation in the new era being built around information technologies. In addition, and as of the mid-1990s, the increasingly adversarial trade relationship of Japan and the United States had reached an apparently new level of antagonism with US threats of punitive tariffs on Japanese-built luxury automobiles and Japanese countercharges of GATT violations. These trade frictions were certainly manifested in public perceptions as well. In the early 1980s, about 60 percent of US respondents and about 50 percent of Japanese respondents characterized US–Japanese relations as good/very good. By 1995 the respective percentages for this characterization were 28 percent and 23 percent respectively (Ladd and Bowman, 1996: 55). From the US perspective, Japan is continuing to play unfairly in international commerce by protecting its home markets while benefitting from freer trade elsewhere. From the Japanese perspective, US products simply are no longer as competitive as they once had been. There is more than an element of truth in both points of view.

General perceptions aside, why specifically have Japan and the United States been at loggerheads? One fairly representative interpretation (Long, 1990) suggests the following sources of friction:

1   The US military buildup in the 1980s created unprecedented budgetary deficits that caused the relative value of the dollar to rise, thereby reducing the United States' export competitiveness.
2   Japanese manufacturers are characterized by a distinctive combination of efficiency and quality control that caused their trade income surpluses to soar.
3   The United States and Japan possessed divergent trade philosophies that stemmed from their respective cultures.
4   US citizens are more prone to consume than to save. The reverse description applies to Japanese citizens.
5   Japan protects its home markets through governmental legislation and corporate arrangements. The United States is committed to free trade policies.
6   The Japanese are aggressive in their governmentally supported attempt to achieve supremacy in controlling international markets. Americans are complacent and export campaigns are not necessarily supported by governmental policies.

The author (Long, 1990: 5) concludes that the combination of these six factors have led Japan and the United States to the brink of a trade war that neither side wants. This conclusion is based on a selected review of earlier policy developments (in the 1980s) and a strong appreciation for philosophical differences about governmental corporate relationships and varying propensities to consume or save. The implication is that if some short-term policies were changed – US deficits reduced, Japanese industrial efficiency imitated, or Japanese consumption propensities increased – the trade friction problems might go away. And perhaps they would. But what if there are more fundamental issues at stake? Then, the short-term manipulation of policies and behaviors might not have much effect. Moreover, an emphasis on short-term phenomena might very well distract attention from the more serious long-term roots of the dispute, and by doing so, make matters worse.

Will a genuine trade war break out in the twenty-first century? Will economic leadership shift from the United States to Japan? These are significant questions without doubt. Yet we tend to pose the questions as if these phenomena had never happened before. American–Japanese trade frictions and the possibility of a shift in economic leadership are anything but novel phenomena in the history of the world's political economy. Not only does the threat of a trade war between the system's two richest economies have a precedent, it also has sufficient precedents to be able to model the general nature of challenges and challengers in the world economy. Instead of basing our answers to questions about trade wars and leadership shifts solely on short-term hunches, we might do well to augment our understanding by considering the long-term evidence on the evolution of these changes with unrivaled and far-reaching significance.

If international competition seems less than intense at this very moment, the next mental reference point might be about 100 years earlier and the decline of Britain in the late nineteenth century. Britain emerged from a 50-year period of industrial revolution and combating the consequences of the French revolution as the pre-eminent economic power in the world. This power was not attributable to traditional control over extensive agrarian holdings but rather to the ability to produce manufactured goods that most other economies were not yet capable of producing and, partially as a consequence, a commanding share of world commerce. Britain remained economically preeminent throughout much of the nineteenth century. Nonetheless, parts of western Europe and the United States were improving their ability to emulate British industrial innovations. By the last third or so of the nineteenth century, two economies in particular, Germany (after 1871) and the United States, were bidding to not only catch up but also to surpass Britain in industrial innovation, especially in steel and chemicals.

One way to greatly simplify what happened over the period from about 1870 to 1945 was an often brutal sorting out of the consequences of these industrial competitions. Would one or both challengers surpass Britain in its relative economic decline phase? Would one or more successful challenger come to blows with Britain as it defended its prerogatives of preeminence after more than 50 years of little economic competition? If both challengers were successful in advancing their relative economic position, would they feel the necessity of fighting each other to determine who replaced Britain as the world's preeminent economic power? All these questions were answered ultimately in the affirmative. Britain and the United States coalesced twice to suppress the German challenge in World Wars I and II. In the process, Britain exhausted much of its resource base and the United States emerged in 1945 as the world economy's indisputable preeminent power without needing to fight its predecessor.

The story of Pax Britannica and its demise has been told many times and in a variety of ways. In the process it has become the prototypical story for political-economic challenges and the rise and fall of economic preeminence. For many, however, the extent to which it is prototypical serves only as a foundation for analogies to processes after 1945. The overtaking of Britain, in other words, is a story about what could happen to the United States. The purpose of this chapter is not to dispute that possibility. There is no question that the economic preeminence of the United States neither can be taken for granted, nor is it likely to last forever. US economic preeminence, after all, already has its challengers.

What is less clear to many observers is that the rise and fall of nineteenth-century British economic preeminence was not the beginning of a sequence of challenges.[1] Britain's position at the end of the nineteenth century was paralleled by Britain's economic position toward the end of the eighteenth century. The difference was that in the earlier case, Britain and its allied coalition was able to defeat its primary challenger. In the latter case, Britain needed a great deal more assistance than it had in the 1792–1815 period and suffered a political-economic eclipse in the 1914–1945 period. But this was little different from what had happened to the United Provinces of the Netherlands in the 1688–1713 period. The Dutch, economically preeminent in the seventeenth century, had needed assistance in fending off a French challenge in the 1680s. They facilitated a radical change in the English monarchy which led to a Dutch–English coalition against France. By 1713, the coalition had become a British–Dutch affair. By the end of the fighting, the Dutch had exhausted their resource base much as their once junior partners were to do two centuries later.

Yet the Dutch were hardly the beginning of the economic leadership transition story. They had supplanted the Portuguese who, in turn, might be said to have replaced the Venetians. The Venetians had supplanted the Genoese who, in their turn, had benefitted from the conquest of Sung China by the Mongols. There is no argument here that all of these actors were engaged in exactly the same process in precisely the same way. Nor did economic preeminence mean exactly the same thing in each successive century. But, there is sufficient similarity and connections to claim that this is a singular sequence of economic leadership, interrupted by intermittent challenges and leadership transitions, that connects Sung China in the tenth century to the United States in the late twentieth and into the early twenty-first century – a millennium later.

To make this story more plausible and to provide just enough information to make some generalizations about its regularities more plausible (the task of Chapter 8), this chapter, and the next one, offer a forced march through about 700 years or so of the activities of economic leaders and challengers prior to the nineteenth century. In the process of leading and challenging, the key participants wrote the political economic history of the world system. They also created the structural circumstances which from time to time encouraged challenges. Their story is important to the argument in the sense that it lays a foundation of basic structures, processes, and practices that we suspect have not necessarily changed as much as many readers might think. To make this argument more coherent, we need to begin with a descriptive, albeit highly selective, review of what transpired in the centuries before 1815, with specific reference to a sequence of economic preeminence and challenges.

Space precludes an examination of all of the challenging activity over the past millennia. Instead, the primary focus will be placed on the western European period between the fifteenth and early nineteenth centuries that immediately preceded the late nineteenth-century challenges of Britain. This analytical decision is not meant to suggest that pre-fifteenth-century behavior was fundamentally all that different from post-fifteenth-century behavior, at least in terms of the economic preeminence-challenger phenomenon. It was not. But the pre-fifteenth-century part of the challenge sequence involves a number of complications that would necessitate a chapter or more devoted solely to the evolution of Sung China and the Italian city states. This is an analysis certainly worth doing but it has been done elsewhere (Modelski and Thompson, 1996) and to do it again would only represent a diversion from our present concerns.

In lieu of a more detailed treatment, a considerably condensed version of the Sung–Genoa–Venice transition will have to suffice. The starting point in this sequence was Sung China in the tenth through twelfth centuries. During this time, East Asia was characterized by a multipolar regional system with China only one of several states. Military pressure from the north gradually drove the Chinese to the southeast which accelerated a number of processes. Most of all, the period was one of considerable economic innovation by the Sung, encouraged by substantial population growth and urbanization, monetization of the financial system, and major improvements in agrarian (rice) productivity. Within this context, Sung agricultural and industrial production expanded rapidly. Iron production, for instance, reached heights not attained again until the British industrial revolution in the late eighteenth century. Tied to these innovations, the Sung developed their transportation infrastructure by developing internal waterways. The political and population movement toward the coast also encouraged the development of extensive external commercial ties via traditional land but also maritime routes. Seaborne trade, especially in the twelfth century, experienced a sizable expansion in scope and volume.

All this innovative economic growth made Sung China the most advanced economy in the world for its time. If it had been able to maintain this growth trajectory, the history of the second millennium might have been rather different. But, throughout the period of rapid growth, Sung China had been under attack by neighboring states. In the thirteenth century, the Sung were finally overwhelmed and absorbed by Mongol forces. The Mongols did not set out to suppress innovative economic growth but their rule, and its associated toll in military campaigns, death, and disease, nevertheless had this effect. The Ming restoration in the fourteenth century, oriented primarily to deal with the continued Mongol threat, was unable to reignite the type of economic growth achieved in the Sung period.

If China had been a world unto itself in this era, the Sung renaissance might have been just another story of economic growth that was not sustained. But China was not isolated in this period. Its rapid growth made it the center of an extended Afro-Eurasian economy that encompassed the Mediterranean. Chinese growth encouraged growth elsewhere in the system. The eastern Mediterranean, and, in particular, some of the small Italian trading cities became noteworthy beneficiaries of this economic expansion. It is not too much of a historical stretch to suggest that the later Italian renaissance owed a great deal to the Sung Chinese renaissance.

One of the peculiarities of medieval Europe were various cities on the southern maritime periphery that were relatively autonomous of nearby land empires. Venice and Genoa became two of the most prominent examples. While part of their early success must be attributed to profits made in ferrying and supplying European Crusaders around the eastern Mediterranean, an important role must also be allocated to Italian participation and control of the western flow of Eurasian trade circuits. This control was manifested in a variety of ways – through trading enclaves in the Middle East to the control of overland trade in western Europe and the opening of maritime routes connecting the Mediterranean to the North Sea. In short, Venice and Genoa became the two leading trading states of the western terminus of Afro-Eurasian trade in the same period characterized by Sung economic expansion.

A key to Genoese and Venetian trading prominence of this period was the alternating relationship of the two Italian cities to the Byzantine Empire. When one or the other city states held the upper hand in controlling European trade to and from the general Black Sea era, the principal overland terminus of the Eurasian Silk Roads, that same trading state would also hold a superior position throughout the Mediterranean–European system. Venice held a quasi-monopoly first by providing vital naval services to the Byzantine Empire but it lost its position to Genoa when the latter backed the winning side in a Byzantine civil war. Supporting the right side in the thirteenth century gave Genoa the predominant position to profit from a byproduct of the Mongol victories. Mongol control of central Eurasia (aside from southeast Asia, India, and Europe) in the thirteenth and fourteenth centuries was beneficial for overland trade. A single empire eliminated many of the costs of engaging in overland trade that stemmed from transiting through multiple political systems subject to variable levels of order.

Yet the benefits of controlling the Black Sea terminus proved to be as finite as Sung innovation and the Mongol imperium. Forced to look for alternative outlets by the Genoese monopoly at Constantinople, the Venetians developed an increasingly exclusive relationship with the Egyptian Mamluks who controlled what was to become the primary terminus of the maritime routes connecting east and west. As the maritime routes flourished in the fourteenth and fifteenth centuries, so too did the Venetians. The Genoese attempted to break the Venetian–Mamluk monopoly on maritime trade entering the western end of Afro-Eurasia. Genoese agents attempted to develop Persian sea power in order to intercept goods heading toward the Red Sea. There were also Genoese attempts to circumnavigate Africa in order to develop an alternative route with access to the Indian Ocean. Yet none of these late thirteenth century efforts were successful. A series of naval wars between Genoa and Venice ultimately led to Genoese defeat and Venetian commercial predominance most clearly manifested in the fifteenth century.

The Sung, Genoese, and Venetian periods of economic leadership, in retrospect, can be said to have been prototypical. The Sung Chinese initiated the process by setting a foundation for a continuous sequence of leadership and challenge from tenth-century China to the late twentieth century and beyond. Prior to the Sung renaissance, there had certainly been dramatic spurts of rapid economic growth associated with politico-military expansion. These same spurts had given way to decline and invited challengers. The difference lay in the temporal gaps between leadership and challenge prior to the tenth century. Successful challengers did not necessarily inherit the leads established by their predecessors. Long periods without significant spurts of growth separated the leaders of premodern times. The Sung introduced a millennium of continuous, albeit fluctuating, economic growth characterized by the periodic spatial movement of modern growth leadership. This spatial movement was hardly random. Nor did it move west because it was predestined to do so. It moved west along the Afro-Eurasian trade routes toward economies that were the most receptive to exploit the opportunities for growth that emerged.

In the twelfth through fifteenth centuries, the small Italian cities demonstrated their receptivity and eagerness to exploit the commercial opportunities available to them. They did not monopolize trade on a Eurasian scale. They did not emulate the Sung renaissance exactly. They could not attempt either given their small size. What they could do was specialize in controlling long-distance trade in the western part of the Afro-Eurasian economy. In this sense, Genoa and Venice were regional prototypes for what was to happen in the fifteenth and sixteenth centuries. First the Portuguese broke out of the confines of the Mediterranean and exported the "Venetian model" outside the region in which it was first developed. They, along with their Spanish rivals, also contributed to integrating the Americas into the very old Afro-Eurasian economy, thereby creating a truly world-wide economy. The sequence continued when the Portuguese effort ran out of steam. The Dutch supplanted the Portuguese only to give way to their English rivals, much as the British were forced to surrender their position of economic preeminence to the United States. The leadership challenge sequence continued, the geographical scope expanded, and, eventually, the commercial thrust of economic leadership returned to the emphasis on production initiated by the Sung centuries before.

With this brief background in hand, it is appropriate to slow the pace and look more closely at the nature of the challenges associated with the Portuguese, Dutch, and first British periods of economic leadership. The assumption is that the contemporary challenge format manifested most familiarly in the late nineteenth century and perhaps ongoing now crystallized in the period between roughly the fifteenth and eighteenth centuries. It did not spring full blown from the Sung experience with its problems with "barbarian" invaders. Nor was the Genoese–Venetian duel exactly like what was to follow although there are clearly some similarities that begin to emerge in this transitional period. The point is that the challenge process, as well as its form, evolved along with the actors most involved and the global political economy whose leadership was in contest.

THE PORTUGUESE CHALLENGE

The Portuguese are rightly credited with playing a leading role in ushering in the "Age of Discoveries", which is another way of saying that Portuguese sailors found an oceanic route by which Europeans could bypass the Middle East on their way to Asia. In doing so, among other things, the Portuguese were also responsible for importing a version of the Venetian model (discussed in Chapter 5) of commercial organization to Asia. What is sometimes overlooked, however, is that the Portuguese had been applying the Venetian or eastern Mediterranean model in Africa for nearly a century before entering the Indian Ocean.

The Portuguese adventures in Morocco definitely had a noncommercial side. An underemployed nobility could play at war sporadically and hope to improve their underfinanced positions through the acquisition of loot along the way. Their sons could win their spurs in religiously sanctioned combat with non-Christians. But there were geostrategic and commercial motivations at stake, too. Several Muslim invasions of the Iberian Peninsula had been launched from Morocco. There may have been some desire to preempt the north African ambitions of Castile. Maritime commercial entry into and exits from the Mediterranean was highly vulnerable to interception and harassment from north African bases.

Moreover, the capture of Morocco was one conceivable way to dominate the wider caravan network of Saharan commerce. Europeans especially needed gold and silver to pay for Asian imports. The production levels of the traditional source, mines in central Europe, were not adequate to satisfy demands. The upper Niger and Senegal river area offered an alternative source. Boxer (1972: 6–7) argues that the Portuguese hoped to make direct contact with the precious metals source by eliminating the north African middlemen. Presumably, therefore, it was not coincidental that the Portuguese chose to first attack Ceuta, which had been a major Muslim trading center and a terminus for the Saharan gold trade, prior to its capture in 1415.

Once in control of Ceuta, Portuguese attempts to expand into the Moroccan interior were consistently frustrated. Emphasis then shifted to moving southward along the coast. Intermittently, attempts were made to capture Moroccan coastal towns. Away from Morocco, the strategy was to establish trading posts in coastal enclaves, predominately specializing in gold and slaves. At the same time Atlantic islands (Madeira, the Azores, the Canaries, and later the Cape Verde islands), characterized by comparatively less indigenous resistance, were viewed as appropriate targets for colonization.

Several aspects of these fifteenth-century activities are particularly worth high-lighting. One is that there is little indication that the Portuguese initially were searching for a route to the Indian Ocean. In the first half of the century, the primary emphasis remained on Morocco and dominating Saharan trade networks. Neverthe-less, a Genoese expedition as early as the late thirteenth century had attempted to find such a route and, historically, there had existed a close connection between Genoese maritime expertise and capital and Portuguese expansion in the Atlantic. The Portuguese thus had reason to be familiar with the concept of an Asian route via the Atlantic but it does not seem to have been a salient goal at the outset. It did become more explicit as the Portuguese pushed their way down the west African coast. Perhaps not initially but eventually the Portuguese began to desire that it would become east African coastline more quickly than it did.[2]

The Portuguese west African activities were conducted within the parameters of a royal monopoly as early as the 1440s. Henry the Navigator, a brother of the King, requested and received a monopoly over trade and exploration in the area in return for the expenses he had incurred in the earliest phase of the movement down the African coastline. What this meant was that Henry could exclude all ships but his own and/or lease the right to trade in the designated area at a price that amounted to 20 percent of the returning goods. It also meant that exploration-trading activities could be monitored closely and controlled.

The Portuguese monarch was not the only power granting trade monopolies in this area. Castile had done likewise and, not surprisingly, Portugal and Castile clashed occasionally over whose monopoly rights took precedence. However, Castile acquired a number of other interests and was usually more interested in the more proximate Canaries than in west Africa. As Portuguese ships worked farther down the African coast, Henry's monopoly was extended.

In the second half of the fifteenth century, European access to Asian goods became more difficult. Venice lost its Black Sea position when the Ottomans captured Constantinople in 1453. The Persian Gulf route was rendered problematic by Ottoman–Persian conflict. The Red Sea route became more expensive as the Mamluks increased their trade levies in anticipation of the Turkish threat. Circum-stances were more than ripe for the discovery of a fourth route that completely circumvented the first three. The Portuguese obliged by finding a way around the African continent, up the east coast of Africa, and arriving in Calicut in 1498.

There is some debate about the original Portuguese intentions in the Indian Ocean. Diffie and Winius (1977) have suggested that they were prepared to engage in peaceful trade with non-Muslims but that Muslim traders encouraged the Zamorin of Calicut to mistrust the new arrivals and to make it difficult for the Portuguese to obtain spices. To overcome Muslim intransigence, Portugal was forced to use coercion.

Curtin (1984: 137) argues more hypothetically that the Portuguese might have tried to trade by Indian Ocean rules – an economic theater which functioned predominantly on free trade lines. Muslim traders were a significant group in this theater but they did not function as a monolithic group. They also had no history of interfering with non-Muslim trade in the Indian Ocean. In this context, the Portuguese conceivably could have paid some form of tribute to local rulers and possibly hedged their security bets by the construction of a few well-placed coastal fortresses. They still could have played by customary local rules. That they did not pursue this approach, Curtin (1984: 138) attributes to Italian instruction on how to do things and a traditional aristocratic preference for coercive techniques.

A third interpretation is that Portugal's principal goal was always to take away a Muslim monopoly over the Indian Ocean flow of spices and transform it into a Portuguese one. This view can be regarded as encompassing two versions – one relatively narrow and one liberal. The narrow version is that the Portuguese envisioned outflanking the Mediterranean distribution points where Muslim rulers were in a position to impose protection fees. The Egyptian Mamluk control of the Red Sea route is the most prominent example. Of course, this meant outflanking the Venetian intermediary role as well. As one early sixteenth century Portuguese writer states: "Whoever is Lord of Malacca has his hands on the throat of Venice" (quoted in Chaudhuri, 1985: 113).

The more liberal interpretation subsumes the narrow version and adds the idea that the Portuguese believed Muslim traders dominated the trade of the Indian Ocean. Not only would a Portuguese trade monopoly outflank Muslim choke points, it would also displace or supplant the group currently controlling the maritime commerce in the Indian Ocean.

Choosing among all these interpretations is difficult because information on Portuguese motivations is not plentiful. It is also difficult because the interpretations tend to overlap with one another thereby making it difficult to completely reject any of the variations outright. What we know is that Asian trade in general was not subject to or accustomed to any maritime hegemony. Strong and weak rulers prevailed on land but on the whole they demonstrated little sustained interest in maritime commerce other than as a source of revenue. There was no Muslim monopoly of Indian Ocean traffic in the Portuguese sense. Egyptians and Arabs dominated in the Arabian Sea connections between India and the Middle East. Muslim Gujeratis were the principal maritime merchants connecting western and eastern India. There was no history of these groups acting in concert before the Portuguese arrived. In fact, some Muslim–Portuguese cooperation did occur from time to time.[3]

Still, the Portuguese arrival in the Indian Ocean introduced some new ingredients into Asian commerce. Muslim–Christian hostility was imported for one thing. Muslim merchants did attempt to make it more difficult for the new arrivals to engage in the Indian trade. European sea power entered a world which had not been exposed in recent times to powerful national fleets, with the sole exception of the Chinese fleets of the early fifteenth century. A third novelty is that the militarily powerful (at least at sea), Christian–Portuguese had little to offer in exchange for the spices they sought. Keeping in mind the precedent set by the trading enclave network developed in northwest Africa and combining the novelties of the Portuguese entry into the Indian Ocean, it probably does not matter whether subsequent Portuguese actions had been fully premeditated or, as is more likely, were subject to some evolution. What they chose to do seems fairly predictable with the advantages of hindsight.

Asian maritime commerce revolved around a set of regional entrepôts or transit ports between Egypt and China. Curtin (1984: 128) nominates Alexandria, Aden, Cambay, Malacca, and Zaitun as the most important. Abu-Lughod's (1989: 252) delineation of three main Indian Ocean subsystems shows how these principal emporia were interconnected. Imagine three concentric and overlapping circles. The first circle had a center south of the Arabian Sea. The second circle was centered below the Bay of Bengal midway between India and southeast Asia. The third circle reached from the second circle's midpoint to the South Pacific east of the Philippines and what is now Indonesia. Alexandria in Egypt was just to the northwest of the first trade circuit which also encompassed Aden and Cambay. The second circuit linked Cambay and Malacca, while the third one connected Malacca to Zaytun.

The Portuguese sought to control as many of the major ports and the activity between them as they could. Military force was concentrated at key points and could be projected to attack points of resistance or defend against attacks at vulnerable points in the system. Asian merchants were required to pay protection fees for the right to move goods at sea. Taxes were levied on merchandise transiting through ports controlled directly by the Portuguese. In addition, the Portuguese crown would maintain a monopoly on Asian goods imported to Europe.

To carry out these ambitious undertakings, the Portuguese created a network of bases and trading enclaves stretching from east Africa to Japan. Goa and Malacca were the principal network nodes with lesser contributions (in the sixteenth century) made by Sofala, Mozambique, Mombasa, Hormuz, Ternate, Macao, and Nagasaki. Attempts to capture Aden were unsuccessful.

It took some time to cobble this framework together but the initial impact was still quite dramatic. An early Venetian perspective, provided by Giolamo Priuli, is interesting in this respect:

> Whence it is that the King of Portugal has found this new voyage and that the spices which should come from Calicut, Cochin and other places in India to Alexandria or Beyrout, and later come to Venice, and in this place become monopolized, whence all the world comes to buy such spicery and carry gold, silver, and every other merchandise, . . . , today, with this new voyage by the King of Portugal, all the spices which came by way of Cairo will be controlled in Portugal, because the caravels which will go to India, to Calicut and other places to take them . . . And truly the Venetian merchants are in a bad way, believing that the voyages should make them very poor.
>
> (quoted in Chaudhuri, 1985: 64–65)

Priuli wrote in 1501 and captured the initial impact of the new Portuguese monopoly. The impact was not permanent. The failure to capture Aden meant that the Portuguese were unable to close the Red Sea route. Their trade licensing system was dependent on a much stronger naval presence than the increasingly overstretched Portuguese could muster. The system also became increasingly subject to corruption. As Scammell (1981: 140) notes, by 1566, twice as much pepper was reaching Levantine ports, much to the relief of the Venetians, as the Portuguese were importing into Europe. But it is equally true that the overall volume of Asian imports to Europe had also increased during this time. All this means is that the efficacy of the Portuguese monopoly eroded. It does not mean that the network disintegrated. The Portuguese remained in place throughout Asia and could scarcely be avoided by the next wave of aspiring European trading monopolists.

THE DUTCH CHALLENGE

Initially, the Dutch challenge of the Iberian political-economic order was much less premeditated than the Portuguese attack on the Venetian–Mamluk lock on the Red Sea route. What became a full-blown challenge began as a provincial revolt in defense of traditional privileges. Developments that occurred during the attempted suppression of the revolt played an important role in chrystalizing the nature of the challenge. So, too, did the strong commercial role played by Dutch shipping that had been developed prior to the outset of the revolt. The latter provided an economic foundation based on bulk freightage. The former shaped the probability that the economic resources would be employed towards the expansion of the Dutch position in the international political economy.

Prior to the 1570s, Antwerp, a southern Netherlands port on the Scheldt River, had become Europe's principal entrepôt. It had assumed the central clearing house functions formerly played by the medieval fairs. Venice and Genoa traded there. For many years, most of Portugal's spices were marketed through Antwerp. A fair amount of Spain's silver and other colonial commodities eventually arrived there. English wool and undyed cloth and Baltic grain and timber were other important spokes in Antwerp's mercantile wheel. Northern Netherlands shipping was particularly salient in carrying Baltic grain but also other commodities such as naval stores on the Baltic–Iberian Peninsula circuit.[4] North Sea fishing was another speciality of the northern Netherlands provinces. The demands of the fisheries combined with carrying role helped to make Dutch ship builders and their techniques the most advanced in Europe. In turn, advanced shipbuilding technology made Dutch fishing and carrying ships the most efficient maritime vehicles in Europe. Geographical positioning more or less midway between the Baltic and Iberian states and at the terminus of the Rhine–northern Mediterranean interior trade route further facilitated the application of their superior marine technology.

Technology and geography are useful things to have on one's side. Rarely are they sufficient. There were, for instance, a number of junctures in the Dutch revolt that might have led to a totally different outcome. The Spanish might have been more flexible in dealing with the traditional provincial privileges and sensitivities of the Netherlands. If there had been no revolt, a systematic and systemic challenge might not have emerged toward the end of the sixteenth century. If Queen Elizabeth had not evicted the "sea beggars" from their English sanctuaries, the seizure of critical Dutch ports might not have been tried successfully in the early 1570s. Without this early sea control edge, the revolt might not have survived as long as it did. Then, too, a successful 1588 Armada would certainly have altered the future trajectory of the Netherlands and possibly the entire world system.

Particularly critical to the forthcoming Dutch challenge, however, was the destruction of Antwerp as the principal European entrepôt and the migration of that function to Amsterdam. It would have been more difficult to maintain Antwerp's economic role in the midst of an imperial civil war in any event. The 1585 disruption wrought by Spanish reconquest, unpaid mutineers, and the interruption of the flow of goods into and out of Antwerp brought by the Dutch rebels' closing of the Scheldt and a blockade of the Flemish coast interacted to ensure Antwerp's decline. The commercial, production, and financial skills and resources, which had been at the core of Antwerp's success, were strongly encouraged to move elsewhere.

As Israel (1989) emphasizes, that elsewhere did not have to be Amsterdam and, in fact, it was not the first choice of many refugees from Antwerp. The Spanish had blocked Dutch access to Iberian markets and commodities after 1585 Spanish troops were expected to succeed eventually in their revolt suppression mission. Amsterdam hardly seemed the most attractive alternative to Antwerp. Nevertheless, Spanish decision-makers helped things along by shifting their military priorities to the French theater in 1590. In desperate need of Baltic products, they also reopened Iberian ports to Dutch shipping. While the military and economic pressures with which they were being confronted were being ameliorated, the Dutch continued their blockade of Antwerp thereby precluding the possibility of its revival. Dutch troops went on the offensive and were able to expel Spanish garrisons in a number of northern towns. Building on the commercial maritime base established throughout the 1500s, the European entrepôt function and its leading entrepreneurs gravitated toward the northern Netherlands with Amsterdam at the center.

The decade of the 1590s witnessed an abrupt outpouring of Dutch traders throughout the world: Russian, the Mediterranean, the Caribbean, West Africa, and Asia. The scale and success of the initial penetrations were variable but the Asian experience was particularly revealing. The expansion of Dutch trade represented, among other things, an expansion of its European redistribution function. The difference was that the Dutch were not content to play the role of regional (European) intermediary. After the 1590s, they sought similar roles throughout the globe. The incentives for expansion were bolstered by the reimposition of an Iberian embargo on Dutch goods and shipping in 1598. If the Dutch could no longer (or not as easily as before) collect goods in Iberian ports brought in from the rest of the world, why not bypass the Iberian ports and go directly to the original sources?

In this sense, the Dutch attack on Eurasian trade was quite similar to the earlier Portuguese effort. Both involved flanking an already established monopoly and imposing a new monopoly that benefitted their own national group and discriminated against others. Inasmuch as the Dutch sought the same goods in which the

Portuguese were interested, the most straightforward strategy entailed seizing and taking over the Portuguese network outright. But this network proved more resistant than the Dutch had anticipated. Hormuz fell fairly early (1622) but Malacca held out until 1641. Most of the other nodes of the Portuguese network lasted much longer. Two of the most prominent, Goa and Macao, survived well into the twentieth century.[5]

An alternative strategy was to push the flanking metaphor a bit further. In the three Indian Ocean subsystems, the Portuguese were the strongest in the first zone they had entered and weakest in much of the third zone beyond Malacca. They also had focused most of their network on and around the main continental entrepôts. In contrast, the Dutch centered their alternative network to the south of the continent in the Indonesian archipelago and at the source of a number of Asian spices. The Dutch also found that they could shorten the voyage around Africa by taking a more southerly route (the "roaring forties") through the Indian Ocean to the spice islands. None of this implied to the Dutch any reason for an increased tolerance of the Portuguese. Attacks on the Portuguese network and harassment of their shipping continued without pause. At the same time, a second network was constructed with the main nodes at Cape Town, Bandar Abbas, Ceylon, Batavia (Jakarta), and Taiwan.

The Dutch plan for dominating Eurasian trade was even more ambitious than the schemes of their Portuguese predecessors. Rather than working within the existing structure of Asian trade, and overstretching themselves as the Portuguese had, the Dutch sought to restructure it around a Batavian center. Batavia should become the principal entrepôt for all trade within Asia and a staging platform for goods to be sent back to Europe. Areas of spice production, in particular, would be controlled as directly as necessary. Asian traders would be tolerated as long as they accepted subordination to the Batavian core market. Other European traders were to be kept out of the Dutch preserve as much as practical.

The main instrument to carry out this plan was the United Netherlands Chartered East India Company (VOC), organized in 1602. When Dutch traders had initially arrived in the Indian Ocean, they found themselves competing against one another, with the Portuguese, and to a lesser extent, the Spanish. English traders had begun to arrive as well. Local rulers and markets responded with increases in prices and tolls. One of the main purposes of the VOC was to reduce the competition among the Dutch. Another was to mobilize some of the same types of resources provided by the Portuguese state: capital, ships, men, and forts. The joint stock approach was a departure from the Portuguese model but the VOC, despite its private corporate status, maintained extremely close links to public decision-makers.

The VOC also took its monopolistic charter even more seriously than the Portuguese in more ways than simply general strategy. After about two decades of disappointing profits, the company's degree of ruthlessness escalated under the leadership of Jan Pieterzoon Coen. Coen attacked the problem at its source by capturing a number of spice producing islands. Their inhabitants were treated harshly, running the gamut from enslavement, deportation, and execution to allowing the most stubborn resisters to starve. Where the Dutch control was direct, output was regulated closely according to demand specifications determined in Amsterdam. Surplus spice production was held off the market or simply destroyed. Spice trees were destroyed to reduce the possibilities of future surpluses.

Another example of the Dutch appreciation for monopoly is provided by the Dutch approach to breaking into the Chinese market. At the end of the 1609–1621 truce with Spain, the Dutch found themselves faced with a shortage of silver. Since the demand for European goods in Asia remained low, silver was essential for European purchases of Asian commodities. Unfortunately for the Dutch, Spanish silver mines in America constituted the principal European source of silver. One possible alternative was Japanese silver. The Japanese were willing to exchange their silver for Chinese silks. However, this Sino–Japanese silk for silver trade was already dominated by Chinese, Japanese, and Portuguese agents. Moreover, the Chinese government viewed the Dutch VOC with considerable hostility due to the Company's earlier mistreatment of Chinese spice traders. The Spanish in Manila and the Portuguese in Macao were viewed as more suitable trading partners.

To resolve their silver/silk dilemma, the Dutch first made an official request to begin trading operations in China. Once the request was denied, a less polite strategy was employed. Manila was blockaded with English assistance. Macao was attacked unsuccessfully in 1622. A third target was Chinese shipping in the vicinity of the south China coast. The idea was to paralyze China's trade until the Dutch were granted not only entry into Chinese markets but also a predominant position in China's external trade. The harassment tactics were successful. By 1624, the Dutch had been authorized to establish their Chinese trading station, Fort Zeelandia, on Taiwan.

Serendipity worked in the Dutch favor as well. Spanish personnel were expelled from Japan for missionary activity in the same year. In 1635, the Japanese were no longer allowed to leave their own islands. Three years later, the Portuguese were also evicted from Japan because of their efforts to expand the numbers of Christians there. The Dutch, who had stayed aloof from missionary activity, almost suffered the same fate but managed to stay in place as the only Europeans permitted to trade with Japan. Thus a combination of coercion and considerable luck helped the Dutch to achieve at least part of the monopoly position to which they had aspired two decades earlier. It did not prove to be a permanent position in all respects. In the 1660s, the Dutch were evicted from Fort Zeelandia and the Japanese banned the export of silver. But the Dutch were able to switch from silver to copper until the Japanese reduced the outflow of that metal as well. The Dutch monopoly as the European trader with Japan continued until the mid-nineteenth century and the arrival of US and other European ships.

Another important aspect of Dutch policy was its territorial expansionist character in areas such as the Indonesian islands and Ceylon. At first, as described in Chapter 5, the Dutch would sign treaties with local rulers to permit fortified trading enclaves and to establish the parameters of the Dutch commercial monopolies. Some of these local rulers became increasingly dependent on these European forts for financial and military assistance. Both subsequently and consequently, indigenous wars, insurrections and labor unrest prompted Dutch military intervention if for no other reason because these developments were bad for business. As a consequence, Dutch pacification efforts yielded more and more territory under direct Dutch control. In some cases, the Dutch explicitly sought the increased territorial control. In other cases, they ended up keeping control because it seemed to provide more certainty and profit for their business operations.

Despite these proclivities, or, in part, because of them, the Dutch lead proved to be as ephemeral as the Portuguese lead had been. By the end of the seventeenth century, the United Provinces of the Netherlands was confronted by two rival challengers – France and England. The thread of that story is picked up in the next chapter.

7

MOUNTAINS OF GOLD
AND IRON

THE ENGLISH CHALLENGE

Summarizing the nature of the English challenge is made awkward by the slow pace of its development and the relatively unusual nature of the eventual outcome. After providing vital assistance to the Dutch challenge of the Iberian order at the end of the sixteenth century, the English backed away from their own direct, mid-seventeenth-century challenge of the Dutch commercial order in the midst of fighting three wars. Yet they emerged ultimately (in the eighteenth century) as the systemic winner almost in spite of their intermittent and hesitant policies.

English nationals had certainly participated in the efforts to break or nibble away at the Iberian monopolies centered in Africa and America in the sixteenth century. But they had done this, for the most part, as private citizens and on a very limited scale. Capital was scarce. Available shipping was limited as were products worth exporting. State support for commercial expansion was extremely limited and more often nonexistent. Elizabeth I might secretly invest in a Hawkins or Drake expedition while at the same time officially condemning English attacks on Spanish commerce in America. The much-vaunted development of English sea power either of the private or public variety had not yet proceeded very far.

England did play an important role in the Dutch revolt. The evidence (Wernham, 1966; Wilson, 1970), however, seems to suggest that the principal motivation was geopolitical. Elizabeth found the concept of rebellion against royal authority distasteful and declined an opportunity to assume a lead role within the Dutch aristocracy. A strong Spanish presence in the northern Netherlands, though, was a different matter for the prevention of the build-up of a potential foreign threat in this nearby locale had become an axiom of English foreign policy. To suppress the revolt, Spanish troops would have to occupy the Netherlands and remain there in force. It was to prevent this development that England assisted the Dutch in the war with Spain between 1585 and 1604.

The withdrawal of English support hinged on the ascension of James I, his pro-Spanish proclivities, and the diminished threat of Spanish success against the northern provinces. There was also an early recognition, at least at the private level, of some of the implications of the rise of Dutch commercial power. On hearing that the Dutch had successfully penetrated the Eurasian market in 1599, English traders in the eastern Mediterranean feared that their access to Asian goods via Aleppo would be undermined (Furber, 1976: 32). Scammell (1981) goes further in suggesting that the English East Indies Company was established precisely because of this fear of Levantine operations being outflanked by the Dutch arrival in Asia.[1] The perceived threat of a future improvement in Dutch–Spanish relations which would work to bar English participation in both Dutch and Iberian markets was another concern of the times.

Once English merchants had been galvanized into initiating Asian operations, they found their way blocked by Portuguese and Dutch resistance.[2] In western India, the Portuguese informed local rulers that they would have to make a choice between the well-established Portuguese and the latest arrivals. Anyone trading with the English would be deprived of contact with the Portuguese. English ships were considered fair game by Portuguese galleons. The atmosphere of intense commercial rivalry from the English perspective is nicely captured in a 1601 comment from the East India Company's first representative in Surat: "I could not peep out of the doors for fear of the Portugals, who in troops lay lurking in the by-ways to give me assault to murther me" (quoted in de Schweinitz, 1983: 76). As a consequence, English merchants in western India were not paid much attention until their ships demonstrated that they could defeat Portuguese galleons in local waters.

The Dutch worked almost as hard to keep the English out of their Indonesian markets. Initially, the English and Dutch worked together to evict the Portuguese from the Spice Islands. Once this was accomplished, the more numerous, better-financed and better-armed Dutch came to regard the English as allies who had out-lived their usefulness. One of the ironies of commercial and imperial history is that the English were more or less forced to concentrate their Asian attentions on western India because the Dutch had not demonstrated much interest in this area in the early seventeenth century. When the Dutch did show more interest in India, the English presence was protected by the dominant Mughal Empire. During this period, English activities were focused largely on Surat, Bandar Abbas (Persia), and Bantam (Java). The Persian foothold was acquired only after the English had provided naval assistance to a Persian army attempting to evict the Portuguese from their Hormuz base (1622).

The early English presence in India was fairly marginal and depended on arrangements worked out with Indian rulers. Indian tolerance was exchanged for revenues and occasional naval assistance, in part, because of the marginal English presence, India and even Asia in general was not a major bone of contention in the Anglo-Dutch confrontation. The Dutch aggressively exclusive policies in Asia were certainly resented. George Downing's 1663 observation on Dutch commercial hypocrisy is a case in point: "these people doe arrogate to themselves St. Peter's powers upon the seas. It is *mare liberum* in the British Seas but *mare clausum* on ye coast of Africa and in ye East Indies" (quoted in Wilson, 1957: 118).

The Amboina "massacre's" long-lived emotional appeal as a rallying cry is another case in point.[3] Nonetheless, Anglo-Dutch conflict was primarily centered on economic activities in Europe and the Atlantic.[4] The core of the conflict was captured succinctly by the mid-seventeenth century English general Monk: "What matters this or that reason? What we want is more of the trade the Dutch now have" (quoted in Mahan, 1890: 107)

During the first half of the seventeenth century, the Dutch had either achieved a dominant commercial position or built upon dominance achieved earlier in the Baltic, the Mediterranean, the East Indies, west Africa, the West Indies, and New England. Everywhere the English merchants turned, they found the Dutch already there in strength and with the ability to undercut or drive out English commercial efforts. It is not surprising that most Englishmen believed that an increase in English trade could only come at the expense of the Dutch. This belief was usually embraced most intensely in periods of economic depression.

English resentment of Dutch commercial dominance was fueled further by the notion that the very roots of Dutch success could be traced back to Dutch exploitation of English resources. One of these roots were the North Sea fisheries lying off the English coast. Fisheries trained sailors, encouraged ship design innovations and shipbuilding, and produced an important product for trade. English fisheries were thus an important foundation of the Dutch maritime orientation. The other resource was partially finished cloth, England's main export. The Dutch completed the finishing process in the Netherlands, realized most of the value added profits and, adding insult to injury, used the product to outcompete English merchants, especially in Baltic markets.

Wilson (1957: 144–145) expresses the essence of this attitude toward Dutch commercial dominance:

> The burden of England's tale of complaint was, in brief, that the Dutch carried away from England and her dependencies little but raw materials and semi-manufactured goods, making large profits in the subsequent stages of manufacture and commerce. The skill of the Dutch in selling back manufactures, necessities and luxuries to their victim was only the second stage of a process plausibly represented as one of double robbery. . . . as long as the Dutch sucked England dry of her stocks of raw materials, there could be no development of England's manufacturing capacity, no opportunity for English merchants to benefit by the most profitable stages of the economic process.

Thus, what Wilson described quite accurately as a lag in technical skill led to a popular rationale emphasizing the dependency barriers to development. The seventeenth century rationale, as in the case of more contemporary dependency theories, was not entirely off the mark. The Dutch, less objectively, were portrayed as monopolistic parasites. To improve the health of the host, the obvious remedy was to eliminate or reduce the parasite's access to the host.

This parasite imagery also fed into one of the central threads of mercantilist thought, the bullion argument. To the extent that the Dutch dominated trade, they drained the countries with which they traded of the money which purchased the goods supplied by the leading European middlemen. The money obtained by trade provided an abundant capital base in the Netherlands to be used for investment in commerce and production. Two byproducts of this abundance were relatively low interest rates and, therefore, operating costs which were extremely useful in beating out the competition (Jones, 1980: 60).

By outperforming their competitors, the Dutch were deemed to be guilty of the twin evils of "sucking England dry" of raw materials and draining its bullion. The Dutch, therefore, became the primary scapegoats for the failure of English efforts to reverse its dependency position. Specific attempts had been made in the early seventeenth century to cut off Dutch access to English fisheries but the English lacked the naval power to enforce their prohibitions and the fishing infrastructure to exploit the nearby natural resource.

Similarly, early efforts to finish English cloth in England failed. The Cockayne Project is perhaps the best-known effort. Between 1613 and 1617, the export of unfinished cloth was prohibited. The monopoly to export cloth was taken from one group and given to another who soon found that they were unable to handle the amount of cloth involved. The Dutch made matters worse by banning the import of finished cloth. The English quickly abandoned this brief experiment in dependency reversal (Conybeare, 1987).

As many as nine diplomatic missions between 1610 and 1636 failed to resolve specific Anglo-Dutch trading disputes. If internal development projects and diplomatic efforts were unsuccessful, it should be expected that repeated emphasis would be placed on political-military techniques to improve England's relative position. The temptation to use force was all the more probable to the extent that the English viewed the Dutch commercial network as increasingly vulnerable. Wilson (1957: 4–5) pinpointed five aspects of perceived vulnerability. First, Dutch trade dominance was manifested in a number of different regions throughout the world but these different regions were becoming increasingly interdependent. Successful interference in one region should have repercussions throughout the network.

Of the many regions in which the Dutch operated, the Baltic and East Indies regions shared an important trade liability. In both cases, the goods extracted from these regions were worth more than the goods the Dutch could bring in from other areas. The one exception to this rule, seemingly in partial contradiction to the mercantilist's bullion argument, was Spanish silver. If Dutch access to the Spanish empire could be reduced, it could not continue to trade as successfully as it had.

A third consideration was linked to the geographical position of the Netherlands. The Dutch were well situated to take advantage of trade between the Baltic and Iberian regions. Yet the English (and the French) were equally well situated to disrupt traffic entering or exiting Dutch ports. This aspect of Dutch vulnerability was compounded by the type of vessels on which Dutch trade depended. The flyboats were large and inexpensive to operate, but they were also slow and not very well-armed. When one adds as a fifth factor the high level of dependence of the Dutch economy, not only on trade as a source of profit, but also on a sufficient influx of food and raw materials to keep the economy functioning, an attack on Dutch commercial dominance seemed feasible.

Several other developments are necessary to understand the bellicose English challenges of the mid-seventeenth century. One development had to do with colonial trade problems. Prior to the rise of Dutch commercial dominance, the English, by default, had enjoyed a natural monopoly of trade with its American colonies (Lloyd, 1984). In addition to their other commercial advantages, the Dutch managed to seize the Portuguese bases in west Africa that supplied the Caribbean sugar plantation slave markets. A second base of operations, in what was to become parts of New York, New Jersey, Delaware, and Pennsylvania, divided the southern English colonies from those in New England. In the 1640s, the Dutch took advantage of the English civil wars to penetrate and dominate the trade between the colonies and England.

The 1648 end of warfare with Spain also permitted the Dutch to regain some of the Spanish markets that had been temporarily lost to English traders. In 1649, the Dutch gained still another commercial edge over England by negotiating an arrangement with Denmark that gave the Netherlands preferential sound toll rates.

While Dutch commercial advantages seemed to be improving on a variety of fronts, the English state had emerged from its civil wars both more willing and more capable of protecting and expanding English trade. The same civil wars had intensified a depressed English economy thereby giving the government more incentive to intervene. One barrier to dealing more forcefully with the Dutch remained. The new English government was now vulnerable in a manner somewhat similar to the Dutch provinces in the 1570s–1580s. The English monopoly had been overthrown but there was no guarantee that an effort to reinstate the Stuarts from within or outside could not be successful. To insure against that possibility, the English government tried to arrange a union with their most natural ally, commercial grievances notwithstanding, the United Provinces in 1651.

The Dutch preferred to avoid what was regarded as an unnecessary entanglement. In response to the English proposal, they offered recognition of the new state and proposed that Dutch merchants should enjoy equality with English merchants in English trade. The equality proposal, however, did not encompass English rights in Dutch trade.

The unappealing Dutch counterproposal led to the passing of the Navigation Act of 1651. Goods originating outside of Europe could enter England only in English ships. Reexports through European entrepôts in non-English ships were banned outright. European goods could be imported only in ships from the country of origin or English ships. Fish caught by English fishermen could only be exported in English ships.

To enforce these prohibitions, English naval vessels began stopping and searching suspected shipping. The Dutch were compelled to provide naval protection for their vessels. The first Anglo-Dutch war broke out in a clash between enforcement and protection-oriented fleets of the respective states.

The conduct of this war and other wars involving commercial motivations are not our direct concern in this study. However, it is worth noting that while war broke out on a partially unintentional basis, war was the logical outcome of the monopoly-breaking ideas entertained by the English. If the Dutch accepted the new English commercial rules peacefully, English trade would benefit. If the Dutch did not accept the rules, the English felt prepared to impose them on the Dutch who were viewed as highly vulnerable by both the English and the Dutch. As the principal Dutch decision maker, Adriaan Pauw, commented when war began in 1652: "The English are about to attack a mountain of gold; we are about to attack a mountain of iron" (quoted in Wilson, 1957: 60).

Three Anglo-Dutch wars (1652–1654, 1665–1667, 1672–1674) were fought in the seventeenth century. The very fact that there were three of them suggests a certain amount of inconclusiveness. The first one did seem to work the way the English had hoped in that the Dutch suffered considerable trade losses. Yet, at the same time, the English, and especially Cromwell, continued to hold out hope that the Dutch would join England in a crusade against the Catholic powers. If the Dutch were damaged too greatly in a war with the English, their alliance value and their willingness to cooperate would be diminished significantly. Geopolitical considerations prevailed over commercial designs and the English decline to push their advantage as they might have.

Anglo-Dutch commercial conflicts remained the same after the war as they had been before. The tactics of the two sides persisted as well. The 1651 Act had proved awkward to monitor. In 1660, a new Act switched the prohibition emphasis from trade in general to specific commodities. Even so, these new restrictions still encompassed about half of England's European and colonial trade (Wilson, 1957). The Staple Act of 1663 required English colonies to purchase all their European goods from England. The Dutch and English trading companies continued to clash in west Africa over control of the slave trade. A series of raids and reprisals took place there between 1661 and 1664.

Nevertheless, the second Anglo-Dutch war began with an English preemptive strike against the Dutch colony in North America. The colony was captured easily in 1664 but other war objectives proved difficult to attain. In the end, English shipping suffered more greatly than did that of the Dutch. The French entry into the war on the side of the Dutch, moreover, helped to reorient English perceptions about who was really the primary enemy. So, too, did French protectionist measures (1664, 1667) against Dutch commerce that impacted on the export of English cloth.

The second Anglo-Dutch war had several outcomes. English commercial interests learned the hard way that they could not expect a short naval war to alter England's trade position in a significant fashion. In one of those intriguing but relatively rare revolutions in perceptions of external threat, France increasingly became identified as the leading threat to both the Dutch and the English. Anglo-French hostility, of course, had a long history dating back to 1066. In the late seventeenth century only one state presented an economic and a military-political threat to the two Protestant states. This overshadowed the more narrow, primarily economic oppression/threat that the Dutch represented to the English and vice versa. For the Dutch, it was clear which threat was closer to home and, therefore, the more serious one.

Other factors facilitated the switch in the identification of the primary enemy despite the fact that the Dutch and English still fought another brief war in the 1670s. One that should probably be given more emphasis than it usually receives is the shift in growth sectors taking place in the last third of the seventeenth century. Wilson (1957: 155) describes the shift as a structural change in English trade. The traditional, extreme reliance on cloth exports was giving way to the reexport of colonial and non-European commodities. But such a shift presupposes increasing supply of, and demand for, colonial products.

From the perspective of the then world economy, the shift meant that earlier preoccupations with fish, wool cloth, and even spices were giving way to US sugar and tobacco and Asian cotton and tea as leading growth sectors in trade. The English were better-positioned to take advantage of this change than were the Dutch who were tied more closely to the older trade products. The French may not have been as well-positioned as the English but they were hardly committed to the more traditional trades. They also appeared to have developed a new appreciation for the benefits of colonial possessions and trading privileges in precisely those areas of greatest interest to the English: North America, the Caribbean, Latin America and India.

We are a long way from being finished with the English at this point but our purposes are best served by shifting the focus to the overlapping French commercial challenges. The French challenges are so closely intertwined with English–British activities that the shift in focus will be more apparent than real.

In this chapter we continue the description of commercial leadership ascensions and transitions begun in Chapter 6. Singling out the French challenges for separate, although not special, treatment is more than merely convenient. The French challenges of Louis XIV and Napoleon serve to bridge the gap between the mercantilistic orientations that predominated up to the late eighteenth century and the relatively new emphasis on industrial production that began to emerge immediately prior to the beginning of the nineteenth century. Thus, these challenges should give us some hints as to whether a challenger model based on the older forms of commercial rivalries is likely to serve us equally well in the nineteenth and twentieth centuries. After laying out the specifics of the French challenges, we turn immediately to these questions of model construction and longitudinal applicability.

THE FRENCH CHALLENGES

Pre-Napoleonic France is an excellent example of a state with oscillating strategic orientations. Fundamentally a rich but not very cohesive, maritime economy, decision-makers would make periodic efforts to expand France's ability to engage in overseas activities. Francis I, for example, disputed the 1493 Papal Bull dividing the non-European world between Spain and Portugal. In 1533, he was successful in obtaining a papal reinterpretation which stated that the 1493 division applied only to territories known then and not lands subsequently discovered. As Knecht (1982: 333) observes, "Francis was thus able to challenge the monopoly claimed by the Iberian powers without fear of incurring spiritual sanctions".

It is not clear that the French were all that concerned by the threat of spiritual sanctions but the reinterpretation did serve to legitimize their exploration and colonial activities in North America. More direct attacks on Iberian territory in the early sixteenth century were restricted largely to privateering interceptions of Spanish and Portuguese shipping in the Atlantic and some interloping in Brazil. For the most part, state encouragement of these activities was present but not overly enthusiastic. The conduct of European wars was always a more pressing preoccupation.

A 100 years later and after a series of civil wars, Cardinal Richelieu sought to revive interest in maritime trade, sea power, and colonization. A classical mercantilist, Richelieu believed the French economy was nearly self-sufficient with the exception of spices and other Asian luxuries. Other economies, however, could not manage without French commodities. The basic problem was that foreigners had carved out a commercial monopoly in French trade (Tapie, 1984: 255). To regain control it was necessary to transport French products in French ships, continue the creation of trading companies with exclusive rights over the territories they conquered or colonized, and encourage shipbuilding and industrial productivity through royal subsidies. Expansion in New France (Canada) continued but Richelieu's more general plans for regaining control of French trade did not go very well. They foundered on the usual constraints faced by French policy makers, including the more urgent demands of European warfare.

The first major French challenge emerged in the last third of the seventeenth century under the direction of Colbert and Louis XIV and was aimed primarily at the Dutch commercial supremacy.

> Nowhere in mid-seventeenth-century Europe did there arise a more acute resentment at being enmeshed in the tentacles of Dutch economic power than in the France of of Louis XIV . . .
>
> . . . the Dutch Republic was perceived as "le magazin general" which, by means of cheap freightage, low interest, the buying up of commodities ahead, and superiority in industrial techniques, had reduced France and all Europe to a humiliating subjection in matters maritime and commercial.
>
> (Israel, 1989: 284)

Since the challenge involved heavy tariff increases on cloth imports, it quickly affected the English, too. Jones (1980: 120) even suggests that the anti-Dutch tariffs were more damaging to the English who were less competitive than the ostensible target of the trade barriers. However, Israel (1989: 284) notes that France was a major market for the Dutch and, therefore, France was in a better position to damage the Dutch trade network than the English had been. Colbert operated from a mercantilistic outlook similar to his predecessor Cardinal Richelieu. His fundamental position was that "commerce causes a perpetual combat in peace and war among the nations of

Europe, as to who shall win the most of it" (quoted in Cole, 1939, vol. 1: 343). Since population and consumption were thought to be constants, commerce was a constant as well. If a weak state wished to become more powerful, it was necessary to reduce the trade proportions controlled by other nations. If successful, the amount of money drained away by foreigners, especially the Dutch, would decrease.

In this respect, Colbert echoed English mercantilism but his own emphasis was more statist. The money drained from France by foreign trade made money less abundant and, therefore, more difficult for taxes to be paid. A state's relative strength depended on its financial base which, in turn, was predicated to a large degree on tax collections.

The Colbertian reform plan was extensive and ambitious. Many of the measures should by now sound familiar:

1   minimize imports by increasing national self sufficiency;
2   support the expansion of all existing industries; develop industries not already in existence, especially those capable of bringing in money from other countries;
3   require any surviving imports to be carried only on French ships and to be imported only by French merchants as much as possible so that profits and freight charges not be kept by foreign middlemen;
4   prohibit the export of bullion;
5   reduce duties on exports; increase duties prohibitively on imports;
6   exclude foreign traders from colonial commerce, especially in the West Indies and Canada;
7   create monopolistic companies to carry and expand French trade to the West Indies, Baltic, North Africa, Levant, West Africa, and East Indies;
8   expand the size of the royal navy and the extent to which it operated overseas in defense of French interests.

Colbert was not simply trying to improve the relative political-economic position of France. According to Clark (1931: 69–70), he believed, incorrectly, that at the beginning of the seventeenth century, not only did France not have a bullion drain problem, it had also been the textile production center for Europe. Thus to restore France to its earlier, mythical centrality, it was necessary to bring about a situation in which the Dutch and the English no longer were major producers of cloth. Spain and England would also return to the days in which all their wool was sent to France. Historical inaccuracies aside, this plan was a much more radical attempt at dependency reversal than was being contemplated by English mercantilists. The English had hoped to improve their position at the expense of the Dutch. Colbert's plans aimed at the "restoration" of French commercial supremacy.

England and the Netherlands recognized the extent of the commercial threat and responded by increasing their own tariffs. The English response was relatively slow due to the crown's pro-French sympathies. French tariff increases occurred in 1664 and 1667. The English tariff increases came in 1678. Most French imports were prohibited through 1685 and then reprohibited in 1689.

The Dutch regarded the second French round of tariff increases in 1667 as a declaration of economic war (Israel, 1989: 287). They were also subjected to increased French pressure in India and the West Indies. The French had proposed a joint effort with the Portuguese to overthrow Dutch control of Asian trade and replace it with a Franco-Portuguese regime. When the Portuguese balked, a French fleet was sent unilaterally to penetrate the southern Indian market [without much success]. In the West Indies, an increased naval presence was being employed to suppress Dutch interaction with French colonial trade. Still, the Dutch chose to respond initially with mild retaliatory tariffs before moving to the stiffer 1671 response of an outright ban on a number of French products, including wine. Several months later, France banned all trade with the Dutch and declared war [one of the war aims came to be the acquisition of the Netherlands although later rejected as impractical]. England joined the war on the French side.

As long as the English remained in the war, the Dutch felt it wiser to suspend seaborne trade. When the English withdrew in 1674, trade resumed but not quite at the pre-1672 level. Israel's (1989: 299–300) comprehensive survey of Dutch commercial primacy argues that primacy was regained in 1674 but that 1672 had represented the zenith of Dutch supremacy. After 1672, a permanent process of positional erosion had set in which was not altered when England and the Netherlands joined forces against France in the 1689–1713 global combat. Rather, the 1689–1713 fighting, in general, reinforced and probably accelerated the decline of the Dutch. After 1713, wartime trade disruptions and losses, increased public debt, a severely diminished navy, and the diffusion of much of its technological innovations combined to ensure that the Dutch would be most unlikely to reverse their downward slide.

The relative decline of the Dutch in Europe was manifested in the Asian trades which had become vastly more competitive. In particular, the British and the French had become the principle European powers in India and China. They had access to relatively more capital. They had more troops and ships. Military force, as it transpired, was to become increasingly critical in eighteenth century India.

Britain and France were also less committed to the "wrong" commodities, namely spices (Bayly, 1989: 66). The commitment to old commodities was matched by a commitment to old procedures. For example, Chinese ports were opened in 1685 but the Dutch chose to rely on their traditional and indirect system centered on Batavia. When they decided to enter the Chinese trade directly in 1729, it was too late. The British were already too well established (Furber, 1976: 124). In addition, the Dutch had been forced out of North America completely, leaving the British and the French to struggle for its control. The same two states were in competition to penetrate the Latin American market as well. In India, China, and North America, the British held the stronger position *vis-à-vis* their French rivals. By the beginning of the eighteenth century, the English East Indies Company had been operating in India for 100 years. It had concentrated in the initially less profitable Indian markets because the Dutch had forced them away from the main source of spices and because the Mughal Empire protected the English from Dutch attacks. If the two European powers had fought over control of Surat in the early seventeenth century, both states would simply have been evicted from the subcontinent (Parry, 1966: 143).

Mughal protection could only be relied upon as long as the Mughal Empire was willing and able to extend it. In the late 1680s, the Company declared war, albeit prematurely on the not-yet declining Empire in an explicit effort to imitate Dutch territorial control practices in Indonesia. The basic strategy was to transform Bombay into a dominant entrepôt on the order of Batavia by channeling all Indian trade through the Company base. The Mughal Empire, however, proved to be too strong for the still relatively weak English forces.

Despite its rashness, the English East Indies Company was permitted to stay in India. A fine was paid. All plunder was restored and the Company promised to behave itself in the future (Furber, 1976: 94–95). Within a few years after the 1689–1713 global war, largely fought outside of India, the Company had begun to shift its focus of activity from western to eastern India. Rising interest in cotton goods and Chinese tea prompted the relocation. Calcutta became the principal base. In 1717, the Company purchased exemption from local taxes in the Bengal–Calcutta area from the Mughal Empire.

French activities in India were always handicapped by intermittent support from home, inadequate sea power, undercapitalization, and a late start. An island abandoned by the Dutch in 1710, Mauritius, was transformed into the principal French naval base in Asia, Ile de France, during the 1730s. But it was not until the period between the 1740s and 1780s that Franco-British conflict in India became acute.

Both sides employed a similar strategy of constructing alliances with Indian rulers to augment their strength *vis-à-vis* the other European company. The alliances led invariably to interventions in succession struggles. For their military assistance, the Europeans were granted control over specified territories and the associated right to collect taxes. In a circular fashion, the development of the institution of sepoy armies in the 1740s, first by the Compagnie des Indies and then by the British East India Company, to bolster the size of their European forces made these tax revenues particularly desirable. They were needed to pay for the increasing military costs that were a byproduct of attempts to expand Indian market share.

The implications of the European competition did not escape the actors most closely involved. The head of the British East India Company in India communicated the following explanation to his London directors in 1751:

> We must recognize that if Europeans had not intervened in these affairs and had left Indian princes to resolve their own quarrels that might have been infinitely more beneficial to trade. But since the French have put themselves in possession of extensive domains and have raised their flag at the bounds of our territory and have striven to constrain our settlements to such an extent they can neither receive supplies nor goods, it has been judged essential to thwart their designs lest their success render our situation worse

during peace than in time of war . . . We shall therefore oppose them to the greatest extent of which we are capable.

(quoted in Furber, 1976: 156)

These observations probably should not be taken entirely at face value. The temptation to intervene in Indian affairs would have been present in the absence of multiple European trading companies. The English company's war with the Mughal Empire in the late seventeenth century is a case in point. But since neither the British nor the French could afford to allow their rivals to gain the upper hand, the European competition accelerated the penetration of the already disintegrating Indian power structure. In 1765, after British Company forces had defeated the Nawab of Bengal, his nominal overlord, the Mughal emperor, legitimized a *fait accompli* by conferring on the Company tax collection and law and order maintenance responsibilities in Bengal.[5] In effect, the Company had become an important subruler within the Mughal Empire. By the 1780s, it was one of the four leading centers of power and the only European one on the subcontinent. As the Mughal Empire continued to decline and regional successors struggled for control, the British East Indies Company found itself in an increasingly good position to succeed as the primary territorial ruler in India.

It is not evident that there was much local British sentiment to abstain from control of India. If nothing else, increased territorial control was too attractive in the Indian setting. Tax revenues could replace the continuing need for silver in Eurasian trade. The Company also assumed control over opium production, which had been a Mughal monopoly. Adequate access to this product was becoming increasingly indispensable for obtaining Chinese tea.

As implied above, the French lost the Indian competition. The British controlled much more trade and shipping in India and were, therefore, better able to sustain the protection costs that had escalated for both sides. Whereas support for the British activities were fairly consistent, especially at sea, the French corporate activities in India had to compete with vacillating orientation at Paris. French governmental elites tended to fall back on European military preoccupation in times of war. By the 1760s, the French strategy in India had become one of preparing for the next war with the British to the exclusion of dwindling commercial considerations (Furber, 1976: 177). In marked contrast, the British were more concerned with developing their Indian–Chinese trade network. By 1783, the French had run out of time and resources in India and were forced to yield to British primacy among the Europeans in Asia.

Much the same thing happened in North America. In that part of the world, Franco-British conflict had been constrained until the 1740s by the geographical barriers between the respective settlements. Colonial expansion on both sides gradually reduced the natural barriers. In the ensuing conflict to protect and extend their colonial monopolies, the British again enjoyed the advantages of a better resource base in terms of population and colonial prosperity, a higher and more consistent priority for colonial affairs, and vastly superior sea power most of the time. Native forces were employed as military auxiliaries but they lacked the weight of numbers, political organization, and military strength of their Asian counterparts. As a consequence, the French defeat came even more quickly in North America than in Asia and was more comprehensive.

The pattern of commercial dominance in the Caribbean and Latin America developed differently. In the eighteenth-century wars, French islands in the Caribbean would be captured repeatedly by the British and then returned after a peace agreement. One reason was that British producers in the Caribbean did not desire increased competition within the protected markets of the British colonial system (Jones, 1980: 222).

Even so, the continued division of the West Indies into French and British colonies, along with a few others flying Dutch and Spanish flags, contributed to the identification of the two states as inescapable commercial rivals (Black, 1986: 135). French and British islands produced the same products, especially sugar. More sugar was produced than could be consumed by the respective metropoles and, therefore, both states were interested in reexporting similar tropical products to the same European and Asian markets.[6]

The impact of these economic structural parallels on attitudes of commercial hostility is hinted at in a 1786 British newspaper argument:

> The demands of each country militate so much against the staple manufactures of both, which are rivals to each other, that the policy of either must be injured by a surrender of the advantages they at present enjoy. Most countries have articles of which we stand in need, and without injury exchange then for ours they have not; but England and France have the same manufactures, are vying with each other for competition.
>
> (Black, 1986: 152–153).

One of the contested keys to penetrating Spanish America was control of the slave trade. The Franco-Spanish alignment of the 1690s had given French merchants preferential access to Spanish colonies. In 1702, a French company was awarded a monopoly for supplying slaves to the Spanish colonies. The British victory in 1713, illustrating how global wars favor the winners, transformed the French monopoly into a British asset. As a result, this positioning placed the British in a situation that was ideal for exploiting the slave trade's demand for inexpensive cotton cloth from India. The continuation of this slave trade *asiento* was to be one of the issues over which the British and the rejuvenated Spanish fought in the 1740s.

The general pattern of Anglo-French rivalry after the defeat of the first French challenge in the 1689–1713 wars was one of near-continuous rivalry and intermittent combat. Between the periods of combat and defeat, the French would recoup and try again as in the 1740s and the late 1750s–early 1760s. The greatest apparent success in inflicting commercial harm on Britain came in the late 1770s–early 1780s French intervention in the US War of Independence. Unfortunately for the French, the success turned out to be more apparent than real. Britain lost important colonies but retained them as trading partners. What Britain really lost then was significant colonial overhead burden. France's military expenditure, on the other hand, increased its debt level substantially. The added pressure on the state's shaky financial system led directly to the overthrow of the French monarchy.

A brief truce in the Anglo-French commercial conflict was declared in the 1780s. In search of revenues, the French government opened its colonies to foreign trade in 1784. In 1786, the Eden Treaty abolished the prohibitions on British imports and reduced the level of customs duties. One official rationale in both the 1784 and 1786 cases was that trade that had been smuggled into France previously could now be taxed. A second French argument for the Eden Treaty was that more wine could be exported to Britain. Presumably, the French negotiators underestimated either the implications of the ongoing industrial revolution in Britain or the need to protect France's own fledgling industries. British cotton textiles flooded into France. French industries suffered to the extent that the Eden Treaty came to be regarded as one of the prominent "sins of the *ancien régime*" (Heckscher, 1964: 20) in the ensuing French Revolution.

The French denounced the Eden Treaty in 1793 shortly before Britain entered the French Revolutionary wars. A navigation act in the same year, modeled on the mid-seventeenth century English precedent, prohibited foreign shipping importing commodities from third countries (for example reexports) and multiplied the dues to be paid by foreign vessels. British imports were once again essentially banned. Smuggling resumed and the prohibitions were enforced selectively. Under Napoleon, however, similar measures were applied even more extensively after the Berlin Decree of 1806. Ships from Britain and its colonies were refused entry into all European ports. In 1807, the Milan Decree announced that all ships that visited British ports or accepted British licensing, the British response to the Berlin Decree, would be confiscated.

The theory behind the Napoleonic Continental System, reminiscent in some respects to English thought in the first two Anglo-Dutch wars, was that the British economy was highly dependent on international commerce. It needed to maintain a steady supply of raw materials and an equally steady outflow of manufactures (Jones, 1980: 290). Since the British controlled the seas after Trafalgar (1805), the option of a marine blockade was out of the question. A European land blockade was conceivable even if it, too, turned out to be more damaging to French economic development than to that of Britain's.[7]

Wallerstein (1989: 94) argues that the French Revolution "occurred in the wake of, and as a consequence of France's impending defeat in the Franco-British struggle for hegemony". Whether or not events can occur as a consequence of other impending events, Wallerstein is certainly correct to argue that the 1792–1815 wars (if not the French Revolution *per se*) ensured Britain's postwar emergence as the system's preeminent industrial/commercial power.

> In so far as the [1815] settlement regulated the transfer of colonial territories, the British government was in a position, in many parts of the world, to take its choice. It had attained, in the field of overseas trade

and dominion, a preeminence over other Europeans even more complete than in 1763, and was determined to safeguard its position by appropriate acquisitions.

. . . The choice was discriminating, there was no rush to acquire territorial dominion for its own sake, no vindictive demand to rob the French of all they had possessed; merely a calculated resolve that sources of revenue or essential materials, valuable markets and major trade routes should be protected against any possible recurrence of French or other interference.

(Parry, 1971: 197)

France kept a few unfortified trading posts in India and regained several sugar plantation islands that had been lost in the Caribbean. The Netherlands regained its Indonesian empire which also had been captured by the British. Spices, as in the case of sugar, were no longer as profitable as they had once been. The British also desired a relatively prosperous, as opposed to an impoverished, Dutch buffer in northern Europe. Yet the British and London in particular were also the beneficiaries of the wartime demise of Amsterdam as a leading financial center. Iberian America was not opened to British trade immediately, despite some inconsistent British aid to Latin American rebels. But within a decade or so after the end of the Napoleonic Wars, Britain had become the principal trading partner of the newly independent South American states.

India was becoming the jewel in the British imperial crown even though a fair amount of territorial consolidation and pacification in the subcontinent remained to be accomplished. To support and protect its Indian presence, the strategic emphasis was placed on maintaining control of a string of naval bases captured during the war: several small islands in the South Atlantic, Cape of Good Hope, the Seychelles, Mauritius, and Ceylon. Singapore was established in 1819 to create an alternative to the recently surrendered Batavia. Malta and the Ionian Islands were kept in the Mediterranean.

Needless to say, the leadership challenge sequence did not end in the early nineteenth century. It has continued up to today. But now we have sufficient information to construct a general model of the process that leads intermittently to violent challenges and global war. The process did not start that way. There were no global wars before 1494. The global political economy had to first become increasingly Europeanized to develop that unfortunate characteristic.[8]

8

CHALLENGES IN THE
ACTIVE ZONE

Based on several strong assumptions about the nature of international political economy, it is possible to construct a multivariate model that differentiates between political-economic challenges that lead to intense, militarized conflicts and those that do not. Ten iterations of challenges over the past millennium provide empirical support for the applicability of the five variable model.

Particularly crucial to this undertaking are the twin notions that all international competitors and all commodities are not of equal importance to this story. Some competitors and some commodities have been and continue to be much more important than others. Just why that is the case requires considerable theoretical justification and elaboration. But the reader is forewarned that this analysis is not about how and why the interactions between any two trading states may become problematic and even dangerous. Instead, the present focus rests exclusively on the most successful economies and their challengers – the actors most responsible for shaping the macrostructure of the political-economic world which we inhabit. Before tackling this subject directly, it is first necessary to lay out as explicitly as possible the assumptions that provide the foundation for the analysis. They are not all equally critical but it will become clear that different interpretations would be likely to emerge if a different set of assumptions was utilized.

ASSUMPTIONS

Theoretical and conceptual distinctions about strategic orientations, technological innovation, and structural hierarchy and conflict will shape the analysis of what is at stake in an analysis of commercial challenges and their significance to the understanding of global politics. And while the primary substantive focus rests on the process of challenge, we must also pay attention to what is being challenged. Therefore, it is necessary to begin with a delineation of the bigger picture in which challengers fit and against which they occasionally rebel or at least seek to reconfigure substantially.

Assumption one: leading sectors

The leading sector concept emphasizes the innovation of new products, processes and ways of doing things. Growth occurs unevenly and at different rates within economies. Some types of economic activities expand fairly steadily and slowly. Some sectors are likely to be stagnating due to lags in incorporating technological change or, more simply, changes in demand. The most significant rates of economic growth are traceable, at least initially, to a few activities that are so transformed by innovation that they experience abrupt and rapid expansion. These sectors thus lead their respective economies, initially, as vanguards of high growth. They also lead in the sense that their growth has spillover or multiplier implications for the rest of the economy. Radically new ways of doing things may be introduced to other sectors. High profits are realized, especially to the extent that the leading sector is monopolized by a single economy. Money for investment purposes becomes less scarce. New industries and jobs are created. Transportation costs are reduced. New markets are found or developed. In sum, leading sectors act as the sparkplugs of economic growth in lead economies (and other, interdependent economies).

Assumption two: the clustering of leading sectors

The advent of new leading sectors are anything but continuous. Instead, they tend to appear in clusters of related innovations that can be described as technological/commercial paradigms about the best ways of doing things. They emerge essentially as mutations on older ways of doing things. Some of these mutations are selected by firms, developed as radical economic innovations and become the genotypes of the new paradigms.[1] The new technology is then used to transport valued commodities over long distances and/or to develop new industries and other types of economic activities. The new products are then exported or reexported throughout the system.

New paradigms, in turn, are characterized by S-shaped growth curves. They emerge, grow quickly and reach mature plateaus. At some point after the attainment of maturity and substantial diffusion, their profit potential begins to erode thereby setting up appropriate conditions for the emergence of another cluster of radical innovations. The average life cycle of leading sectors is about two generations or 50 years in duration.[2]

Assumption three: lead economies

If leading sectors are the sparkplugs of their respective economies, lead economies are the sparkplugs of the world economy. They are found at the very apex of the world economy's technological gradient. For finite periods of time, these economies constitute the principal source of innovation and new technology, and, therefore, the active zones of the world economy, as long as firms headquartered within these national economies continue to pioneer in the development of the new technological/commercial paradigm. The phenomenon of lead economies is thus predicated on the spatial concentration characteristic of radical economic innovation.

As the principal innovator of new products/processes, the lead economy determines the initial rate at which the fruits of innovation appear on the world scene. Its reward is that it profits most from the monopoly rents associated with pioneering economic activities. As imitation, diffusion, and increased competition develop and as the once novel products/technology become more routine, these monopoly rents diminish accordingly. The economic leadership of states thus rises and falls with their ability to corner the market in radical economic innovation.[3]

Assumption four: the historical sequence of lead economies

The historical sequence of lead economies focuses on shifts in the location of the world economy's most active zones of rapid growth beginning with the first breakthrough to a modern form of economic growth in Sung China (McNeill, 1982; Jones, 1988; Modelski and Thompson, 1996) through Genoa, Venice, Portugal, the Netherlands, Britain, through to the latest leader, the United States. Table 8.1 matches the growth leaders with their rough period of growth leadership.

This list represents something more than just a roster of significant economies. It constitutes a lineage of first movers in commercial-maritime/industrial activities that are linked through time as successive leading innovators and as principal inheritors of its predecessors' information base.[4] Thus, at a given time, these economies lead their competitors in developing radically new ways of doing things but they also are building upon and/or diverging away from the advances made by earlier leaders. These influence flows (involving technological transfers, preferential trading arrangements, and investments among other things) approximate the hereditary principle often associated with evolutionary approaches in biology in the sense that traits are "inherited" or passed on from one generation to the next. While space does not permit a discussion of this understudied phenomenon at this time, the lineage has undergone extensive evolutionary change in terms of the types of economic activities undertaken and the related alterations in domestic constitutional fitness and institutional coevolution.[5] In many respects, this lineage is fundamentally responsible for the spread and diffusion of liberal political systems by generating conducive political-economic niches in which these types of ideas could survive and thrive.

Assumption five: hierarchy and mobility on the technological gradient

An economy's innovativeness plays an important role in determining where that economy is placed on the world economy's general technological gradient. Over the past millennium, a few economies have virtually monopolized invention and innovation for finite stretches of time. The economies of other states are found further down the gradient. Some economies create production niches for themselves

Table 8.1 Global lead economies

Lead economy	Lead commodities or Sectors	Approximate timing
Northern Sung	Printing; national market formation; rice; iron	10th–11th centuries
Southern Sung	Maritime trade	11th–12th .centuries
Genoa	Champagne fairs Black Sea trade	Early 13th century Late 13th century
Venice	Galley fleets Pepper	14th–15th centuries
Portugal	African gold Asian spices	Late 15th century Early/mid-16th century
Netherlands	Baltic trade late Asian trade	Late 6th century Early/mid-17th century
Britain I	West Indies products Asian–American trade	Late 17th century Early/mid-18th century
Britain II	Cotton textiles, iron Railroads, steam	Late 18th century Early/mid-19th century
United States	Steel, chemicals, electrics Aviation, automobiles, electronics	Early 20th century Mid 20th century

Source: Modelski and Thompson (1996)

just below the peak where they engage in relatively sophisticated production on a fairly narrow scale. Lower ranking economies must work with lower quality technology. The lowest technological level tends to be occupied by subsistence level economies.[7]

Mobility up and down the gradient has been a crucial factor in the history of the world's political economy. Ambitious entrepreneurs and decision-makers who find themselves in lower ranking economies will strive to move up the gradient by accelerating development processes. Acceleration can be accomplished through internal processes of development or by capturing the technological bases of more advanced rivals.

Similarly, the decision-makers of highly advanced economies must cope with the threat of movement down the technological gradient. Most at risk in this sense is the lead economy which must remain constantly innovative if it is to maintain its edge over all its rivals. The difficulties associated with, and the improbability of, constant innovation make it unlikely that the lead economy of any era will keep its lead indefinitely. The internal resistances and barriers to staying continuously on the technological frontier are compounded, thanks to uneven development, by the strong likelihood of challenges from rising powers.

Assumption six: the duality of fundamental strategic orientations

One of the historical axes of political-economic behavior at the élite level of world politics is the classical geopolitical distinction between territorial and maritime-commercial powers. Territorial powers tend to be preoccupied with questions of expansion and defense in their immediate neighborhoods or regions. The army is the favored military instrument in a territorially oriented power. The economy tends to lack cohesion, is often based on agrarian output and the exploitation of raw resources, and is subject to slow growth. Politically, land powers have tended to be authoritarian and dominated by landed aristocracy.

In contrast, maritime-commercial powers favor their navies and avoid outright territorial expansion as much as possible in order to pursue commercial expansion. Politically, maritime-commercial powers have tended towards some level of pluralistic tolerance and allow some possibilities for domestic political competition and the circulation of decision making offices. Commercial-maritime economies may be small or large but they are highly cohesive, often centralized around a dominant city and strongly oriented toward external trade and industrial opportunities.[7]

Major powers and their strategies tend toward one extreme or the other but only a few states, if any, will match the pure geopolitical ideal type exactly. There are also some states that vacillate or wobble in their geopolitical orientation. These states tend to possess many of the basic attributes of territorially oriented powers. From time to time, however, their economies may also be characterized by significant bursts of innovation. Not coincidentally, their decision-makers may develop some selective appreciation for the advantages of maritime strategies (trade, navies and extra-regional activities). These intermittent appreciations, nevertheless, must compete with ever-present and well-entrenched land or continental strategies and their advocates. For the most part, the more decisively maritime-commercially oriented systems have managed to escape this internal strategic debate thanks only to internal wars in which élites preferring territorial strategies have been defeated. This development is particularly pronounced in the cases of Portugal, the Netherlands, Britain, and the United States. It appears to have been less true in the cases of Southern Sung and Genoa which never resolved their domestic disagreements on this issue.

Without exception, lead economies have emerged from the maritime-commercial power column. This development should not be surprising. To lead in inter-continental economic activities, a significant maritime transport infrastructure and orientation is absolutely necessary. Economic leads, among other things, are necessary to pay for the sea power. The sea power, among other things, is necessary to defend the economic lead.

It is often argued that industrialization has undermined the significance of the land versus sea power distinction.[8] However, the position taken here is that the basic geopolitical duality has retained its significance throughout the twentieth century and will probably continue to do so into the twenty-first century, subject, of course, to continuing changes in the ongoing fusion of sea and aerospace technology. Nonetheless, it is rather difficult to resolve this contentious issue in a paragraph or two. Suffice it to say that twentieth century examples of overcommitment to land-based strategies are found as recently as the World War II experiences of Japan and Germany and the Cold War strategy of the Soviet Union.

However, the advent of intensified industrialization did mean that non-sea powers could also become leaders in economic innovation whereas the earlier commercial innovations had required a considerable maritime orientation and capability. This transformation in technological emphasis muddied the waters somewhat in terms of the relationship between strategic capability and economic innovation. Prior to the nineteenth century, economic innovation and strategic capability of the long reach variety went hand in hand. Leading economic innovators possessed leading navies. After the eighteenth century, the linkage persisted but only partially. Some economic innovators, and so far the most important ones, maintained an edge in global reach capabilities but it could no longer be assumed that leadership in economic innovation would lead to leadership in global strategic capability.

Assumption seven: the aspiration to monopolize

In differentiating commercial-maritime and territorial orientations, we must be careful not to exaggerate the implications of distinctively different orientations for coercive behavior and conflict. For instance, one image that we have is that those states that specialize in commerce are more likely to follow the dictates of economic logic and eschew war as much as possible. Rosecrance's "trading state" model highlights this expectation quite nicely when he (Rosecrance, 1986: 24–25) argues that interdependence and efficiency considerations dictate the acceptance of specialization, divisions of labor, and the avoidance of trade-disrupting conflict.

Yet perhaps the most serious flaw with this conventional, liberal image of a stable, peaceful division of labor among competitive units is that the most successful trading states have been monopolists. In the early years, they vigorously sought commercial monopolies and, once they had been created, fought equally vigorously to keep them. Commercial monopolies outside Europe eventually became territorial monopolies in the form of colonies. From the seventeenth century on, production monopolies, based to a large degree on pioneering technological innovation, became increasingly important in their own right and as a significant foundation for exports, thereby feeding back to commercial predominance. Throughout the past 500 years, attempts at monopolizing the possession of global reach capabilities (sea and aerospace power) have been utilized to protect and advance the other types of monopolies.

Part of the problem may be that trade and territorial conquest, as practiced in history, need not be quite the conceptual opposites they may seem. In territorial conquest, one group of people attempts to dominate another group of people living within some specific area. The would-be conquerors seek a monopoly of political-economic control within the territory to be acquired.

In trade, the basic idea is to exchange commodities at the best or most profitable terms of trade that can be realized. Buying low and selling high is the time-honored strategy. Of course, stating the maxim and creating or exploiting conducive opportunities are two different propositions. One way to achieve the selling high goal is to stockpile large quantities of commodities and then manipulate the selling price by controlling supply. Another way is to reduce or eliminate the competition as much as possible. Competitors increase risks and uncertainty. Competitors may have access to superior resources. They may drive harder bargains. They may simply work harder. At the very least, the existence of competition is likely to increase the purchase prices or decrease the selling prices of the commodities on which the competition is focused.

To the extent that one group of people manages to eliminate their competition in a given commodity trade, market, or region, the outcome will approximate a monopoly of economic control that is easily translated into political-economic advantage. Historians customarily refer to this distinction between territorial and economic control as formal and informal empire (Gallagher and Robinson, 1953). Both depend on monopolies of some sort – territorial, commercial, production, or global reach. Historically, the four types of monopoly have tended to become intertwined even though each type's relative utility will vary in value and fashion over time.

Naval monopolies are critical for acquiring and protecting among other things, commercial monopolies. The early trading states sought territorial monopolies, too, but they either restrained themselves or found themselves too weak to make as much headway as they might otherwise have preferred. Gradually, however, commercial monopolies, or the desire to obtain and maintain them, gave way to territorial monopolies. Commercial monopolies provide a useful resource base for political influence and intimidation. The more valuable the commodity that is involved, of course, the greater is the potential for profit and wealth accumulation. The greater the demand for the commodity, the greater is the dependence of consumers on its transporters.

As industrialization became increasingly more prominent, the emphasis shifted to exploiting technological advantages and breakthroughs by creating new products for export. Technological pioneers enjoy high returns on their investments. States with technological leads become prosperous and more independent. As a consequence, Gilpin (1987: 99) is hardly guilty of overstatement when he stipulates quite bluntly that "every state aspires to be a monopolist and enjoy monopoly profits or rents". Few states may actually be successful in creating situations from which they can enjoy monopoly rents. Nor are the monopolies ever likely to be permanent. Nevertheless, the few states that have succeeded even temporarily have done so in a spectacular fashion, only to be replaced in an even more spectacular fashion by another leader and another set of monopolies.

CHALLENGES

Genuine challenges to the world's political-economic status quo constitute a significant class of behavior in world politics. This set of activities remains underappreciated despite its close links to some of the most vicious wars of the past half-millennium and the political-economic restructuring that occurred in the midst and the aftermath of these contests. One reason for the underappreciation of this phenomenon has to do with their relative frequency. Serious challenges simply do not take place all that often. Yet a more important reason for the underappreciation is our reluctance to differentiate various types of political-economic competition (Frederick, 1989). The competition of élite states has been a routine hallmark of world history. Some of this competition has been coercive in nature. Much less routine is the intermittent propensity for some ascending states to attempt radical revisions of the system's structure. These attempts constitute a distinctive class of competitive behavior for they are revolutionary in terms of the goals of their instigators and the outcomes of the efforts, or at least potentially so. More often than not, the challenges fail but these failures do not preclude some fundamental and highly significant changes in structure.

The types of structural challenges in which we are most interested pertain to the global system and the rules and networks that govern transregional and transoceanic economic transactions. There is no denying that global and regional affairs have tended to be intertwined, especially in the era of European predominance. This is, in fact, another reason for underappreciating the challenge phenomenon. They have been interwoven with struggles over strictly regional stakes. Since we do not often take the trouble to distinguish the regional activities from the global ones, European inheritance squabbles end up being given the same weight as schemes to partition and subordinate the world economy. Yet while regional and global affairs have been related, their relative contribution to an understanding of the world's political economy is not equal.[9]

Global challengers attempt to alter radically the organization of transoceanic/ transregional interactions. At some earlier point, structural rules have been created by the leading global power and its allies. Leadership attributes were developed and manifested in a global war fought, in part, to determine whose version of world order would prevail. Challengers then come either from the ranks of previous losers in global wars or newly ascendant states that were not in a position to share in the benefits associated with the status quo's allocation. Existing rules and privileges are perceived as barriers to further ascent in the political-economic hierarchy. As a consequence, the constraining obstacles to upward mobility must be eliminated.

The very nature of success in a world political-economy built around the monopolization of innovating practices encourages challenges. There are a number of advantages earned by the pioneering activity engaged in by the technological leaders. Pioneering producers enjoy production monopolies and monopoly rents until competitors learn how to imitate the manufacture of the new products. Nor do pioneering producers, who create new markets, have many incentives to allow their manufacturing secrets to be copied. Commerce works along remarkably similar lines. Pioneering traders, that is specialists in commodity exchange who discover new ways to break into old markets or to create new markets, enjoy territorial monopolies initially and will seek to defend those monopolies from interlopers as long as possible.[10] Yet it is most unlikely that the ability to fend off interlopers will be infinite. As the perceived vulnerabilities of the pioneers become more noticeable, the temptation to take advantage of the vulnerabilities increases accordingly. Moreover, the very nature of the system, and especially movement up the gradient, requires the upwardly mobile to attempt to break into the territorial and proprietary preserves of the established leaders. Ensconced élites in any type of system rarely surrender their privileged positions without a struggle.

Yet since the most technologically advanced states define the world political economy's status quo – that is, its rule of economic interaction – they also establish who will benefit most in the prevailing political-economic order. To break into this system of exclusive privileges requires some degree of challenge.[11]

Another way of looking at this challenge phenomenon is to view them as part of an evolutionary process. What is at stake is an opportunity for leading actors in the system to select organizing principles and leadership for the world economy from a variety of competing formulas and agents. Selection from variety is a hallmark of evolutionary processes. So, too, is mutation. The tendency toward the temporal and spatial clustering of technological-commercial innovation, another component in the opportunity for selection from variety, and consequent uneven development generates periodic mutations and thereby alters the distribution of "fitness" for economic leadership. But, historically, superior fitness alone has been insufficient in bringing about political-economic change. Superior fitness, or possession of the attributes of superior competitiveness, must be demonstrated in order to determine which actor and which particular types of "fitness" is, in fact, optimal. Challenges provide the opportunity to select winners and losers by allowing or forcing winners to demonstrate their superiority over losers.

Two more essential ingredients in the challenge formula include the probability that an established monopoly will decay thereby inviting attack and that new aspirants to monopoly positions will emerge. Established monopolies deteriorate for a variety of reasons. Resources become exhausted. Managers become mired in standardized operating procedures that no longer match changing environments. Tastes and demand change. A hot commodity at one time period loses its growth potential in a later period. New leading sectors and new ways of doing things emerge. As a number of formerly successful entrepreneurs have discovered, it is frequently difficult to transfer investments in the old growth sector to a new one fast enough to keep up with competitors who are not handicapped by commitments to old products and old-fashioned ways of doing things.

One of the ironies of the history of monopolies is that the reasons for the decline of commercial and production monopolies seem very similar. The problems that the Dutch commitments to Indonesian spices encountered in an eighteenth century more geared to placing a premium on Indian textiles and Chinese tea resemble very much the late nineteenth-century problems experienced by the British in the emergence of the steel, electricity, and automobile sectors. Whether we view the late nineteenth-century British as reluctant, distracted, relatively uninterested, or committed to other sectors, it is fair to say that the British were slow to develop competitive competencies in these new sectors.

As a consequence, monopolies are quite likely to be finite propositions because earlier innovational success does not guarantee continued innovation leadership. On the contrary, early successes may make later successes less probable. A mixture of complacency and psychological preference for what is known and tested as opposed to uncertain and untested new ways of doing things, combined with just enough continuing profit to make abandonment of old leading sectors seem irrational, increase the probability that innovation centers will shift over time.

The temporary nature of monopolies or, more simply, decisive leads is further enhanced by waves of would-be challengers. The tendency is for a period of relatively successful monopoly/lead to give way to a period of intensified rivalry. Alternatively expressed, a period characterized by the ascendancy of one group gives way to a period characterized by attempts at catching up by competitors and would-be competitors. Rivals may come from newly emerged groups seeking at first to improve their competitive position. Rivalries may also be of a longstanding nature. For one reason or another, one group pulls ahead without completely eliminating its competitors. Some of these old competitors survive to renew their rivalries either because they have been able to improve their own resource bases and/or because they have been able to wait long enough for the former winners to lose some of their advantages.

The persistence of challenges, therefore, can be explained most easily by observing that the very existence of exclusive monopolies, and especially eroding or weakening monopolies/leads, make challenges not inevitable but certainly more probable. In order to markedly improve one group's position within the division of labor, it is necessary to reduce, eliminate, and/or supplant exclusive arrangements established earlier by another group(s). Successful challenges do not end the tendency toward monopolistic behavior; they only establish new monopolies.

Conflict will be further accentuated to the extent that the groups in confrontation seek to perform the same economic function or market the same commodities in the same space. Agents of upwardly and downwardly mobile economies are especially susceptible to this form of conflict. So are economies that are structured in over-lapping fashions. Since the high growth sectors of any given era are apt to be relatively limited, it is the most advanced economies that are most likely to become intense competitors. It is these same economies and their states that are most likely to contend for systemic leadership.

Finally, another defining attribute of a global commercial/industrial challenge is its eventual explicit and premeditated quality. Challengers need not fully appreciate the extent to which they are engaged in an assault on the politico-economic status quo at the outset. Whether quickly or gradually, though, this lack of awareness disappears for some parties. By some point, challenger decision-makers will have assessed their international environments and reached the conclusion that a strategy of vigorous commercial competition and confrontation is essential to their ability to improve the status of their state in the international pecking order. We are not talking about accidental collisions in commercial space between two or more expanding and competing rivals. Accidents may happen but in a full-scale, global challenge the challenger has determined who it perceives to be thwarting its upward progress. That is the most overt challenger has identified who its principal political and commercial enemies are and that these enemies need to be swept aside. If the confrontation becomes reasonably intense, the identification of the principal enemy is likely to be reciprocated by the targeted and threatened system leader.[12] It should not be surprising if a conflict spiral sets in and the nature of the conflict begins to spill over into other spheres. As commercial conflicts become proximate geopolitical threats, accommodation becomes even less likely and intensive conflict more probable.

The committed challenger normally has also assessed the target for points of maximal vulnerability. To nibble away at the fringes of the status quo is not the hallmark of an ambitious and impatient challenger. Accordingly, the commercial attack of the challenger will be focused initially in specific commodities and regions as opposed to an across-the-board campaign. Only if the competition persists for some time and the challenger begins to think in terms of conquest strategies will the rivalry begin to take on an omnibus quality. Of course, if the declining leader's deteriorating position accelerates due to its own choices, perceived vulnerability will increase and so, too, will the scope of the challenger's attack.

In the last analysis, it is the very nature of the global political economy and the activities of its leading actors, combined with the probability of change, then, that makes challenges probable. What is left relatively open is who challenges whom, when are challenges more likely to occur, what forms are these challenges likely to assume, and what sort of challenges are most likely to succeed or fail. But even these questions can be at least partially answered.

The likely target of challenge is not an ambiguous proposition. Unlike the pattern in warfare in which ascending states fight their way up through their regional neighborhoods before they take on the system's most powerful states, commercial challenges are aimed immediately at the leading commercial power. The challenges may or may not take years to achieve a high intensity level. They may or may not be restricted within regional arenas. But contenders need not fight their way through a series of preliminary bouts with lesser commercial powers before taking on the incumbent leader. On the other hand, the forms challenges assume may range from the economic equivalent of guerrilla warfare/piracy to full-scale global warfare. Low intensity challenges peck away at the fringes of the status quo. High intensity challenges attempt to mount an overthrow of the prevailing status quo and the imposition of a new one slanted, quite naturally, in the challenger's own favor.

The more intense challenges, it is hypothesized, are differentiated from the less intense quarrels by five variables: proximity, similarity, threat/frustration perception, strategic orientation, and innovation. Figure 8.1 illustrates the proposed inter-relationships among the variables.

While we tend to think automatically in terms of dyadic challenges (that is the Venetian–Genoese Wars, the Anglo-Dutch Wars, the Anglo-German rivalry and so forth), challenges do not necessarily come only in the form of one challenger pitted against an incumbent power. The existence of several simultaneous challengers or potential challengers is more likely given the temporal and spatial concentration of innovation, its uneven diffusion, and the eventual erosion of monopoly leads.

144

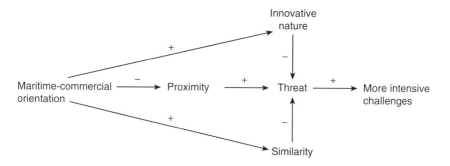

Figure 8.1 A more intensive challenger model

However, not all challenges will necessarily be perceived to be equally threatening by the incumbent target. If for no other reason, threatened leaders simply do not have the resources to take on several challengers simultaneously. Therefore, some prioritizing inevitably occurs with the outcome that some challenges are deemed more menacing than others.

The most threatening challenges are those that are explicitly premeditated, proximate, and forthcoming from dissimilar types of states with predominately different strategic orientations. Challenges come in different hues of intensity. The most dangerous challenger is one that has decided that its upward mobility on the technological gradient can be attained only by completely supplanting the incumbent leader. Coercive strategies become increasingly attractive and, as they do, economic challengers come to be viewed as strategic threats by their explicit targets. A less dangerous situation involves the view that upward mobility is thwarted by a too powerful incumbent whose superordinate position needs to be reduced. A good illustration is provided by the mid-to-late seventeenth-century contrast between the positions of England and France *vis-à-vis* the Dutch. The French wished to eliminate totally Dutch commercial supremacy in Europe. The English thought the Dutch controlled too much trade and desired a greater proportion of it for themselves. Partly as a consequence, the French attempted to conquer the Netherlands. The English fought three largely inconclusive wars with the Dutch, only to end up allying with them against the greater perceived threat posed by France.

Another element conducive to high threat projection and perception is the physical distance between challenger and challenged. The history of economic leadership has been marked by long-term tensions over the survival of maritime-commercially oriented enclaves in the face of threats of conquest from adjacent territorially oriented empires. The subordination of the Phoenician seaports to land-based empires is an old example. Sung China, Genoa, Venice, Portugal, and the Netherlands all eventually succumbed to conquest by adjacent territorial powers. Thus, given a choice between two or more challengers and other things being equal, the one closer to home is apt to be viewed as more threatening. This should be all the more the case if the nature of the threat has less to do with intensified commercial competition as opposed to the possibility of outright conquest by invading armies.

Overlapping with these considerations of proximity and strategic orientation is the idea of similarity in terms of regime type, ideology, culture, and race. We need not buy into the assumptions of democratic peace arguments to accept the plausibility of the generalization that attributes that create psychological distances between groups have the potential to make conflicts more intense. Greater suspicions of the other side's motivations and greater distrust of their behavior are concomitants of viewing competitors as somehow alien. Different regime types (democracy versus autocracy), different cultures (Catholic versus Protestant), different races, and different ideologies (Communism versus Free Enterprise) have potential to create complications that further exacerbate material conflicts.[13]

An additional consideration is linked to the innovation clustering tendency. We might expect conflict to be greatest in situations in which a challenger and incumbent leader compete primarily within the same commercial-technological cluster. For the challenger to make substantial headway, the leader's monopoly position must be overcome in some way. For example, if it was a question of who would control Asian trade with Europe, it was clear that any challenger had to come to terms with the leader's previously established, entrenched commercial network. Even if new routes could be created, there would still be some expectation of conflict over control of the major network nodes (for example, Mallaca).

Alternatively, we might anticipate that a challenge situation in which the challenger was clearly ahead in the race to dominate the next technological cluster might be a relatively more pacific contest (at least between the challenger and the declining incumbent) than a situation involving conflict over leadership in an existing cluster. In such circumstances, the declining leader might choose to acquiesce, albeit reluctantly, to the new leader if other threatening factors were relatively absent.

A variation on this theme is incumbent exhaustion in the defense of its position against the attacks of one challenger leaving few reserves to combat additional challengers. Something like this happened to both the Dutch and the British. The Dutch were worn down by the wars with Louis XIV. Their British ally emerged as the biggest winners of that global war struggle and as the heirs to Dutch political-economic dominance. More than 200 years later, it was the British turn to concede preeminence to their American ally after British resources had been exhausted in the two world wars of the twentieth century.

Table 8.2 specifies who challenged whom and the outcome of the challenges. The basic pattern has been one of territorially oriented powers mounting the most serious militarized challenges and maritime–commercial states succeeding to the earlier established leading positions of other maritime–commercial states. The migration of the active zone from Sung China, after successive conquests by Jurched and Mongol warriors, to the eastern Mediterranean initially benefitted Genoa most. The decline of the Mongol empire proved facilitative for the Venetian ascendancy over Genoa. Portugal succeeded Venice. The Dutch succeeded the Portuguese. The British succeeded to the Dutch position and were replaced in turn by the United States.

Table 8.2 Principal challengers and outcomes

Iteration	Outcomes
1	*Chin (Jin) Empire* conquers Northern Sung; Sung withdraw to south
2	*Mongols* conquer Southern Sung
3	Genoese ascent over other Italian city states (especially Venice)
4	*Venetian* ascent over Genoa
5	*French I* challenge defeated; Portuguese ascent over Venice
6	*Spain* conquers Portugal; Dutch ascent over Portugal
7	*French II* challenge defeated; British ascent over the Netherlands
8	*French III* challenge defeated; British leadership renewed
9	*German I* challenge defeated; US ascendancy stalled
10	*German II* and *Japan I* challenge defeated; US ascent over Britain
11	Soviet challenge apparently stillborn; the extent of Japanese challenge still unclear

Of course, the pattern is not really as clearcut as the preceding paragraph suggests. The problems for generalization purposes are the early Asian and eastern Mediterranean outcomes, the Spanish conquest of Portugal, and the nature of the British–Dutch transition. Yet these "exceptions to the rule" also highlight some of the nonlinear aspects of evolutionary change in world political economy. The Sung economic mutations met the traditional fate of rapid growth experiments based, in part, on maritime trade; they were ultimately absorbed by adjacent land empires. That might have been the end of the lineage development if it had not been for the relatively unusual configuration of western Europe which facilitated the emergence and survival of small trading states.[14] That same configuration initially allowed the long duel between Genoa and Venice to go on until an exhausted Genoa was pushed westward in the late fourteenth century. Thereafter, the distinctive duality of western European politics – the tension between expanding land empires and small but rich maritime powers – began to emerge and assert itself in the late fifteenth century.

In some respects, the Spanish conquered the Portuguese center without technically capturing the Portuguese network. The decision to maintain the separation of the two empires is an indication of a rather major qualification of an otherwise successful capture-the-center strategy long appreciated by expanding territorial empires. Another source of qualification is the almost immediate onslaught of the Dutch challenge. Thus, the Spanish were never able to fully enjoy the customary profits associated with a period of unchallenged leadership of the world economy.[15] The mid-seventeenth-century English challenge of the Dutch was not sustained in the high intensity format symbolized by three Anglo-Dutch wars. Instead, two things happened. First, the English and the Dutch both recognized the French threat as the paramount one. For the Dutch in particular, the French threat was quite acute and certainly highly proximate. Second and very much while the Dutch were preoccupied with the French menace, a leading sector shift in the world economy moved against the Dutch specialties in favor of English specializations in US and Asian reexports. Britain emerged from the 1688–1713 fighting in an increasingly commanding

Table 8.3 Testing the challenger model

Iteration and challengers	Non maritime commercial orientation	Proximate	Not similar	Not more innovative	Score
1 China	Present	Present	Present	Present	4
2 Mongols	Present	Present	Present	Present	4
3	Genoa versus Venice – not applicable				
4	Venice versus Genoa – not applicable				
5 France I	Present	Present	Present	Present	4
Portugal	Absent	Absent	Present	Absent	1
6 Spain	Present	Present	Absent	Present	3
Netherlands	Absent	Absent	Present	Absent	1
7 France II	Present	Present	Present	Present	4
Britain	Absent	Present	Absent	Absent	1
8 France III	Present	Present	Present	Present	4
9 Germany I	Present	Present	Present	Absent	3
United States	Absent	Absent	Absent	Absent	0
10 Germany II	Present	Present	Present	Absent	3
Japan I	Present	Present*	Present	Present	4
United States	Absent	Absent	Absent	Absent	0

Note:

Iterations 1 and 2 involve one regional leader confronted by a single challenger. Iterations 3 and 4 involve the competition between two regional challengers. Thus, the first four iterations are not fully comparable with those that begin with the fifth iteration.

*Japan is coded as proximate to Britain in iteration 10 because the focus of contention was commercial dominance in east Asia in which Britain had been the leader and Japan a proximate challenger.

commercial position. The Dutch emerged from the same global war crucible as a financially exhausted, junior ally. The successful British transition was thus predicated more on defeating the French challenge than on directly confronting the declining Dutch. Rather than view this period as an exception, it should be seen as conforming quite well to the challenge model presented earlier.

But just how well is the challenger model supported by the historical experience? A crude test is summarized in Table 8.3. The objective is to postdict which challenger will mount the more intensive challenge of the incumbent leader. Ideally, we would examine every possible contender for the role of challenger. A more simple approach is to focus on the main actors involved in the 10 completed iterations. The model that is outlined in Figure 8.1 emphasizes maritime-commercial orientation, proximity, similarity, and whether the challenger is more technologically innovative than the incumbent. In Table 8.3, the main actors involved in each iteration have been assigned scores in the following way. One point is assigned if the actor does not possess a maritime-commercial orientation, is proximate, is not similar in terms of governmental structure, and/or is not more technologically innovative (that is, is more proficient than the incumbent in the next growth wave's leading sector focus). No points are assigned if the actor fails to satisfy a criterion.

Not all iterations involve multiple principal challengers and, therefore, a model discriminating between more and less intensive challengers is not very helpful in some instances. But most of the modern iterations after the fifth one, encompassing the 1494–1945 period, are characterized by two or more challengers. The one exception is the Napoleonic challenge. Nevertheless, the model does pick the more intensive challenger by a wide margin in every applicable instance. This outcome does not mean the model is fully validated. For example, the crude and fairly subjective test does not tell us anything about how the predictor variables are interrelated. Nor does it tell us what relative significance each variable possesses. The outcome would not be all that much different if we dropped either the proximity or the similarity variable from the "equation". All we can say at this point is that the model seems to be reasonably congruent with the historical experience so far. However, a more parsimonious set of variables is not inconceivable. More detailed analyses of the individual challenge iterations is clearly needed.[16]

THE CHANGING CIRCUMSTANCES OF CHALLENGE

Challenges constitute opportunities for evolutionary change by forcing selection from the variety of ways to organize the world political economy. Yet the process of challenge is also characterized by evolutionary change. Two examples provide some further illustration of this point. One has to do with challenger strategies; the other with the types of business organizations that have predominated at various stages.

There are three basic types of challenging strategy although challengers, as suggested in Table 8.4, may mix them in practice. The first type, the "capture-the-center" strategy, is the most traditional one. As demonstrated in the Chin and Mongol attacks on the Sung and the French attacks on northern Italy in the fifteenth century and the Netherlands in the seventeenth century, the focus of conflict is fixed on whether the challenger can seize the lead economy. It is assumed that seizing the center will deliver the leader's commercial networks as well.

The capture-the-center strategy, prior to 1815 at least, was associated exclusively with the Chin and Mongol conquerors of the Sung dynasties in eastern Asia and

Table 8.4 The historical evolution of challenger strategies

Iteration	Active zone	Territorially-based autocracies	Maritime-commercial powers	Strategies
1	Northern Sung	Chin		Capture-the-center/imperial expansion
			Southern Sung	
2	Southern Sung	Mongols		Capture-the-center/imperial expansion
3			Genoa Venice	Alternative network development/ flanking/skirmishing
4	Genoa		Venice	Alternative network development/ flanking/skirmishing
5	Venice	France I		Capture-the-center/imperial expansion
			Portugal	Alternative network development/ flanking
6	Portugal	Spain		Capture-the-center/imperial expansion
			Netherlands	Alternative networkdevelopment/ flanking/skirmishing
			England	Alternative networkdevelopment/ flanking/skirmishing
7	Netherlands	France II		Capture-the-center/imperial expansion
			England	Skirmishing/alternative network development/ subsystemic protection at home and in colonies
8	Britain I/II	France III		Alternative network development/ subsystemic protection and regional/imperial bloc formation (capture-the-center contemplated)
9	Britain II	Germany I		Industrial competition/alternative network development
			United States	Industrial competition/subsystemic protection and regional expansion
10		Germany II Japan I		Industrial competition/subsystemic protection through regional/ imperial bloc formation
11	United States	USSR		Subsystemic protection through withdrawal and regional/imperial bloc formation
			Japan II?	Industrial competition/subsystemic protection at home and regional bloc formation?
		China?		

Spain and France in western Europe, neither of which can be characterized as either small or particularly maritime in orientation. Both cases involved large land powers attempting to absorb adjacent maritime centers. Only the Spanish effort was successful and that outcome probably owed a great deal to the unusual Portuguese vulnerability after the Moroccan intervention debacle.

A second strategy involves avoiding a direct attack on the center and instead attacking the global network and/or creating an alternative network. Small maritime states have been particularly more likely to pursue, and logically so, the alternative network strategy. The Portuguese, for example, simply outflanked the Venetian–Mameluke spice network in the early sixteenth century. In the seventeenth century, the Dutch first established an alternative Asian network to that of the Portuguese and then proceeded to engage in a war of attrition on the Portuguese operations. The pre-World War I German case may not have been as premeditated as some of these earlier alternative network development iterations but the outcome turned out to be similar in form although much less successful.

The third strategy, carving-out-a-subsystem, entails creating a smaller scale, usually regional system within the larger global system. The subsystem is organized around a regional leader but it need not be autarkic or completely autonomous. The scope of the challenge, therefore, is delimited in terms of territory and ambition, but it remains a challenge as long as the subsystem is created at the expense of the incumbent system leader. The more prized the territory, the greater the perceived threat to the leader's position. The more coercive and expansive the effort, the greater the perceived threat to the status quo.

Historical examples are Napoleon's Continental System, the US Monroe Doctrine in principle and the western expansion of the United States in practice, and the schemes for a German-dominated *MittelEuropa* and the Third Reich's implementation of its version. The Soviet-led withdrawal of part of Eurasia from the US-led world economy is another, now presumably dated example. Clearly, then, the three types of strategy sometimes overlap in practice. Both may be tried simultaneously, in sequence, or one at a time. Pre-World War II Japan represents a relatively pure case of the carving-out-a-subsystem type. And it is this type of strategy or the alternative network creation strategy that should be the most likely of the three possibilities to predominate in the twenty-first century because one remarkable characteristic of the evolution of challenger strategies has been a noticeable trend toward convergence of a form of "best practices".

Table 8.5 illustrates another one of the more noticeable transformations in the past 1000 years. We have already commented upon the trade-to-industry transformation. Two other aspects of these evolutionary shifts are the interrelated changes in the type of firms and the continuing shift in the predominant focus of economic activities.

Trading companies initially highly dependent upon the regulatory powers of their home state governments have given way to transnational corporations (TNCs) that are increasingly difficult to regulate or even monitor on a national basis. It could be argued that this type of shift is so profound that there is little room left for comparing earlier behavior with more contemporary activities. Yet there are two

151

Table 8.5 Historical periods of capital accumulation and organization of companies with international activities

Historical period	Main source of capital accumulation	Main type of international firm associated with each period
Merchant capitalism (pre-1770s)	Eurasian/colonial trade	Trading companies often reliant on a state-granted monopoly position
Industrial capitalism (1770s–1940s)	National industry	National firms organized around factory systems and companies securing raw materials for national industries moving toward national/international cartels to secure monopolistic positions in the early twentieth century
Global capitalism (1940s–	International networks of production, trade and finance	Oligopolistic transnationals

Source: Based on Cantwell (1989: 16–17) with modifications

facets of this shift worth keeping in mind when assessing the profundity of the changes.

One is that while the TNCs may have become difficult to control, for the most part they have not yet become genuinely transnational in identity, ownership, management, or home-basing.[17] Despite genuinely transnational production and sales, we still tend to identify TNCs in terms of their national identities just as nationalists continue to be alarmed by the intrusive and expansionary corporate activities of other nations' firms. The desire to protect home markets from foreign domination has hardly abated. Nor have suspicions that the expansion of foreign participation in our own domestic markets will lead to increasing domination in the future quite disappeared either.

As long as international economic behavior continues to take on national colors, whether accurately or not, it may be enough to permit or facilitate the fusion of economic and geopolitical competition that helps to transform trade conflicts into military conflicts. Automobile components, for example, are manufactured in so many different parts of the world that it is increasingly difficult to characterize specific automobile models as having a national origin. There are also significant trends toward increasing multinational investment, production and retailing alliances among automobile producers. Even so, consumers and politicians alike still discern a national difference between Ford and Mazda or Chrysler and Mitsubishi. Until that ability to identify firm nationality changes, it is unlikely that the operational complexities introduced by the advent of global capitalism are sufficient to eliminate the rivalries of national leaders and challengers in the world economy.

If anything, the nineteenth-century shift toward national industries made challenges of the pre-1815 variety more rather than less likely. Certain states continued to lead in innovating new industrial processes and products. The positional advantages and material rewards associated with innovational leadership made the temporary gaps between technological leaders and followers even more acute. The urge to catch up, indeed the perceived need to do so, became even more paramount in decision-makers' eyes. In spite of the hegemony of liberal ideas to the contrary, there seems to have been little diminution in the tendency to equate upward mobility on the technological gradient with national security. Since movement up that gradient meant the national development of nearly identical sectors of production and, assuming some limits to the demand for the products of diffused production capability, conflicts over exports and export markets became more rather than less likely.[18] Intensive trade wars could (and can?) still become shooting wars as long as it remained (remains?) difficult to disentangle commercial from geopolitical threats.

Up to the nineteenth century, and even into the first half of the twentieth century, commercial monopolies had been delimited by territorially demarcated spheres of influence. For periods of time, trade in some parts of the world belonged to the Portuguese, the Spanish, the Dutch, the French, or the English. These commercial spheres and the associated trade routes, as we have said, were protected by forts, colonies, and armies and navies. In order to obtain a larger share of this long-distance trade, newcomers had to take it away from more established powers. They either had to seize their predecessor's networks, make them obsolete by outflanking them, or create separate systems within which the more established powers were prevented from participating. Any of the three strategies or some combination of them usually led very quickly to military conflict.

Did this change in the nineteenth century? After all, controlling the sources of various types of stimulants (spices, sugar, tobacco, tea) were no longer the key to the world economy's leading sectors. Now it was transforming cotton into textiles, building railroads, or developing new chemicals and processes for making steel. But where and by whom was the cotton to be grown? Who would consume the textiles once they were produced? Where and by whom were the railroads to be built? Who would gain the lead in developing these products? Who would gain the technological edge in marketing them around the globe? Whose militarized networks would provide protection for these long-distance activities? Who would reap the benefits associated with political-economic preeminence and predominance? The basic nature of the game was not substantially altered by the shift from commerce to industrial production in the sense that the important questions remained the same, and so, too, did their answers.

CONCLUSION

The more things change, the more they remain the same or so the celebrated French saying goes. To be sure, not every dimension of challenge has remained unchanged. But as long as there is a tendency for a single national economy to lead the rest of the system in developing and marketing critical or leading commodities and sectors, the international political economy will be subject to periods of instability, challenge, and leadership transition. This observation assumes, naturally, that the lead achieved by one national group is finite in duration and that the commodities and sectors that are most critical change as well for it is the likelihood of temporary leads in fluctuating categories that is particularly conducive to instability.

Permanent leads and permanent leading sectors leave no room for challenge. The absence of declining or vulnerable leaders would offer no status quo defenders to target. The absence of change in the definition of leading sectors would offer no windows of opportunity for upward mobility. Therefore, it is the existence and centrality of leaders in specific categories that make challenges likely because mobility, if not growth, continues to retain some elements of the mercantilist age's zero sum quality, not all of which was strictly a matter of perception.

But where does that leave our earlier expressed interest in the Japanese challenge of the US order? That Japan is in the process of mounting a challenge there can be little doubt. The more interesting question is what type of challenge is it likely to be? Is it likely to be of the more intensive militarized variety or will it be one of the less intensive kinds? The answer to that question hinges on the answers to several auxiliary questions related to the long-term challenger model developed earlier. The most important questions would include the following:

1   Will Japan and the United States continue to vie for dominance of information technologies, or will one state pull decisively ahead? If the United States should leap ahead, Japan's challenge might recede with the retention of the world economy's active zone in North America. If Japan pulls ahead, the world economy's active zone will have moved west and US pretensions to economic leadership will appear increasingly anachronistic. On the other hand, should the technological competition continue indefinitely with no decisive winner, we should anticipate continued and perhaps increasing tension between the two competitors spilling over into every conceivable sphere of interaction.

2   How long will the Japanese–US trade conflict remain basically dyadic in structure? Over the past millennium, dyadic contests have become less frequent while triadic contests have become more common. A united European actor might change the nature of the challenge circumstances. More probable, however, is the possibility that East Asia might recreate western Europe's experience of intermittent balance of power conflicts with expanding aspirants for the role of regional hegemon. It now has the prerequisite structural configuration with large imperial autocracies on the mainland and high growth, commercial-maritime trading states offshore. A resurgent Russia cannot be ruled out completely as a major player. A more likely scenario, however, would depict a Chinese threat against Japan. The historical model outlined previously would suggest that the emerging Japanese–US confrontation would be likely to give way to a united front against the greater mutual threat from the Asian mainland. Even so, it might be difficult to predict which ally would be more likely to emerge the more exhausted from such a conflict. Nor is there any certainty that still another iteration of sea versus land power conflict would lead to a sea power victory. As

before, the outcome might very well hinge on the sea power coalition's allies on the Eurasian mainland (Modelski and Thompson, 1988; Gray, 1992).

3   How dissimilar or distant will Japan and the United States appear to one another in coming years? A similarity index pairing these two states would encompass a mixture of relatively positive and negative scores depending, of course, on when and in what relative context the scores were computed. There are obvious cultural and racial differences that have negatively affected US–Japanese relations in the past. These are unlikely to disappear. After World War II, the United States imposed a democratic constitution on defeated Japan that may or may not stick. A deteriorating international environment once before pushed Japanese domestic politics in a nonliberal direction. The problem remains, however, that we may need to calculate the similarity–dissimilarity computation in terms of third parties. The short-term emphasis stresses the absolute dyadic distance but in the long term, the question may be one of relative dyadic distance. As noted, the perceived distance between Japan and the United States might diminish in the presence of a third party threat.

Thus, knowing something about previous iterations of the struggle over political-economic predominance does not reveal exactly how the next iteration is likely to play itself out, or even if there will be another iteration.[19] How the next iteration might work depends on a variety of factors and processes that are difficult to predict with any certainty. The open-endedness of political-economic evolution must once again be highlighted. At the same time, knowing something about previous iterations at least gives us a better, long-term handle on what to look for than the short-term preoccupation with reading the ahistorical and ambiguous tea leaves of current events alone is capable of providing.

Part IV

STRUCTURAL CHANGE
AND EVOLUTION

BRITAIN AS A SYSTEM LEADER IN THE NINETEENTH AND TWENTIETH CENTURIES

There must be something distinctive about international relations that generates such grossly varying interpretations of what is believed to be going on at any given point in time. Some of the reasons are obvious. Even though most people do not possess much information about the subject, everyone has an opinion. Yet international relations can encompass extremely complex processes and, for that reason alone, analysts will tend to disagree about how best to capture and package the complexity. But there is more to wildly dissimilar interpretations than simply world politics' complexity, the deficit in information, and the surplus number of opinions about it. There is also the question of attitudinal predisposition toward various analytical choices. In earlier chapters it has been assumed that a historical structural interpretation of Britain's systemic leadership in the nineteenth century was one of the least noncontroversial assumptions that could be made. This is not really a safe assumption. There are analysts who refuse to accept the notion that Britain ascended (again) to the peak of the global political economy after 1815 and then proceeded to lose its leading position toward the end of the century. These same analysts even see Britain in a stronger position immediately after World War I than before. Clearly, there are some quite explicit disagreements here.

In this chapter a modest thesis about different predispositions is developed, with particular emphasis on the question of structure. This thesis can be illustrated by looking specifically at arguments about how we should best interpret Britain's status in the world system between 1816 and 1945. Seventeen antistructuralist criticisms of structuralist interpretations are extracted from the literature and examined critically from an avowedly structuralist position.

MARTIAN AND VENUSIAN PREDISPOSITIONS

One school of thought in world politics contends that international relations is fairly structured. There is a hierarchy of élite actors based, in large part, on their respective shares of technological innovation, economic resources in general, and military capability. However, the hierarchy is neither constant nor stable in the long term. The structure changes when élites move up (ascent) and down (decline) the hierarchy as they either improve their relative economic standing or experience positional deterioration. International conflict – who fights, who wins, and who loses – is to some considerable extent influenced by these structural changes. When the structure is reasonably stable and one state predominates over the rest, a condition that is most likely immediately after an intensive struggle over succession to the apex of the hierarchy, conflict is less probable. When the systemic leader's position is challenged by newly ascending or reemerging competitors, conflict becomes more probable.

Calling this structural interpretation a school of thought glides over the many disagreements among the analysts who subscribe to the general outlines. For instance, structuralists disagree about which actors are élites and why some actors should be given special weight in analyses. They disagree about which international conflicts are important and why they are important. They disagree about the role of political economy and the sources of power and influence in the world system. Disagreements about actors, conflicts, and central processes lead to varying historical scripts and calendars so that there may be major conflicts of interpretation between any two structural interpretations.

The reader should keep in mind that the structuralist position advanced here is couched primarily in the terms of one structural framework – the leadership long-cycle perspective illustrated in Chapter 1. It cannot be expected to speak for all approaches to historical structural interpretation. In particular, the leadership long-cycle perspective distinguishes between global and regional structures. Global politics are about the management of long-distance, interregional commerce and other interactions. Global powers are those actors with sufficient global reach to engage in long-distance commerce and applications of military force. Historically, this has translated primarily into sea power. Regional powers are more locally oriented and are more likely to specialize in military power that emphasizes land applications are useful for the extension of territorial control. In contrast, trading states, armed with sea power, are limited in their interest in, and capability to, control extensive territory around the world.

The most critical actor in this framework is the world power. This actor is the leading global power. Its foundation for global leadership is established by its initial control of major economic innovations in commerce and industry. These innovations are crucial for long-term economic growth and tend to be generated in clusters that are highly spatially and temporally concentrated. One example is the late eighteenth-century's Industrial Revolution emphasis on ways of producing cotton and iron products which gave way to an emphasis on steam and railroads in the mid-nineteenth century. Britain led in these two technological waves only to be displaced in subsequent waves focusing on electricity, chemicals, and automobiles in which Germany and the United States took the lead in the late nineteenth century.

In the leadership long-cycle framework, a new world power emerges at the end of a period of global war fought at least, in part, over which state's decision-makers will have the opportunity to make a policy for the global system. It has demonstrated its authority during the global war by putting together and leading a coalition of states to defeat the opposing coalition. The world power also emerges from the global war as the world's leading sea power – a military capability that was useful in winning the global war and that will be useful in enforcing the consequent global order.

Yet none of this hierarchy lasts forever. The world power loses its monopoly on economic innovations and its leading sea power position. Its position is challenged by other global powers that seek to ascend to the lead position. Ultimately, in conjunction with other factors – such as growing concentration in the world system's primary region – another bout of global war is fought to determine who will become the next world power. The last two rounds of global war were fought in 1792–1815 and 1914–1945.[1] In between these periods of global combat, Britain ascended to, and declined, as the system leader or world power.

A directly opposed school of thought exists. It denies that world politics is structured. Or, if it is, that it is impossible to measure relative positions among the élite actors. Position and influence hinge on too many intangible factors that have no fixed interpretation. The resources states deployed in one instance may have no or little impact in another instance, region, or point in time. For instance, strategic bombers may have one kind of impact in a highly urbanized setting and quite another in a jungle terrain. The only thing that really matters is whether decision-makers are successful in achieving their goals in specific applications of power. And success in this context is as much a function of such attributes as cleverness, will, reputation, bluff, and idiosyncratic behavior on the part of other actors as it is a function of material resource foundations.

Even more to the point, the contrary position is that Britain did not possess the appropriate attributes for systemic leadership, that its sea power was of limited utility, and that its economic resources that were most applicable to world politics had little to do with industrial innovations. Britain's success was instead predicated on its empire – in marked contrast to arguments that maritime powers are supposed to eschew territorial entanglements – and finance. But successful as it might have been, Britain never had the sort of global predominance depicted in structural perspectives. Moreover, it is argued that the structuralists have it backwards. Structuralists argue that Britain was strongest in the early nineteenth century and in decline in the latter half of that century. Antistructuralists contend that Britain was strongest immediately after World War I, both relative to the preceding century and in comparison with its rivals.

These schools of thought produce seemingly night and day or, to be more *au courant*, Venusian and Martian interpretations of international relations. What an analyst from one school calls black, another analyst labels white. Nowhere is this more obvious than in the interpretation of the British role in world politics in the period between 1816 and 1945. The structural school portrays Britain as the leader of the successful coalition against Napoleon, the leading economic producer of the first half of the nineteenth century, and that century's preeminent sea power. Toward the end of the nineteenth century, other states, most prominently Germany and the United States, began to catch up with, and surpass the British economic lead. Britain, in relative decline, was forced to retrench in order to deal with the new competition. World Wars I and II were fought, in large part, to decide who would succeed to the systemic leadership role once occupied by a Britain no longer capable of defending its former leading position.

The antistructural school of thought contends that this interpretation of British leadership and decline is nonsensical. Britain was never that powerful in the first two-thirds of the nineteenth century and only became influential in European politics toward the end of that century – at the same time that the structural school perceives Britain in a freefall economic decline. Britain, according to this antistructural view, was successful because European circumstances had changed in such a way as to create an opportunity for British balancing that had not prevailed before the 1890s and because British decision-makers exploited the opportunity in defense of their widespread empire. Not only did Britain emerge the winner in World War I, its post-war position was superior to any position attained by Britain in the previous 150 years. That is, Britain did not experience any meaningful decline before 1939. Consequently, British behavior cannot be explained in terms of something that never happened. Things fell apart only in the 1930s because the Soviet Union and France would or could not play their traditional roles and because British decision-makers made the wrong choices, not so much due to relative resource weaknesses but more as a function of missed opportunities and a lack of will. It was World War II and its aftermath, the destruction wrought by the Axis powers and the postwar behavior of colonial subjects and Cold War allies, especially the United States, that "did in" the British Empire.

While these interpretations come across as Martian and Venusian reconstructions of what transpired between 1816 and 1945, they are not necessarily as far apart as they seem. At least, it can be argued that the structural interpretation is not quite as incompatible with the antistructural point of view as the antistructuralists would have us believe. The incompatibility that is apparent reflects a perennial blind spot in the structural perspective and a fundamental misunderstanding/blind spot (or perhaps more than one) on the part of the antistructuralists. To the extent that the disputed interpretation revolves around whether capability absolutely determines power and influence, it is not clear that anyone is in disagreement. The question then becomes more one of why antistructuralists believe that structuralists think that structure dictates outcomes in both the short and long term.

These disagreements are not inherently a function of different disciplinary ways of doing things. The same disagreements are found within history and political science as well as between representatives of the two disciplines. The real distinction separates what might be termed humanities approaches versus social scientific ones. While historian antistructuralists are likely to be more comfortable with the humanities (and perhaps it is fair to say that historian structuralists are not as uncomfortable with social science as historian antistructuralists), it does not follow that political science antistructuralists are also likely to feel discomfort operating in a social scientific form of discourse. On the contrary, antistructuralists predominate in social science research focused on international relations.

We first attempt to clarify these generalizations about the distinctions between historians and political scientists and then proceed to an extended example focused on 17 antistructural assertions about the roles and status of 1816–1945 Britain.

Making distinctions about historians and political scientists

The exchange among Elman and Elman, Levy, Haber, Kennedy and Krasner, George, Ingram, Schroeder, and Gaddis is quite useful in establishing differences of approach, attitude and instinct between diplomatic historians and political scientists who study international politics.[2] Their arguments are summarized in Table 9.1. Historians focus on specific problems such as why did France retreat at Fashoda or why did Britain not intervene in the American Civil War? The stories they tell are based to a considerable degree on a description of what took place in 1898 or 1861–1865. Generalizations about what people do are uncommon, in part, due to a heightened sensitivity to fluctuations in context. Things are never quite the same from episode to episode. That rule of thumb, in its own turn, is due, in part, to the perception that individual personalities loom large in these event stories. It is not Germany that acts in the late nineteenth century but Bismarck and Kaiser Wilhelm and

Table 9.1 Attributes alleged to distinguish history and social science

Attributes	Historians	Social Scientists
Approach	Orientation toward specific problem	Orientation toward general problem
Explanation	More narrative based	More theory-based
Generalization	Rare	Frequent
Change	Contingent on particularistic principles	Operates on universal principles
Agency	Individual-oriented	Behavior-oriented
Temporal emphasis	More distant	More current
Argument complexity	High?	Low?
Attitudes toward:		
Objectivity	Impossibility recognized	Impossibility resisted
Causation	Uneasy	Straightforward
Context	Highly sensitive	Highly insensitive
Evidence	Focus on the example	Focus on representativeness of sample
Past	Valued in its own right	Instrumental for future
Prediction	Disinclined	Insistent
Theory	Useful for explanation	Source of explanation
Theory and history	Theory exists to explain history	History exists to test theory

a cast of other very specific characters who formulate and execute German foreign policy. To be able to come to grips with the complexities surrounding distinctive events and personalities, one needs access to various sorts of material, but, for diplomatic history, governmental archives of memorandums and reports are thought to be indispensable. If, for no other reason than that governmental archives are slow to be opened, historians are focused on events that have happened in the past. But, of course, historians need no special excuse to appreciate the past for its own sake.

Historians try to avoid arguments about whether complete analytical objectivity is conceivable and proceed with their analyses as honestly as they can. Given the perceived complexity of events and personalities, the very notion of causality is often suspect. In particular, simple causal arguments must be wrong if only because they are too simple. Evidence is obviously important but it cannot be disentangled from its specific context and, in any event, it tends to be evidence about why X did or thought Y at time Z. Theories may or may not be useful in illuminating some dimensions of a specific story. Alternatively, specific stories may be useful in discrediting certain theories. But there is no question that theory is and should be subordinated in the search for greater historical understanding.

In marked contrast, political scientists are oriented toward more general problems. They seek to explain arms races or wars as a categorical phenomenon, not the outcomes of the Anglo-French naval arms race or World War I. If asked to explain a specific case, the first instinct should be to identify what the particular case represents in general because theories only offer explanations about general phenomena, not specific events. In their own research (as opposed to answering pesky questions about current events), political scientists are supposed to begin with theories and then move toward cases that can help assess the relative utility of the theories that exist. Explanation is accomplished if general theoretical propositions (or hypotheses derived therefrom) receive empirical support. Prediction is important in this context because that is how political scientists test the degree of conformance between what is expected theoretically and what is observed empirically. This meaning of prediction is not the same thing as forecasting future probabilities based on extrapolations from current trends – a fairly rare practice which nevertheless seems particularly vexsome to historians.

Political scientists, in general, prefer generalizations that apply universally. Spatial and temporal modifiers and exceptions are thought to be undesirable because they represent factors that simply have no specific meaning or have yet to be theorized about successfully. Conceivably, we could take this approach to any particular period in history but more recent problems and cases are usually preferred to more distant ones. Empirical data tends to be more readily available as long as we do not insist on going too far back in time. The knowledge that is gained by explaining relatively current phenomenon seems more relevant and is, therefore, more likely to be both funded and appreciated. Moreover, there is always the suspicion that the farther back in time one goes the more key parameters must have changed. Since we do not know much about those key parameters or, alternatively, because the existing key parameters have more policy relevance, it is more prudent to work with relatively recent phenomena.

Objectivity is thought to be both possible and highly desirable, or at least conceivable, for political scientists as long as our values are made explicit and somehow kept out of the analysis as much as possible. Causation is taken for granted and parsimonious causation is better than complex causation. The focus is on the interaction of variables, not personalities operating in specific contexts with proper place names. The existence of the past cannot be denied. Path dependencies are acknowledged at least in the abstract. But, in general, history should be subordinated to the quest for better theory.

Having repeated these distinctions found in the literature, it must be noted that the descriptions of historians who study international relations sound more accurate than the descriptions of political scientists who study international relations. The reason for that is that historians are a much more homogeneous population than are political scientists. Levy (1997: 23) is correct to point out that we need to stick to describing central tendencies. The only problem is that it seems easier to discern central tendencies characterizing historians than it is to make generalizations about political scientists. After all, there are a goodly number of area specialists, philosophers, institutional historians, ideologues, journalists, and wannabe policy-makers within the social science fraternity/sorority. Quite often, their approach may seem to more closely approximate the historian's way of doing things than that of the mythical social scientist's. One possible solution to this problem is to contrast historians with social, as opposed to political, scientists. It does not solve all the problems of overgeneralization or inaccurate generalization, but it helps to reduce some of the errors. It may also eliminate a sizable proportion of the political science population from the comparison.

Even so, the attributes denoted in Table 9.1 should best be viewed as opposing polarities on continuums along which individuals may be located. For instance, there is some variance among historians on the extent to which their analyses are narrative-based. Some historical treatments are sheer narrative. Other historians would be aghast if someone accused them (rightly or wrongly) of narrative-based explanation. The same thing holds for social scientists who vary by how much theory and what sort of theory (for example, single hypothesis, middle range, grand) is introduced into their inquiry. So, we can imagine a narrative/theory-based scale on which individuals place themselves according to how they approach their subject matter. At one end is pure description and the other pure theory. Undoubtedly, very few analysts always work at the polar ends of the continuum. Nor need we assume that analysts are always consistent in operating at the same scalar point as they move from topic to topic. But some rough level of consistency can probably be anticipated.

While each of these various attributes that are being attributed to historians and political scientists suggests a different scale, it is unlikely that analysts place themselves on each possible scale differentially. It is more likely that they, not unlike attitudinal attributes, cluster. We can, for example, easily visualize a historian who is strongly narrative-bound, highly impressed by contingent relationships among major personalities and extremely uneasy about how causation works. There are also historians who are more comfortable with generalization, causation, and theory. On the other side of the ledger, there are social scientists who abhor the thought of nonuniversal principles, cannot or prefer not to think in terms other than simple causality, and believe that predictive success is the only criteria, besides parsimony, by which to judge theoretical arguments. Then, there are social scientists who have a healthy respect for context, can tolerate some level of contingency, and do not expect to find universal principles or laws.

What does all this speculation have to do with the disputed role of structure in world politics? At the risk of some overgeneralization, the thesis advanced here is that the two "types" of historians and social scientists used as examples in the paragraph above tend to view the role of structure differently. The type A historian (narrative-bound, emphasizing contingency and personalities, and uneasy about causation) and the type A social scientist (seeks universal principles, simple causality, parsimony and predictive success as the primary evaluation criterion) are least likely to embrace structural ideas. For these types of analysts, structural arguments simply do not fit their versions of reality. They generate cognitive dissonance and, therefore, are likely to be ignored or dismissed out of hand. And, the more closely an analyst approximates the ideal A type, the more dismissive he or she is likely to be.

Some type B historians (relatively comfortable with generalization, causality, and theory) and at least some type B social scientists (relatively sensitive to context, contingency, and nonuniversal generalizations) are more apt to appreciate structural arguments because structural ideas generate less cognitive dissonance for these types of analysts. Instead, it is the analytical products of type A analysts which give them generic discomfort.[3]

Of course, there are exceptions to these generalizations. Most important, there are few pure type A and B analysts. Most historians and social scientists are found scattered on points somewhere in between the A and B continuum poles within their respective "disciplinary" domains. Fortunately or unfortunately, depending on our point of view, we would also have to admit that both analytical populations are skewed toward the A points. Type B analysts are clearly in the minority everywhere. There is also the irony that type A historians have absolutely no lines of communication to type A social scientists and vice versa since they represent polar opposites on still another scale but type B analysts at least have some obvious potential for profitable, mutual interaction.

Nonetheless, the proposition advanced here is that the differential clustering of scholarly attitudinal predispositions is one prime reason for Martian and Venusian versions of international relations. Type A and B analysts are inclined psychologically to see different things going on in the real world. As a consequence, their interpretations give the appearance of emerging from completely different planets.

A case in point is the debate over the utility of structural interpretations of international relations. It must be repeatedly emphasized that this debate goes on within history, within political science, and between historians and political scientists. It is not derived from inherent differences between disciplines, but is derived from inherent differences that exist among historians and political scientists about how best to approach their preferred subject matters.

Yet if type A and B products create genuine cognitive dissonance for the other type of analyst, on what basis can we communicate across types? That is an interesting question for which we are not inclined to provide an optimistic answer. It is not clear that successful interaction across types of analysis and analysts is feasible. Still, we need to make the effort to try because there is something to be gained. Structuralists can learn from antistructuralists where their arguments seem weakest. Presumably, antistructuralists can learn the same lessons. There is also some strong probability that the two points of view are simply talking past one another. They give the appearance superficially of totally rejecting the other side's basic assumptions and conclusions. But, abstractly speaking, there are ways to accommodate seemingly diametrically opposed views and profit from the exchange. Whether all or any concerned will, in fact, perceive profit is another question entirely. In the next section of this chapter, the emphasis switches to a point-by-point examination of selected assertions made by antistructuralist historians primarily about the work of structural historians on interpreting Britain's status in world politics in the nineteenth and twentieth centuries. There certainly were other ways of organizing the material. For instance, we might just as easily have focused on antistructuralist social scientist's critiques of structural social scientific work. Or, we could have focused on antistructural historians' problems with structural social scientific analyses. But setting up the structure of the exposition as a matter of historians criticizing historians helps to illustrate the argument that these cleavages are not necessarily inherent to disciplinary distinctions alone.

While the critical assertions are aimed at the work of specific historians, no particular effort will be made here to defend the specific works under attack. Rather, the emphasis is placed on responding generically to the claims as a structurally oriented social scientist.

Specific assertions on the part of the antistructuralist school

Table 9.2 lists the 17 assertions in one set. They were not selected randomly. Rather, the rationale was to develop a set of statements that summarized as fairly as possible the antistructuralist positions on questions of particular interest to structural interpretations of Britain's nineteenth- and twentieth-century roles. In addition, the assertions were organized to move from more general to more specific statements and, as much as possible, to move chronologically over the 1816–1945 era.

There is a limit to how exhaustive one can be in assembling these assertions. Needless to say, antistructuralist analysts have advanced other assertions. Table 9.2's list should thus be viewed as a both a representative and a purposive sample.[4] While it is difficult to respond to the set of assertions as a group in a meaningful way, it should make more sense to take them one at a time.

1 Structural approaches to world politics and the 1816–1945 role of Britain are exercises in economic determinism (McKercher, 1991: 756; Neilson, 1991: 696).

Table 9.2 Seventeen antistructuralist assertions about Britain's role as a system leader

1 Structural approaches to world politics and the 1816–1945 role of Britain are exercises in economic determinism.

2 Structural arguments that portray Britain as a relatively special case and one that exemplifies categorical systemic leadership are exercises in Anglocentrism that rivals US exceptionalism. Long-cycle structuralism goes even further by developing a model of progressive cycles predicated on the United States as the mature end-point and then projecting backwards to reinterpret the Portuguese–Dutch–British leadership sequence as an evolutionary maturation process, not unlike the transition from tadpole to frog.

3 Since many of the components of power and influence that matter most are too intangible to measure systematically, it is impossible to create rank orders of states in the international system.

4 Since no weapon is inherently superior to other types of weapons, even the most simple types of capability counting are meaningless and, therefore, demonstrate the impossibility of comparing the relative strengths of states.

5 In the 1792–1815 global warfare, Britain was no match for France on the continent. The advantages of sea power in this type of confrontation are exaggerated for sea powers are inherently limited as to the damage they can inflict on continental opponents. What was most important to the outcome was coalition of European states that formed to defeat Napoleon. If the ostensible new system leader could not decide the Napoleonic outcome with its own resources and instead only profited from the work accomplished by land powers, in what sense can it be regarded as a system leader? Moreover, the subsequent limitations on British influence in Europe were more due to the strategic limitations of sea power than to decline. For instance, British sea power could not be expected to impose order within Europe or to fully contain Russia within Eurasia. Contrary to the emphasis placed on sea power by the long-cycle approach, Britain's global reach was based more on the Indian Army than on the Royal Navy.

6 Britain "flourished in peculiar historical circumstances". Britannia could rule the waves in the nineteenth century because no other state cared to challenge it.

7 If Britain was so powerful in the mid-nineteenth century, why were its interests threatened by Russia? Why could Britain not deter the outbreak of the Crimean War?

8 Britain at its peak never equaled Rome.

9 No great power, certainly including Britain, is or ever was omnipotent.

10 At the turn of the nineteenth and twentieth centuries, Britain retreated from the Americas and made new arrangements with Japan, France, and Russia to share its security burden. These developments cannot be attributed to British relative decline. Rather, they demonstrated British strength in international politics.

11 It was German policy and not German power that led Britain to identify Germany as a threatening adversary.

12 The emphasis on British relative decline in manufacturing and trade ignores the critical role played by Britain's leadership in providing investment capital and international finance after 1870. In any event, wealth in Britain continued to be based on land ownership. For much of the nineteenth century Britain remained a preindustrial state, run by aristocrats, bureaucrats, and bankers, and not industrialists and merchants.

13 "Britain had the money, the technology, the industrial capacity and the will to maintain the underpinnings of deterrence [in 1914]."

Table 9.2 (*cont.*)

14 Britain and Germany twice found themselves fighting wars which neither of them expected or desired. Throughout the nineteenth and early twentieth centuries, Britain's challengers were France and Russia. At different times, Austria and Germany acted as Britain's continental allies to contain the threat of French and Russian expansion. Britain's decision to go to war in 1914 was thus not predicated on balancing against German expansion. Rather, it was based on a fear that a Franco-Russian victory would lead to their shared domination of Eurasia and a subsequent joint bid for global supremacy. Britain had no choice but to bandwagon with the side that was likely to win, in hopes of restraining their future appetites.

15 Global relations do not determine relations in the system's core region (Europe between 1494 and 1945). Global relations are derived from relations in the system's core region. If global wars were fought only between states with global reach and about global relationships, they would have had little impact on the world's great power clashes.

16 World War I can only be seen as a triumph for Britain. In the 20 years following the war, Britain was as strong, if not stronger, than it had been in the preceding 150–200 years.

17 Britain was great because of its Empire, not despite it. One interpretation is that the real British problem was its failure to create a tightly integrated Empire in 1919 (or before) that could generate the resources necessary to compete effectively in international politics. If we counted the population and resources of the empire as opposed to the United Kingdom, we would construct a much different impression of the relative position for "Britain" as well as little evidence of relative decline. This failure of imperial integration was compounded by the losses experienced in World War II. But the real sources of the demise of the British Empire was colonial agitation for independence after World War II and the pernicious policies aiming at decolonization and the destruction of the empire by Britain's US ally.

The antistructuralist school repeatedly describes structural approaches as economic deterministic in nature. Yet it is interesting to note that antistructural analysts do not describe themselves as power/influence/prestige/will deterministic. As a consequence, we sense that the "economic determinism" charge is some sort of coded denigration as, indeed, the determinism accusation is usually meant to be derogatory and dismissive as opposed to a neutral description of a school of thought. Whatever the case, most structural approaches are far less deterministic than their critics claim. Structural approaches do, however, tend to privilege economic variables in their theoretical hierarchies, that is, it is usually assumed that economic variables have more influence on political variables than the other way around. That assumption neither rules out reciprocal influences (political variables influencing economic variables), nor does it attribute all the variance in political variables to economic causation. Rather than determinism, the bottom line is that actors are more likely to have greater influence when their relative economic position is greater than when it is lesser. That leaves a great deal of theoretical room for the operation of other processes and relationships.

A case in point is Kennedy's (1987) argument. Since many of the antistructuralists to which this chapter is a response have focused on Kennedy as a main target of their

Table 9.3 Paul Kennedy's theory of structural change

---

1 The central dynamic of change in international politics is driven primarily by developments in economic growth and technology. These developments, in turn, bring about changes in social structures, political systems, military power, and the hierarchical position of actors.

2 The pace of change is nonuniform due to irregularities in the unevenness of growth, technological innovation, entrepreneurial invention, and other intervening factors such as climate, geography, and war.

3 Different regions and states have experienced faster or slower rates of growth due to shifts in technology, production, and trade as well as to their variable receptivities to adopting new modes of increasing wealth.

4 Military power ultimately depends upon economic wealth derived from an infrastructure integrating production, technology, and finance. Uneven economic growth, therefore, significantly, impacts the relative military power and strategic position of states.

5 Great power warfare has been closely related to the rise and fall of major actors. The new territorial order established at the end of each great power coalition war, in which victory always goes to the side with the greatest material resources, confirms longer-term shifts in economic capabilities and the redistribution of international power.

6 A peculiar set of historical and technological circumstances facilitates the emergence of states that are enabled to acquire, temporarily, a disproportional share of wealth and power.

7 While the relative erosion of disproportional wealth and power is inevitable, the pace of erosion can be accelerated by attempts to maintain commitments that exceed the diminishing means to sustain them.

Source: Rasler and Thompson (1994: 143–44)

scorn, it is appropriate to look at just what this particular structural version actually argues.[5] Essentially, Kennedy contends that economic and technological growth is a central dynamic in international relations, not the only dynamic conceivable. Moreover, the way this central dynamic operates gives a temporary advantage to one state for a period of time which it loses eventually. The rise and fall dynamic also impacts ultimately on military power and is closely related to the probability of great power warfare. The propositions outlined in Table 9.3 hardly read as if they were a manifesto of economic determinism. What determinism is present is a long-run determinism. In the long run, states and decision-makers cannot evade their structural constraints. Nothing in the argument suggests that states and decision-makers cannot be creative in ignoring and/or sidestepping their structural constraints in the short run.

As it happens, the antecedence of some economic variables deemed important to the creation of structure and hierarchy over some important military-political variables has been established empirically. Rasler and Thompson and Reuveny and Thompson have repeatedly found that indicators for economic innovation (growth rates in leading sector production) and concentration (shares in leading sector production) antecede naval concentration (shares in sea power capability) and warfare (military spending/GNP or military personnel/total population).[6] These relationships characterize both the British era of leadership prior to 1914 and the US era after 1945. Naval concentration and warfare do feed back into the economic realm in significant ways but these reciprocal influences do not diminish the causal priority and primacy of economic innovation and concentration.

Nevertheless, the principal Achilles heel of structural approaches is that the lion's share of attention is devoted to the rise and fall of the economic foundation and not enough attention has been directed at what might be called the capability-influence gap that the antistructuralist emphasize. Thus, in the long run it can be argued that capability (the resources an actor possesses or can access) roughly approximates influence (whether actors obtain the outcomes they desire). However, that does not also imply that capability equals influence in the short run. The primary value of the antistructural school of thought (from a structural point of view) is to point out that a rapidly deteriorating relative economic position need not spell immediate political disaster. Eventually, relative decline "catches up" with decision-makers and they will find their options so circumscribed that retrenchment becomes nearly inevitable. In the British case, though, relative economic decline set in some time in the second half of the nineteenth century and it might be said that British policy did not fully adjust to its deteriorating economic position for another century. Hence, there is clearly a lag between declining position and fully delimited options that is both material and perceptual in nature. In the interim, there is much room for nimble strategy and adroit maneuvering. And it very well may be true that decision-makers are not necessarily the first to realize or to admit that their nation's capability foundation is in the process of eroding. The perceived rate of decline is always a matter of debate. Therefore, it should not be surprising if, on occasion, decision-makers speak and act as if they are unaware that their former preeminence has slipped away from them. Some would even say that is part of their job description.

2 **Structural arguments that portray Britain as a relatively special case and one that exemplifies categorical systemic leadership are exercises in Anglocentrism that rival US exceptionalism (Martel, 1991: 674). Long-cycle structuralism goes even further by developing a model of progressive cycles predicated on the United States as the mature end-point and then projecting backwards to reinterpret the Portuguese–Dutch–British leadership sequence as an evolutionary maturation process, not unlike the tadpole to frog process (Ingram, 1999b).**

There are elements of Anglocentrism (and other types of exceptionalism) in structural models of international relations but, if so, it is probably due primarily to the prominence of the British example in relatively recent history. On the other hand, Ingram contends that the long-cycle approach is US-centric because the authors in question knew what the US system leader looked like and whiggishly traced its presumed antecedents back in time through the British and the Dutch to the Portuguese (Ingram, 1997, 1999b). The criticism is that the authors in question presumed a development process at work. If it is known what the mature product looks like, it is then necessary to find the less developed precedents. Since Ingram does not believe there is a development process at work in the first place, arguments to the contrary are viewed as figments of overwrought social science imagination. As it happens, the leadership long cycle perspective that Ingram was criticizing now (Modelski and Thompson, 1996) traces the origins of contemporary (or most recent) US leadership to origins in Sung China 500 years before the Portuguese breakthrough into the Indian Ocean. The argument is that the long-wave type of modern economic growth first manifested in Sung China a millennia ago (see, for instance, the partially parallel argument of the historian William McNeill, 1982) can be tracked forward in time continuously via the successive growth experiences of the Northern Sung, Southern Sung, Genoese, Venetians, Portuguese, Dutch, British, and the United States. While isolated episodes of long-term growth can be discerned before the Sung period (that is before the tenth century CE), the continuous succession of growth leaders cannot be traced before the tenth century. Therefore, it is presumed that something changed in the parameters of the world economy around the tenth century. Does that mean leadership long-cycle analysis has become Sung-centric?

Are these cycles progressive? Is there a maturation process involved? These are highly debatable issues. What is less debatable is that while an evolutionary process is thought to be at work, there is no assumption that either progression or maturation are inevitable. Whether they have occurred are empirical and theoretical questions. In actuality, the evolutionary assumption is that change is open-ended. There need not be a next leader, nor is any specific leader necessarily an improvement on its predecessors in all spheres. As we make the transition between any two leaders, the naval technology may or may not have improved, the underlying leadership resource base may or may not have expanded, the global wars may or may not have become more extensive and deadlier, the scope of leadership operation may or may not have been enlarged, and the level of global order established may or may not have been extended. Over the last 1000 years, in contrast, all these criteria have changed for better or worse. For example, leadership in the global political economy no longer depends on slavery as it once did. That is certainly a progressive feature. However, the potential lethality of another global war seems markedly less progressive.

There are no tadpoles in the Sung–US leadership sequence; they are all frogs of varying size and capability performing somewhat similar roles in the global political economy.[7] The United States has never been the ideal role model on which the long-cycle theoretical apparatus rests. On the contrary, what is amazing is that after 1000 years of change, the global political economy stumbles along with much the same form of political leadership with which its "modern" era started.

More interesting is Gunder Frank's (1998) charge that all, or almost all, the current theorizing about structural change is highly Eurocentric. His argument is that the center of the world economy was located in eastern Asia until about 1800 and, then, centrality shifted only briefly (for about 200 years) to western Europe and North America. It is now shifting back to eastern Asia according to Frank's Sinocentric perspective. But, putting aside the question of the accuracy of Frank's location of the world economy's center in the 1500–1800 period, the world's center of economic innovation was once clearly located in the Near East some 5000 years ago. If this argument is made must we then call it a Sumerocentric point of view?

The answer is probably "yes" and the general point is that we create models based, in part, on our interpretation of international "realities". Where else are our models to originate? To accuse a perspective of harboring some type of centricity, then, does not have much meaning unless it is implied that the interpretation fits only that patch of geographical territory at some point in time and no other or, alternatively, exaggerates the appearance of some territory's attributes or behavior into a general model. The antistructural critique comes closer to the latter than the former but since it is denying that the structural perspective fits the British experience in the first place, the implications of "Anglocentricity" are left vague.

There is also the perhaps amusing question of who is more genuinely anglocentric – one group that sees British ascent and decline as a phase that other states have experienced in history or another group that argues that Britain is difficult to compare with other similar political units and, in any event, never declined until it was stabbed in the back by its US ally? Or is the root question one of whether emphasis should be placed on Britain as opposed to the British Empire? This question of state centricity versus imperial centricity will emerge again (see p. 183–85).

From a structural point of view, one highly appropriate question is whether the center of the action is identified correctly. From an antistructural point of view, there presumably is no center to identify correctly or incorrectly. The question then revolves around whether an empirical case can be made for or against some group's alleged centrality.

3 Since many of the components of power and influence that matter most are too intangible to measure systematically, it is impossible to create rank orders of states in the international system (Martel, 1991: 677).

If the components of power and influence are mainly intangible, a rank order of states in the international system would be rather difficult to construct. However, the adherents to the antistructural perspective seem a bit confused on this issue. While they stress the intangible, they also insist on the continued preeminence of Britain up to 1914 and even, amazingly, to 1939. The antistructural position (McKercher, 1991: 751, 783; Neilson, 1991: 696, 725) is that Britain was the only global or world power prior to the two world wars. All other possible contenders were either isolated and/or confined to regional theaters.[8] Hence, one gathers that it is possible to at least rank-order the geographical scope of influence. Antistructural analysts (McKercher, 1991; Neilson, 1991) also claim that Britain was the world's leading sea power and financial power at a time when structural analysts are describing Britain as a declining power. Does that imply that it is possible to rank-order sea and financial power but not other types of capability?

4 Since no weapon is inherently superior to other types of weapons, even the most simple types of capability counting are meaningless and, therefore, demonstrate the impossibility of comparing the relative strengths of states (Martel, 1991: 678).

Frankly, this statement is most peculiar. Taken on its face value, it is clearly untrue.[9] History is replete with examples of people with iron swords defeating other people armed only with bronze swords, of people with faster-firing rifles defeating other people with slower-firing rifles, and of people with the capability to hurl projectiles farther defeating people with less hurling capability. Without any doubt, some weaponry is inherently superior over other types of weaponry. Other things being equal, an eighteenth-century ship captain engaged in a sea battle would rather have a 50-gun ship-of-the-line than a frigate with 25 guns. That is exactly how the concept of ships-of-the-line emerged as the number of guns escalated and lesser-gunned ships could no longer engage competitively in the front line of the fleet. Over time, this escalation in artillery numbers expanded to encompass armor thickness and how far the artillery could fire its shells. Wooden ships gave way to iron/steel ships just as galleys had given way to sailing ships in earlier blue water clashes. Dreadnoughts made predreadnought battleships obsolete because Dreadnought artillery could engage and destroy predreadnoughts before the older-style battleships could bring their guns to bear on the opposition. Carriers took this idea one step further by launching aircraft to attack ships that were not in sight. Once that principle became dominant, battleships were forced to yield their front-line status.

The point remains that it is quite conceivable to quantify weaponry capability as long as one is reasonably careful.[10] Historically, decision-makers have spent some time counting their opponent's ships of the line, battleships, carriers, attack submarines, and so on – and not without reason. The outcome between an encounter between any two ships equally armed and armored may be difficult to call without reference to crew training, skill, and luck. But a fleet with twice as many first-line ships as an opponent's is normally more likely to win a battle between the two fleets. Similarly, a state with more front-line ships than all of its opponents combined is a better bet to become the world's leading sea power than is a state with only 10 percent of the naval capability pool. However, no one presumably argues that sea power is guaranteed to be of much use in combat waged in interior deserts, mountains, or jungles.[11] Nor is anyone arguing that a battleship equals an infantry battalion. And it cannot be assumed that the possession of weapons means that those weapons will be utilized at all or wisely. There are, indeed, limitations to weaponry quantification and the uses to which it may be applied. Yet these limitations do not prevent us from separating major from minor powers or system leaders from followers.

5 In the 1792–1815 global warfare, Britain was no match for France on the continent. The advantages of sea power in this type of confrontation are exaggerated for sea powers are inherently limited as to the damage they can inflict on continental opponents. What was most important to the outcome was the coalition of European states that formed to defeat Napoleon. If the ostensible new system leader could not decide the Napoleonic outcome with its own resources, and instead only profited from the work accomplished by land powers, in what sense can it be regarded as a system leader? Moreover, the subsequent limitations on

British influence in Europe were more due to the strategic limitations of sea power than to decline. For instance, British sea power could not be expected to impose order within Europe or to fully contain Russia within Eurasia. Contrary to the emphasis placed on sea power by the long-cycle approach, Britain's global reach was based more on the Indian Army than on the Royal Navy (Ferris, 1991: 732; Martel, 1991: 680; Ingram, 1999b).

There should be no question that the statements concerning the limitations of sea power in confrontations with continental opponents and the need for coalitions of sea and land powers to suppress an attempt at regional hegemony are correct. However, none of these arguments are alien to structural perspectives which are ordinarily highly sensitive to the distinctions between sea and land power. It is helpful to emphasize, as does leadership long-cycle theory, that there are really two different games at play. One group of states has specialized in long-distance trade, sea power, and the avoidance as much as possible of continental (in this case, read European) entanglements. Another group of states has specialized in territorial expansion within Europe and developing its instruments of land power. While not all major powers (since 1500) clearly belong exclusively to one species or the other, the most lethal wars have been fought when the leader of the sea power group has organized a coalition of states to suppress the regional hegemony of a European land power (for example, Spain, France, and Germany).[12]

Particular emphasis must be placed on the coalition organization function of the system leader. To the extent that the system leader has specialized in sea power, there are very real limitations on what it could do militarily against an entrenched land foe. This is the classical whale versus elephant dilemma (Thompson, 1995). They cannot get at each other very well or conclusively. Either the whale must enlist its own elephants or the elephant must enlist its own whales. In modern history, the whale coalition leader has always triumphed over European elephants, in part, due to a two-front strategy combining sea and land power against a would-be hegemon relying largely only on land power.[13] Once the coalition has been victorious, the coalition leader has not emerged as the world hegemon. Rather, an aspiring regional hegemon has been defeated thereby suppressing a potential threat to the global system of long-distance trade and advanced technological production. It is this global system over which the system leader is preeminent due to its coalition leadership but also due to its near-monopoly position in controlling long-distance trade and advanced technological production. Preeminence in the global system does not necessarily translate into influence in and over regional affairs. Moreover, that global preeminence is likely to be maintained longer to the extent that the system leader is able to avoid entanglement in regional politics. Even so, no global system leader has managed to isolate itself from regional problems for very long. Its own position is likely to erode. Equally likely is the emergence of new competitors and challengers.

Britain did not win the Napoleonic Wars single-handedly any more than the United States won World War II on its own. It has instead been the task of system leaders to cajole, subsidize, and, if necessary, intimidate fellow global war coalition members. At the same time, sea power has been critical to the process of wartime coalition leadership in terms of moving troops and supplies, their own and those of others, as necessary. They also must deny the same maritime benefits to the other side. These are tasks that Britain became quite proficient at in its heyday.

Sea power is also critical in acquiring and maintaining the system leader's global network of bases around which imperial territorial control tends to cluster and expand. System leaders do not initially plan on constructing extensive territorial control but ever since Venice it has proved difficult to avoid this byproduct of success. The Indian Army did prove critical in maintaining and expanding the territorial frontiers of the British Empire in a relatively inexpensive way. However, the utilization of the Indian Army was greater in the second half of the nineteenth century as opposed to the first half. From a leadership long-cycle perspective, Britain had already peaked in the first half of the nineteenth century. The deployment of the Indian Army along the turbulent African and Asian frontiers thus was more a matter of hanging on to positions already achieved than a matter of constructing new sources of wealth and global power. But if one views the Empire as the source of wealth and power, it is the second half of the nineteenth century and the continuing imperial expansion that seems more critical. This disagreement seems to be a matter of assumptions and interpretations, and not one of disputes over the facts of the nineteenth century.

6 Britain "flourished in peculiar historical circumstances". Britannia could rule the waves in the nineteenth century because no other state cared to challenge it (Ferris, 1991: 733).

From a structural perspective, there was little that was peculiar about Britain's flourishing in the nineteenth century. The general situation that Britain exploited to its advantage has been iterative. One state has developed an overwhelming lead in sea power and commercial/industrial innovation. At the end of a period of intensive global war, its main competitors are weakened or exhausted. It is not that competitors do not choose to challenge the system leader's post-war maritime authority, they either cannot or dare not do so. But this type of situation is finite. Competitors eventually begin developing their capability to challenge at sea and in the market place. Hence, the Pax Britannica was no more "artificial" or illusory than the Pax Americana that some skeptics attribute to the temporary effects of the aerial bombardment of German and Japanese factories. The generalization is that system leaders improve their edge over their competitors even more by exhausting them in an intensive global war. At a minimum, time is required to recover. In that interim, the system leader is less likely to be challenged in the management of the global system's preoccupation with long-distance trade and advanced technological production. This interim situation does not mean that the international system will be completely peaceful or that the system leader's governance will be effective, widespread, or even visibly manifested in regional affairs. It does mean that a conclusive global war is likely to be followed by a period of time characterized by a significant absence of serious challenges to the political-economic status quo.

7 If Britain was so powerful in the mid-nineteenth century, why were its interests threatened by Russia? Why could Britain not deter the outbreak of the Crimean War? (Martel, 1991: 682).

There are two easy responses to this assertion. One is that Britain was most powerful at sea in the mid-nineteenth century. The Balkans and the Crimea are not easily accessed by sea power. Therefore, Russia could contemplate predominately land attacks on the Ottoman Empire. A second answer is that the Crimean War took place in the mid-nineteenth century. It did not take place for some 35 years after the end of the Napoleonic Wars despite earlier opportunities for Russian–British antagonism in the Near East.[14] In structural perspectives, the system leader's position erodes and challenges become more probable. In the case of the Crimean War, the challenge turned out to be less than formidable. So, too, was the response of the coalition organized to deal with it. Nonetheless, the Crimean War did not represent the same type of threat as that posed by the Germans in 1914. The Crimean War was part of the some 160 years of Eurasian sparring between Britain and Russia–the Soviet Union. It did not represent an attempt to establish European regional hegemony along the lines of a Philip, Louis XIV, Napoleon, or Hitler. Nor was it a full-fledged assault on the global order.

8 Britain at its peak never equaled Rome (Martel, 1991: 681).

Precisely. The analogy is completely wrong. For a time, Britain led the global system in long-distance commerce and advanced technological production. Rome was a regional land power and traditional imperial hegemon. It engaged in long-distance trade as a function of its wealth but it never specialized in it or the ancient equivalent of the global system. It also ran into political-economic trouble once its territorial expansion had reached its technological limits. In contrast, Britain became the ruler of an extensive territorial empire only after it had specialized in trade, and, in large part, it became an imperial ruler to defend its trading prospects. Whether all or much of that extensive territorial empire facilitated British prosperity or became a drain on its resources remains a contested proposition.

9 No great power, certainly including Britain, is or ever was omnipotent (Martel, 1991: 682).

Without doubt this is true. But then no one ascribes omnipotence to Britain in the nineteenth century or to system leaders in general. While it seems true that system leaders have become increasingly powerful over the last few centuries, and that Britain was more powerful in its second term as system leader (nineteenth century) than in its first term (eighteenth century), omnipotence was never very likely in a system of multiple states.[15] One would first have to transform a system into a single state/empire along Han–T'ang–Mongol–Ming lines to attain some level of omnipotence. With the exception of the Mongol experience, such unification has only been successful at the regional level. The territorial unification of the global system is an awkward subject and, in any event, would involve a rather awesome, transregional undertaking that may have been contemplated from time to time, but only rarely attempted and never so far by a system leader.[16]

10 At the turn of the nineteenth and twentieth centuries, Britain retreated from the Americas and made new arrangements with Japan, France, and Russia to share its security burden. These developments cannot be attributed to British relative decline. Rather, they demonstrated British strength in international politics (Martel, 1991: 683–684, 686; Neilson, 1991: 698–704).

British decision-makers are to be credited for unusually insightful deal-making in the period roughly between 1890 and 1910. Devising new grand strategies to meet new sources of threat is rarely accomplished smoothly or easily. If we knew more about the construction of grand strategies, it might even be possible to argue that devising new grand strategies to meet new sources of threat is rarely accomplished. Still, it is difficult how else we might interpret the need to pull back from extended positions that had been acquired in less threatening circumstances than as a function of relative decline. At one point in time, Britain was prepared to contain France within Europe, to contain Russia within Eurasia, to contain the United States within the Americas, and might have been prepared to also attempt to contain Japan within east Asia. The first three containment plans variably preoccupied the British throughout most of the nineteenth century. The French gradually became less of a perceived threat within the European theater although they still raised problems in Africa and Asia. The Russians remained a problem but were weakened severely by the Russo-Japanese War and domestic tensions, permitting a temporary detente in the Anglo-Russian cold war or Great Game. In the Americas, the British gradually yielded to the greater local capability of the United States during the second half of the nineteenth century.

Had the Japanese ascent begun much earlier in the nineteenth century, there probably would have been a British attempt to contain the expansion of their regional influence. The Japanese timing, however, was such that they had begun to become increasingly significant at a time when Britain was in the market for an Asian ally. That in and of itself may not seem so remarkable unless it is considered in the context of the British preference to avoid alliances throughout the nineteenth century. Only when a combination of new threats and competitors had emerged and its own relative position had declined were British decision-makers prepared to change their way of doing things. They did not have to seek out alliances from a declining position but alliances, accommodations, and military retrenchment were options to pursue given the changing circumstances. British decision-makers might also have attempted to maintain their earlier containment strategies and simply added Germany to the list. This is precisely where relative decline enters the picture in the sense that decision-makers seemed to sense they could no longer continue doing business as usual. Their relative resources were not up to the expansion in challenges, despite the fact that at least two of their longtime rivals' potential for generating threat had been curtailed in the first decade of the twentieth century.

11 It was German policy and not German power that led Britain to identify Germany as a threatening adversary (Martel, 1991: 685).

This statement constitutes another curious assertion. In political science 101 terms, threat equals capability multiplied by intentions. It is agreed that the British were agitated by perceived and real German intentions, but they would have been much less agitated by a Prussian state of the early nineteenth century funded by an agrarian economy. In the late nineteenth century, Germany was one of two states with the potential to overtake and surpass the British lead in technological innovation. That potential was very much a part of British threat perception.[17]

12 The emphasis on British relative decline in manufacturing and trade ignores the critical role played by Britain's leadership in providing investment capital and international finance, especially after 1870. In any event, wealth in Britain continued to be based on land ownership. For much of the nineteenth century Britain remained a preindustrial state, run by aristocrats, bureaucrats, and bankers, and not industrialists and merchants (Ferris, 1991: 73; Martel, 1991: 686; McKercher, 1991: 751; Neilson, 1991: 721; Ingram, 1999b).

Without question, Britain remained the leading source of capital and investment even after (or especially after?) its relative economic foundation had begun to deteriorate. So had the Dutch before them. Some structural theories (Wallerstein, 1984) go so far as to argue that there is a lock-step order to economic preeminence: (1) agro-industrial; (2) commercial; and (3) financial. And as numbers (1) and (2) give way, financial preeminence lingers on. Be that as it may – and while it is clear that industrial and commercial preeminence can lead to financial preeminence, it is less clear that it must always do so in the same way – it is also not clear how lingering financial preeminence challenges structural perspectives.

As for the assertion about land-based wealth, there may be something of an ecological fallacy operating here. Wealth inequalities within Britain were and presumably remain to some extent linked to land holdings. Even wealth gained in technological endeavors might be exchanged for aristocratic titles and land. But, surely, the argument is not that Britain's spectacular international activities were predicated to whatever degree on the exploitation and mobilization of agrarian resources in England, Ireland, and Scotland ?

The issue concerning the nature of ruling élites is an interesting one but it is not an issue that has been studied comparatively (across different system leaders). Shifts in ruling élites within system leaders have occurred in every case since the Sungs and usually subject to considerable lags. That is, fundamental changes in the nature of a system leader's predominant economic activities predate equally fundamental shifts in what sorts of élites have influence over decision-making. As a consequence, the national prioritization of interests and policies tends to change more slowly than one might otherwise expect. In what respects these transitional lags make systematic differences in foreign policy behavior deserves more study. But since no structuralist argument portrays British decision-makers as being former merchants or industrialists, it is also not clear exactly what the criticism is about.

13 "Britain had the money, the technology, the industrial capacity and the will to maintain the underpinnings of deterrence [in 1914]" (Neilson, 1991: 724).

Why then did World War I ensue? This is hardly the place to review the multiple causes of World War I but one important element that has been neglected too often was the structural disarray. The international hierarchy was challengeable and in the process of being challenged. Britain was no more able to deter Germany in 1914 than it was in 1939. Nor had the British–the Dutch, or the Portuguese been successful in preventing the outbreak of war in 1792, 1688, or 1579–1580. To the extent that one finds similar structural circumstances at play in these episodes, there would appear to be a generalizable phenomenon at work. Declining system leaders are less efficacious at deterring attempts at regional hegemony than are system leaders that have not yet begun to decline. The ultimate irony of deterrence in this context is that it is most likely to be successful when it is least necessary and least likely to be successful when it is most necessary (Thompson, 1997/1998).

14 Britain and Germany twice found themselves fighting wars which neither of them expected or desired. Throughout the nineteenth and early twentieth century, Britain's challengers were France and Russia. At different times, Austria and Germany acted as Britain's continental allies to contain the threat of French and Russian expansion. Britain's decision to go to war in 1914 was thus not predicated on balancing against German expansion. Rather, it was based on a fear that a Franco-Russian victory would lead to their shared domination of Eurasia and a subsequent, joint bid for global supremacy. Britain had no choice but to band-wagon with the side that was likely to win, in hopes of restraining their future appetites (Ingram, 1999b).

This is an interesting hypothesis that mixes some established facts and entirely unverified conjecture. As a hypothesis, it cannot be ruled out as entirely implausible. Yet, so far, it lacks any supporting evidence. It would also seem even more plausible as an explanation for Britain entering World Wars I and II on the side of Austria and Germany or not entering at all, and not, as they did, on the sides of France and Russia. If the motivating force was fear of a Franco-Russian victory, why contribute to its probability? Why not sit on the sidelines and hope for an outcome beneficial to Britain more or less as Britain did in 1861–1865, 1870–1871, and 1904–1906?

Ingram is quite correct to point out that France and Russia were Britain's principal rivals and challengers throughout much of the nineteenth century. The United States could be added to this group of challengers as well.[18] It is also true that as a general rule system leaders, given their maritime capabilities, have needed continental allies in order to be successful in Eurasian politics and war. However, something changed towards the end of the century as German capabilities and potential expanded from its earlier Prussian form. British decision-makers, accurately or inaccurately, ultimately chose to look upon Germany as its principal foe and made separate arrangements with the Americans, the French, the Japanese, and the Russians to deescalate their traditional rivalries with Britain. German behavior after 1890, and especially after 1914, certainly contributed to this major power realignment of rivalries. It is possible that the realignment might have been a temporary expedience of great power politics and, in some respects it was. The British rivalries with Russia and Japan later resumed, but while Britain and France, and Britain and the United States, continued to compete and quarrel, they were increasingly less likely to go to war with one another after about 1904. The strategic nature of their nineteenth-century rivalries had come to an end.[19]

15 Global relations do not determine relations in the system's core region (Europe between 1494 and 1945). Global relations are derived from relations in the system's core region. If global wars were fought only between states with global reach and about global relationships, they would have had little impact on the world's great power clashes (Ingram, 1999b).

The relationship between the global political economy and the system's core region is indeed an important one. One leadership long cycle argument (Rasler and Thompson, 1994) is that between 1494 and 1945, power concentration tendencies in the global and European systems were dissynchronized. When power was most highly concentrated in the global arena, power within western European tended to be deconcentrated. As global concentration eroded, European power concentration increased. These tendencies were hardly coincidental. Global wars, for instance, accelerated global concentration while contributing to deconcentrating western European power, especially as manifested in defeating a regional hegemonic aspirant. Moreover, the rise of regional hegemonic aspirants seems to have been encouraged to varying degrees by declining system leaders, who are seen as weakening obstacles, increasingly vulnerable, and potentially capable of being supplanted. Thus, there is no argument that global and/or regional relations are autonomous. They are inter-dependent and tend to become highly fused intermittently in periods of crisis.

Global wars, in particular, represent periods of acute regional and global fusion. They are wars fought simultaneously over questions of regional and global governance. For instance, World War I could be said to have been an outcome representing the convergence of several ongoing rivalries. The Anglo-German rivalry was predominately global in nature. The Franco-German and Austro–German–Russian rivalries were mainly regional (western and east–southeastern Europe) in nature. World War I was a global war, or more precisely, the first phase of the 1914–1945 global war, but its onset cannot be explained solely in terms of global relations (or the Anglo-German rivalry). Yet even though global wars constitute

Table 9.4 Britain's decline in naval power and leading-
       sector production

	Naval power share	Leading sector share
1780		0.292
1786	0.360	
1790		0.455
1796	0.363	
1800		0.534
1806	0.419	
1810		0.603
1816	0.660	
1820		0.549
1826	0.582	
1830		0.643
1836	0.482	
1840		0.583
1846	0.493	
1850		0.546
1856	0.505	
1860		0.500
1866	0.475	
1870		0.519
1876	0.434	
1880		0.430
1886	0.479	
1890		0.333
1896	0.467	
1900		0.245
1906	0.392	
1910		0.146
1916	0.424	
1920		0.100
1926	0.336	
1930		0.082
1936	0.273	
1940		0.075
1945	0.350	
1950		0.093
1960		0.087
1970		0.070
1980		0.039

Sources: The naval capability shares are taken from Modelski and
Thompson (1988); the leading sector shares are taken from
Thompson (1988)

regional–global fusions and are brought about by multiple factors, they still play a crucial role in creating opportunities for the emergence of new global leadership – among other consequences. That is why, especially from a global perspective, World War I was inconclusive.[20] New global leadership did not emerge fully until after the conclusion of World War II.

16   World War I can only be seen as a triumph for Britain. In the 20 years following the war, Britain was as strong, if not stronger, than it had been in the preceding 150–200 years (Ferris, 1991: 773, 739–740; Martel, 1991: 657, 692; McKercher, 1991: 751, 783; Ingram, 1997: 56–57, 59, 1999b).

World War I was certainly a triumph for Britain and British coalition management but the triumph, in turn, hinged on the coalition that was constructed marshaling greater and more effective resources than were available to the central powers' coalition. It eventually did put together a superior resource base but the outcome was not inevitable. Nor was the outcome attributable to a Britain that had maintained its preeminence up to and through 1914. Without US intervention, a stalemate or worse had been conceivable in view of the Russian collapse. Britain survived World War I but not without a great deal of help from various quarters.

The assertion that Britain was stronger in the interwar years than at any time during the nineteenth century is one of those statements that seem rather peculiar. From either a British or imperial security perspective, there were few immediate external threats in the immediate aftermath of World War I, but that aftermath was an incredibly short-lived period. One does not even have to invoke short- versus long-term distinctions to point out that a postwar decade or less of relative strategic security is hardly an appropriate or compelling slice of time for evaluation. It could be pointed out that this same period was characterized by various *internal* threats to the perseverance of the British Empire and that former allies (Italy and Japan) soon became external threats. World War I also made a significant dent in British financial preeminence, both in terms of capital lost directly to war purposes and the opportunity for competitors (most notably, the United States) to make headway in places such as Latin America that had once been British financial preserves.

Yet what is most striking about the statement of British relative strength in the interwar years is that it simply is not very accurate in terms either of economic production – a point with which the antistructuralists would probably agree but not care – but also in terms of naval capability. As demonstrated in Table 9.4 and Figure 9.1, the British relative position between 1919 and 1939 was the poorest it had been over the preceding 150 years. Whatever else might be said about the war to end all wars, World War I did nothing significant to arrest or reverse the long-term, relative, economic and naval decline of Britain. In terms of Britain's financial position and even the cohesion of the empire, World War I only accelerated the disintegrating British position.

17   Britain was great because of its empire, not despite it. One interpretation is that the real British problem was its failure to create a tightly integrated empire in 1919 (or before) that could generate the resources necessary to compete effectively in international politics. If we counted the population and resources of the Empire as opposed to the United Kingdom, we would construct a much different impression of the relative position for "Britain," as well as little evidence of relative decline. This failure of imperial integration was compounded by the losses experienced in

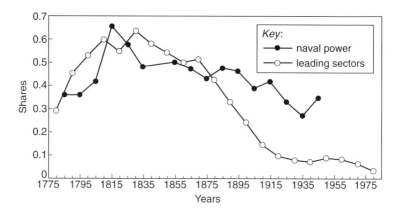

Figure 9.1 British relative decline

World War II. But the real sources of the demise of the British Empire was colonial agitation for independence after World War II and the pernicious policies aiming at decolonization and the destruction of the Empire by Britain's American ally (Ferris, 1991: 736; Martel, 1991: 693; Ingram, 1997: 56–57, 59, 1999b).

It is sometimes argued that Germany in the early part of the twentieth century was more concerned with keeping up with the Soviet Union and the United States than it was in succeeding to the British position as a global system leader. Territorial expansion in the Ukraine was supposedly the central European answer to the gigantic scale of the future superpowers. If so, the charge that the fundamental British strategic error was the failure to create a tightly integrated empire when it had the chance may belong in the same vein of thought. However, there are two problems with the argument. First, the British Empire may not have been founded "in a fit of absence of mind", as Martel (1991: 690) states it, but it was not entirely premeditated either. Much of the time territorial gains were resisted by British decision-makers and while local agents of expansion may have known what they were doing, London decision-makers often did not seem to know what to do with the scattered and intermittent *fait accomplis* on some distant border of the empire (Thompson and Zuk, 1986).

This ostensibly timid approach to empire-building could be criticized as a missed opportunity. Whether it was or was not, though, imperial expansion was never the primary goal of British foreign policy, nor was expansion necessarily considered an indicator of foreign policy success. As long as Britain had an edge in producing valued industrial commodities and distributing valued commercial goods – and were not entirely precluded from competing for foreign markets – territorial possessions beyond the minimum necessary for a global network of support bases were more a liability than an asset. The British were hardly the first to grapple with this policy problem. Similar debates are found in the annals of the Venetians, the Portuguese, and the Dutch. The usual pattern was an initial avoidance of territorial acquisition followed by a gradual deviation from the avoidance policy. By the time an empire was fully established by a trading state, the state in question had already lost its competitive edge.[21] Then the question usually became whether to retreat behind the imperial tariff/mercantilistic walls as opposed to continuing to compete at a growing disadvantage in more open markets.

The second angle on the full unification of the British Empire was that significant parts of the Empire were not interested in a more integrated union. It is an irony of considerable proportions, given the strong Canadian identity of the members of the historical antistructuralist school, that Canadians led the resistance to tighter union in the early twentieth century. The first British Empire and the first British stint as a global system leader fell apart over a quarrel about how tightly the Empire should be managed. There was also an element of British relative decline in the last quarter of the eighteenth century which complicated its ability to hang onto its empire. It is doubtful whether the second British Empire could have been reconsolidated after an extensive period of nineteenth-century relative decline. Too many of the constituent parts were eager to go their own way.

A third way to look at this imperial thesis, ironically, is provided by one of the anti-structural critics. Ingram (1999b) argues that nineteenth-century Britain was a dual monarchy – one centered in the British Isles and the other centered on the large south Asian peninsula. As such, "Britain" lacked the insularity attribute usually associated with systemic leaders and customarily attributed to the Britain situated off the shore of western Europe. The Asian part of the British Empire forced Britain to engage in Eurasian politics and to compete with Russia in southwest and central Asia for primacy.

Anglo-Russian relations and rivalry in the nineteenth century were certainly predicated, in part, on the need to defend Britain's position in, and the approaches to, India. However, Anglo-Russian rivalry actually began over Baltic commerce in the eighteenth century and was later extended further south to the struggle over the disposition of the Ottoman Empire and access to the Mediterranean and Indian Ocean. But Britain's position in south and southwest Asia, the Middle East, and North Africa were also subject to dispute with other rivals, such as France and Germany. One point is that Britain's Indian position did not uniquely privilege the Russians as Britain's principal rival. The identification of Britain's principal rival fluctuated between 1815 and 1914, depending on who was in power in Britain and what sort of foreign policy problems seemed most pressing.

A second point is that Britain's imperial commitments in Africa and Eurasia expanded throughout the nineteenth century. In 1815, at the onset of the second British period of systemic leadership, British commitments to defend far flung possessions were relatively limited. That strategic flexibility gradually vanished as Britain increasingly resembled Ingram's dual monarchy. It is precisely in this respect that Britain's imperial successes detracted from its ability to perform systemic leadership roles. But then the problems Britain encountered in the late nineteenth century were only partially related to its noninsularity in Asia.

As for the American stab-in-the-back thesis, we have seen this sort of phenomenon emerge as a form of explanation in a variety of circumstances. Usually, it involves groups that have lost position and resources and prefer to blame some perfidious external or internal agent for its problems. If only they had not been so preoccupied or trusting, the losses might have been prevented by taking more forceful action against supposed allies or fellow countrymen. In this particular case, the problem seems to be that the incumbent global system leader organizes a successful coalition sometimes only to be supplanted by a former junior ally. The English did this to the Dutch in the 1688–1713 period and the Americans did this to the British in the 1914–1945 period.

If the reality of relative decline is denied then perhaps falling back on stab-in-the-back pathologies is one way to make sense of the world. It is not a very accurate portrayal, however, of the way in which new global system leaders move aside old global leaders and their privileged arrangements. In the Anglo-American case, as in the Anglo-Dutch case, the incumbent leader and its eventual successor had been strategic rivals before they coalesced to deal with a mutual threat. In the Anglo-American case, the two states maintained a commercial rivalry after they had ended their strategic rivalry in the first decade of the twentieth century They continued to be commercial rivals in the aftermath of World War II but the rivalry had become increasingly asymmetrical thanks to British decline and American ascent. Hence, there is no question that US policy contributed to the demise of the British Empire. The only question is why this should be viewed as a stab in the back after nearly 200 years of hot and cold rivalry? In the final analysis, perhaps it only betrays some antediluvian sentiments about the desirability of Anglo-Saxon solidarity or a wish to express some considerable disappointment about the payoffs of ostensible special relationships. It would be interesting to compare these sentiments with what the Dutch, in particular Dutch authors with experience in Jakarta, China, or India, had to say about the British a generation or so after 1714.

CONCLUSION

Is it possible to successfully rebut the antistructuralist assertions? We think the answer, not surprisingly, is affirmative. Readers will have to arrive at their own conclusions and, no doubt, the evaluations will need to proceed on an assertion-by-assertion basis. Whatever else is clear, it should be apparent that working out the answers to the British role in nineteenth- and twentieth-century world politics remains contested. One book chapter will not resolve the contest.

Is it possible to persuade the antistructuralists that they are wrong? Probably not, if the argument about analytical predispositions is accurate, but then hope springs eternal. There are some very real disagreements. Should economic and technological variables be given priority over the intangible skills of strategists? Can international hierarchies be measured, compared, and tracked over time? Did Britain possess the prerequisites for global leadership? Did Britain actually play a systemic leadership role, and when, and where? Did Britain experience relative decline? Does relative decline explain British behavior very well? All these questions deserve more attention.

Yet there are also some disagreements that are wholly unnecessary. Structuralists make assertions about the long term. Antistructuralists tend to make counter-assertions about the short term. These particular arguments are not playing on the same field. If we can get them playing on the same field, antistructuralist interpretations have potential for delimiting more sharply the assertions of structuralists about the capability-influence relationship. The converse holds as well. Structuralist interpretations have potential for delimiting the assertions of antistructuralists about the capability-influence relationship. Whether Martians and Venusians can find an efficacious way to communicate productively between their two planets remains to be seen. Regrettably, the likelihood of such a meeting of the minds seems slim.[22] That does not seem to be the way cognitive dissonance operates in academia, or elsewhere.

Yet communication, persuasion, and conversion between and among different camps are not the sole goals of our collective endeavors. We are all trying to make sense of historical reality. That must remain the primary goal. If we choose radically different assumptions about how best to go about achieving that goal, so be it. If consumers of our attempts at grappling with explaining historical realities select only those products that have been constructed in accord with their own assumptions, so be that as well. Ultimately, we have no choice but to proceed along lines of inquiry that make the most sense to us as individual analysts. Still, it will not hurt to keep an eye out for what alternative approaches are doing. We all might learn something in the process.

10

THE ANGLO-AMERICAN RIVALRY BEFORE WORLD WAR I

The Anglo-American rivalry remains something of a puzzle for historical structural analysts. Here we have two states. One represented the very apex of the world system's power structure, the other at some point its most probable successor. They had fought each other but only in wars that had long preceded the point of power transition. Not only did they not fight as the United States was catching up with Britain, they ended more than a century of hostile relations and became first informal allies and then formal allies. Still later, they developed their famed special relationship. Why? If structural change does have some explanatory power, one would have thought the very opposite would have occurred.[1] Moreover, there was simply too much at stake for something on the order of Anglo-Saxon sentimentality to account for this otherwise peculiar behavior. Thus, the shift in the Anglo-American relationship from hostile rivalry to amicable cooperation raises important theoretical questions about structural explanations in world politics.

If the Anglo-American relationship is something of an anomaly for historical structural analysis, it is the precise opposite for liberal perspectives on international relations. One way to view the story is to highlight the gradual convergence of two democratic and economically interdependent states and populations. As their institutions and economies converged, their populations are thought to have become more comfortable with one another's similarities, aided and abetted by a common language and history. Similarities breed empathy, trust, and alliance. Dissimilarities lead to suspicion and conflict that are unlikely to be resolved away from the battle-field.

However, there is a problem with this approach. Anglo-American relations between 1783 and say, 1914, were interspersed with a stream of crises that might have led to war. Only one did and that one, too, might have been headed off as were the others without coming to blows. There is no need to discount institutional and economic convergence entirely but it is certainly awkward to try to explain a phenomenon that seems to have predated the development of the explanation. Something else other than democracy and interdependence may be important to this (and other) case(s).

Finally, it is axiomatic in realist perspectives on international relations to presume that rational choice provides a reasonable guide to élite decision-making. Decision-makers scan their environment, contemplate their alternatives, and choose a course of action that appears to be most beneficial and least costly. The choice leads directly to behavior.

There is another way of looking at these situations. Instead of emphasizing fixed opportunities/constraints, alternatives, and preferences in the short term, it may be more useful to focus instead on changing opportunities/constraints, changing alternatives, and changing preferences in the long term (Modelski, 1996). These two interpretations need not be mutually exclusive but one (rational choice) gives great weight to human agency while the other, more evolutionary approach emphasizes the context of changing circumstances and trial-and-error behavior on the part of decision-makers struggling to cope with those changing contexts.

Which vantage point best serves us in understanding the course of the Anglo-American rivalry? Did decision-makers first create crises and then choose to shy away from militarizing them? After more than a century of conflict, did decision-makers abruptly determine that the rivalry was no longer beneficial or too costly and thus decide to end it? Or, do these images suggest more conscious human agency in the processes of rivalry than is warranted?

Thus, the Anglo-American rivalry is interesting for several reasons. It is, of course, a significant case in its own right. What was it about? Why did it end? What factors, if any, governed its escalatory and deescalatory processes? How important, if at all, were spatial and positional factors? Yet the Anglo-American case also serves as a sort of multihued, stalking horse for reexamining selected aspects of theory in world politics. To get at these questions, we need to first briefly outline the history of the rivalry before we can return to more general questions about rivalry, structural change, and decision-making.

AN OUTLINE OF THE RIVALRY

For some readers, the idea of a great power rivalry between Britain and the United States may seem odd. The usual association when the Anglo-American dyad is mentioned is that of a special relationship in the twentieth century (Russett, 1963; Bartlett, 1992), not a rivalry. Then, too, the United States is not conventionally counted as a great power until after the war with Spain in 1898. About the same time, the United States began to enter into a celebrated period of *rapprochement* with its long-time adversary, Britain. Does it make sense, then, to talk about an Anglo-American rivalry, and particularly one in the nineteenth century? The answer is "yes" for several reasons. One reason is that the 1898 date for US great power status has always been a bit late. While it is true that the United States never played much of a role within the nineteenth-century European regional system with which the other great powers were so closely associated, it was an actor of some importance on North, Central, and South American issues throughout the nineteenth century. Consequently, the likelihood of a US response to a European probe somewhere in the Americas or the implications of US continental expansion entered intermittently into the calculations of the decision-makers in London, Paris, Madrid, and even St. Petersburg.

More to the point, the United States held a fairly consistent ranking in the rivalry schedule of the most powerful of the global powers. Throughout most of the nineteenth century, Britain's principal rivals were France, Russia, and the United States. The priority of the first two oscillated with France sometimes in first place, only to be edged out by Russia from time to time. The United States always seemed to remain in third place. Yet the point remains that its third place rival status long preceded its anointment as a great power.[2] If the Anglo-American rivalry in the nineteenth century was not a full-fledged great power rivalry, it was at least something more significant than merely a long-running dispute between the leading global power and an upstart minor power.

The root of the Anglo-American rivalry was traceable to one salient geopolitical fact. From 1783 through at least the late nineteenth century, the two strongest states in North America were Britain and the United States. They were contiguous states on what gradually became the long Canadian border. Both had interests in territory that was either controlled by the other state or aspired to by the other party. Both were involved in a competition for regional preeminence initially in North America and later in Central and South America. The story of the Anglo-American rivalry cannot be reduced solely to schemes of territorial expansion and containment and the competition for regional preeminence but neither is it possible to make much sense of it without tracking the history of these key processes.

Formally, the international relationship between the United States and Britain began in a definitely hostile mode as a result of the War of American Independence (1775–1783). Neither side was likely to look kindly on the other after nine years of bitter warfare and European intervention on the side of the victorious colonials. The British were unaccustomed to losing substantial portions of their Empire. The continued existence of the United States as a revolutionary but relatively weak republic in a world of monarchies was hardly guaranteed. The immediate postwar problems were further aggravated by the failure of both sides to honor their treaty obligations. The United States did not treat its prewar debts or the welfare of the Loyalists exactly as promised. Britain maintained several fortifications in the northwest territories long after they should have been withdrawn from US soil. Conflicts over trade were immediate because Britain chose not to open its imperial markets in Canada or the West Indies to US commerce. Conflicts over maritime law (impressment and the rights of neutrals) quickly appeared with the outbreak of European war in 1792–1793.[3] Only the late eighteenth-century tensions with France distracted US attention temporarily from the preoccupation with British intentions and behavior. A second war in 1812 only underscored the reciprocal hostility of Britain and the United States. But it was hardly an implacable hostility since the one post-1783 war outbreak might have been defused given better communications or different players on one or both sides.

Table 10.1 attempts to summarize the history of US–British rivalry by specifying a number of episodes that historians describe as having had some prospects of

Table 10.1 Anglo-American crises after 1783

Date	Issues	Comments
1793–1794	Canadian frontier posts shipping restrictions	Britain conciliatory due to war with France and desire to keep North American supplies flowing; United States fears economic repercussions, a loss of customs revenues, and disintegration of the Federal state should war break out; also angry at French shipping restrictions
1807–1808	Attack on Chesapeake	Britain initially conciliatory but United States imposes trade embargo that turns out to be too costly to US economy
1812–1815	Maritime restrictions impressment; Canada; US trade embargo	British concessions came too late to avert US declaration at a time when Britain was involved heavily in the Napoleonic Wars; the British are eager to end the war in 1814 lest European hostilities resume
1837–1838	US private assistance to Canadian rebels	US government attempts to punish neutrality violations; neither side wishes to fight
1838–1841	Maine–Canada boundaries Canadian official on trial in United States; slave trade tensions	Canadian official acquitted; Britain at war elsewhere; negotiations successful
1845–1846	Control of Oregon and Texas	Britain did not value Oregon highly; poor economic conditions discourage war in Britain; both sides make concessions
1854–1856	Central US canal; fishing rights	Britain involved in Crimean War and chose to press grievances
1861	US boarding of Trent	United States conciliatory in early stages of civil war
1862	Intervention in American Civil War	British decision hinges on outcome of battle which North wins rendering intervention option less meaningful
1895	Venezuela–British Guiana boundaries	US securities' values dive; British Guiana not valued highly; Germany showing support for Boers at same time; Britain surprised by crisis outbreak and conciliatory towards the United States

Sources: Bailey (1958); Burt (1961); Horsman (1962); Bourne (1967); Campbell (1974); Jones (1974); Wright (1975); Small (1980); Christie (1982); Brauer (1984); Field (1984); Chamberlain (1988); Jones (1992)

escalating to war. Ten periods of crisis are delineated in 1793–1794, 1807–1808, 1812, 1837–1838, 1838–1841, 1845–1846, 1854–1856, 1861, 1862, and 1895. The specific focus of each crisis shifted along with its geographical emphasis. Rather than dwell on the details of each confrontation, it might be more profitable to discuss them as a group in terms of escalation and deescalation tendencies.

CONFLICT ESCALATION PATTERNS

The pattern of conflict escalation in the Anglo-American rivalry was characterized by several features. One has to do with the expansion of US foreign policy ambitions and the initial British commitment to contain US expansion. Each crisis would usually end in, or lead to, some type of settlement of the issue at hand. A few years later, another crisis would emerge over something relatively new. An underlying reason for the repetitive pattern is that US interests progressively expanded throughout the nineteenth century. Once expansion into the northwest territories was resolved, new tensions arose over the acquisition of Florida in the south. After Florida came Texas and Oregon in the southwest and northwest. After Oregon came Central America and a possible pan-isthmus canal. After Central America, came civil war-related issues and then fishing and sealing rights, followed by boundary disputes in South America and Alaska. The nature of conflict within the rivalry thus evolved in step with the evolution of US interests. The rivalry persisted in part because one party's goals and ambitions were hardly static between 1783 and 1900. The resolution of one outstanding issue did not, and probably could not prevent the emergence of a relatively novel one a decade later.

Another important aspect of the Anglo-American rivalry was the British commitment to the containment of American continental and extracontinental expansion. This is the other side of the American expansion coin. Without an intention of systematically resisting US expansion, the serial nature of Anglo-American crises, no doubt, would have taken a less continuous form. Nevertheless, the British containment policy was marked by two major features of its own. First, the application of containment was at best intermittent and often reactive. British foreign policy interests were genuinely global; activities in the Americas were only rarely given primary consideration. When it came time to fight or blink over the possession of a specific territory, British decision-makers were often conciliatory.

At least three general reasons for the flexibility can be advanced. In a number of cases, they did not feel the territory in question was worth fighting over. When the crises emerged, British resources were often already committed to ongoing wars in Europe or imperial wars in Asia or Africa. Thirdly, British decision-makers were always conscious of their vulnerability in North America. Neither British maritime trade, Canada nor the West Indies would be easy to defend from US attacks. The United States, as had been demonstrated twice before, was a difficult target to attack and defeat permanently. The Americans could always retreat and the British repeatedly had problems projecting their power on land (Maslowski, 1994). An attack on the United States might also encourage a European attack on some part of the British Empire. The "lessons" of the American Revolution were still worrisome to British decision-makers several generations later.

The US side of this particular dimension of the rivalry is that the United States was rarely prepared to either attack or to defend itself against an opponent with high military capability. US decision-makers, after spirited debate, had early decided against creating a blue water navy that might attract a British preventive attack. The size of the nineteenth-century army was always small except during the civil war half-decade when other policy concerns were more pressing. As Maslowski (1994: 207) notes, the nineteenth-century geographical expansion of the United States was predicated on moving against opponents ("Indians, Spain, and Mexico") who were even weaker in military capability. Most of the time, this fundamental weakness precluded too much belligerence when confronted in a dispute with Britain.

The nature of interaction between an often distracted Britain and a United States with very limited military capability, as a consequence, combined verbal bluster and diplomatic negotiations in which both sides were prepared to contemplate and threaten war but usually willing to back down from the brink. The awkward flavor of the interaction is captured by Stratford Canning's notes in an 1820 meeting with British foreign minister Castlereagh, just prior to Canning assuming the ambassador post in Washington:

> Pacific-conciliatory-forbearing – cannot oppose them with success on inferior local points – national animosity a considerable part of their strength and therefore in our interest to soften or abate it – By their own confession, made during the discussions on the fisheries they would *for the present* give up to us on any point for which we were ready to go to war, but a continued thwarting they would not brook . . . In angry discussing we have all to lose, as they are always ready to go the furthest in insolence – once committed, we cannot recede, and hence the great delicacy of treating with them; but when it is not worth our while to call out our whole strength, they must always have an advantage over us.
>
> (quoted in Bourne, 1967: 7–8)

At times, domestic politics could complicate this awkward relationship. On the US side, Anglophobia was a useful card in party politics, and one used similarly to the employment of references to the Soviet Union during the Cold War. Nevertheless, the political utility of attacks on Britain, the nineteenth-century version of an evil empire, seems to have waned toward the end of the nineteenth century. Campbell (1974: 10) suggests that the one Anglo-American war after 1783 was "determined by American party rivalries". The basic problem was that if the Republicans backed away from their intransigent stance *vis-à-vis* opposition to British trade and maritime practices, they would have lost too many votes to the Federalists to stay in power. But elsewhere the same author (Campbell, 1974: 55–56) argues that the peaceful outcome in the 1838 crisis was facilitated by the election of a more conciliatory US president and his appointment of an equally more conciliatory secretary of state. Presumably, then, US domestic politics could at various times facilitate escalation or deescalation of Anglo-American tensions. Perhaps the single most important factor was the gradual erosion of élite and popular distrust of British motivations. When the collective levels of distrust were strong, US decision-makers were faced with one more constraint on their behavior but this one, unlike military weakness, made it difficult to be publicly conciliatory without risking domestic losses of support.

The nature of nineteenth-century, domestic politics on the British side of the equation seemed to have been more likely to facilitate deescalation. More than one British decision-maker, especially into the middle of the nineteenth century, complained about the indifference of the British population to North American issues and the consequent difficulty of arousing support for tougher stances with the Americans. But since these same decision-makers were often less than eager themselves to adopt inflexible positions about low priority foreign policy problems, it is not clear that public opinion generally had much of an independent influence.

The second aspect of British containment policies in North America was that they faded away roughly midway through the rivalry. The inclination to contain was particularly prominent in the first half of the nineteenth century but after the United States had achieved its essential bicoastal form in the 1850s, it had become clear that containment was no longer a realistic aspiration in North America. It also had become increasingly clear that Canada could not be defended successfully from a determined US attempt at conquest. The American Civil War may have postponed the full realization of these assessments. If the United States was split in two, new possibilities of restricting the expansion of US influence would be possible, but that hope was to be dashed within a few years of internecine warfare and the eventual likelihood of a Northern victory. By the end of the 1860s, British efforts at containment in North America had ceased. British decision-makers were prepared to concede regional preeminence to the United States in North America. Some 35 years later, the scope of the preeminence acknowledged by the British had been extended to Central America and in politico-military terms, to South America.[4]

Unlike other lengthy clashes over regional preeminence (for example, France and Germany), there did not appear to be much in the way of residual bitterness on the part of the losing side. Part of the reason is presumably linked to the gradual diminishment of US interests in seizing Canada which emerged roughly in step with British concessions of US North American hegemony. The idea of absorbing Canada continued to rise in US political debates until the very end of the nineteenth century. Fenian raids across the border occurred sporadically, but somewhere between the late 1830s and 1860s, the appeal of acquiring Canada had lost much of its political luster. No doubt, it helped that there was so much territory elsewhere with which to be preoccupied.

It also helped that British decision-makers were removed from the local scene. Canadian élites seemed much more concerned about the threat of a dominant United States than did their British counterparts. In many ways, British élites later welcomed the extension of US dominance throughout the Americas immediately prior to World

War I. Part of this welcome was tinged with more than a strong dose of inevitability. Referring specifically to US fleet expansion, for example, Lord Salisbury commented (in early 1902): "It is very sad, but I am afraid America is bound to forge ahead and nothing can restore the equality between us" (cited in Gooch, 1994: 288).

Not only was the positional transition deemed nearly inescapable, it also made good sense to let someone else provide the local policing and debt collection services in Latin America as long as access to US markets remained open to British firms and capital.

In this respect, spatial issues were important to the persistence of the rivalry. They kept it alive from decade to decade throughout the nineteenth century. Yet the rivalry fundamentally was not about Anglo-American differences over who was to possess what territory. Rather, territorial disputes were simply the most concrete manifestations of the positional struggle over predominance in the North American region. Once the positional maneuvering had been resolved, territorial or spatial disputes could and did continue to occur but they were no longer as dangerous as they had once been. Without a positional dimension at stake, spatial issues between major powers become easier to resolve.

THE RAPPROCHEMENT

By 1904, Britain had abandoned preparing for a war with the United States (Dobson, 1995: 17). Shortly after the turn of the century, a US President had more than once publicly proclaimed the very low probability of war with Britain. In 1905, Theodore Roosevelt, not especially known for his pacific attitudes in international relations, wrote the following to a minor British minister:

> You need not ever be troubled by the nightmare of a possible contest between the two great English-speaking peoples . . . In keeping ready for possible war I never even take into account a war with England. I treat it as out of the question.
>
> (cited in Perkins, 1968: 106–107)

A few years earlier, Rudyard Kipling could make sport of the Anglo-American rivalry as something to be taken less than seriously:

> France has Germany; we have Russia; for Italy, Austria is provided; and the humblest Pathan possesses an ancestral enemy. Only America stands out of the racket; and therefore, to be in fashion, makes a sand-bag of the mother-country, and bangs her when occasion requires.
>
> (cited in Perkins, 1968: 5–6)

Sometime around the turn of the century, then (roughly between 1895 and 1905), the United States ceased banging the sandbag and Britain came to reluctant terms

Table 10.2 Selected Anglo-American trade data

Year	British exports to the United States	As % of total British exports	British imports from the United States	As % of total British imports
1830	6.1	16.1	–	–
1840	5.3	10.4	–	–
1850	15	21.1	30	29.1
1860	22	16.2	45	21.3
1870	28	14.0	50	16.5
1880	31	13.9	107	26.0
1890	32	12.1	97	23.0
1900	20	6.9	139	26.6
1910	31	7.2	118	17.4

Year	US exports to Britain	As % of total US exports	US imports to Britain	As % of total US imports
1790	7	35.0	–	–
1800	19	26.8	–	–
1810	12	17.9	–	–
1820	24	34.3	24	32.4
1830	26	35.6	24	34.3
1840	55	42.6	33	31.7
1850	71	48.3	75	42.4
1860	169	49.4	138	38.3
1870	248	59.3	152	33.8
1880	454	53.4	211	31.0
1890	448	50.2	186	23.0
1900	534	36.8	160	18.1
1910	506	28.1	271	17.0

Sources: The British and US trade data are based on information reported respectively in Mitchell (1980) and Mitchell (1993)
Note:
British exports and imports are expressed as million pounds sterling; US exports and imports are expressed as million US dollars

with the implications of US ascendancy. It is certainly possible to argue that the rivalry continued past 1905. Relations between the United States and Britain deteriorated on several occasions, especially in the 1920s and immediately after World War II. The two competed most prominently in terms of naval and commercial/financial leadership. Yet even when relations between them were poor, there is no evidence that either side ever contemplated reversing the earlier decision to discount the possibility of an Anglo-American war (Dobson, 1995; Orde, 1996). So, even though Anglo-American competition continued on a variety of fronts, the strategic rivalry had ended by 1904–1905, if not before.

What happened to terminate the rivalry? One hypothesis relies on the complications of economic interdependence. Increasing economic interdependence escalates the costs of war to both sides of a dispute and, therefore, is thought to inhibit the likelihood of a dispute escalating to the battlefield. Groups that benefit from the trade

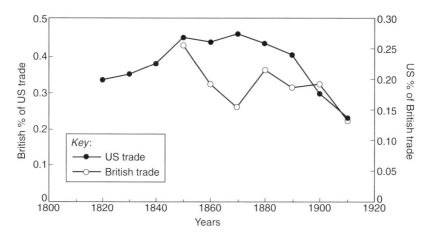

Figure 10.1 US–British trade as proportions of their total trade

will favor the maintenance of amicable relations and will presumably lobby their respective governments to avoid any possible disruption of the profitable commerce. Decision-makers, especially in commercially oriented states, are likely to be responsive to these business élite preferences and the potential for economic hardship. The greater the level of interdependence, then, the greater is the probable inhibitory effect on war escalation.

The problem in the case of the Anglo-American rivalry is that economic interdependence was fairly high throughout the history of the rivalry. Much of the time, the two states were the best customer of the other (Campbell, 1974: 5). Only after 1875 did colonial India edge out the United States as Britain's principal export market. Therefore, economic interdependence was more or less operative almost constantly from the onset of the rivalry. The qualification to its constant presence, though, is the fact that economic interdependence had begun to decline qualitatively and quantitatively prior to the *rapprochement* around the turn of the century. The peak in economic interdependence actually preceded the American Civil War (Bagwell and Mingay, 1970).

Table 10.2 shows the alterations in absolute and proportional export and import tendencies. Figure 10.1 simplifies the comparison by comparing the proportion of total trade accounted for by the other member of the rivalry. From the British angle, the trend is uneven with cotton imports declining in mid-century and then declining again more or less after 1880. On the US side, the British account for nearly a half of US trade between 1850 and 1870 but decline steadily thereafter to about a 23 percent share in 1910.

While it may be difficult to argue that Britain and the United States were becoming more interdependent in economic terms, the changes in their economic relationship may have been more significant in another respect. At the beginning of the nineteenth

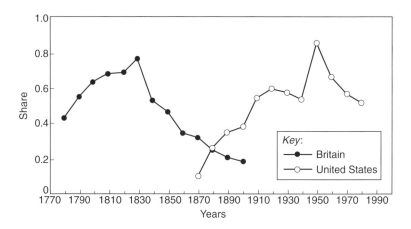

Figure 10.2 The British–US transition in leading sector leadership

century, the United States provided food and raw materials in exchange for manufactured goods to an industrial Britain. By the end of the century, the United States had reversed its position of economic dependency rather spectacularly. Not only had it moved out of the periphery, it had moved toward, if not into, the very center of the world economy as the new leading edge industrial producer. Figure 10.2 shows that an ascending United States passed Britain in relative decline as the world's lead economy around 1880.[5]

This transition should have aggravated Anglo-American relations and, in some respects, it did. Not surprisingly, there were alarms within Britain that US firms were becoming the corporate representatives of the world's new dominant economic power, elbowing aside the long reign of the British as the world's workshop. Four factors seemed to have reduced the threat to the possibility of friendly Anglo-American relations. First, US economic ascendance initially was oriented primarily toward serving its own large, domestic market. The intensity of Anglo-American conflicts over markets in turn-of-the century Afro-Eurasia were less sharp as a consequence. Then, too, as with naval expansion, the apparent inevitability of US economic ascendance as the première active zone in the world economy helped the adjustment process somewhat.

Third, the inevitability of the US economic ascendance was rendered less than a sure thing by the gains made by the German economy. But German–British commercial rivalry throughout Afro-Eurasia was sharply contested. If we had to pick between the lesser of the two evils, the German economic threat was deemed the more immediate one and one that could and should be confronted. In this sense, Britain chose to focus on the German commercial and military threat. While the German threat was not fabricated, it was not the only choice British élites might have made.

Finally, and perhaps one of the most significant elements in the Anglo-British equation, is that, economically, United States élites no longer felt inferior to the initially more advanced British economy. The persistent imagery of American reluctance to be the "cock-boat in the wake of the British man-of-war" had relevance for more than one sphere of international relations. US decision-makers were reluctant to join British diplomatic initiatives as potential junior partners. The transition in economic positions worked to reduce what Perkins (1968: 121) has summarized as "US touchiness and British arrogance", albeit at some risk of simply reversing the national attributes. Perkins' (1968: 122) argument that it was the erosion of the traditional pattern of economic interdependence with Britain as patron and the United States as client that made some difference definitely appears more applicable than the conventional insistence on deepening interdependence.

Thus all patterns of interdependence should not be expected to produce the same results.[6] In the case of the Anglo-American dyad, the classical form of economic interdependence may have contributed to the hesitation of decision-makers to go to war. It is hard to be definitive because the lack of enthusiasm can be explained in a variety of ways. However, the patron–client dependency form of interdependence probably had to be eliminated before *rapprochement* could be entertained.

The economic interdependence argument overlaps with the idea that birds of a feather flock together. Unlike familiarity, similarity is thought to breed proclivities toward alliance. The conceptual overlap is well captured in the following 1857 *Manchester Guardian* editorial:

> Of all foreign powers, there is none with whom we are so anxious to keep on good terms as our transatlantic cousins. Their language, their race, their institutions should render them our natural allies. Our commercial relations with them are of such incalculable importance that the least sign of a seriously hostile spurt on either side must overcloud the peace and endanger the comfort of millions of our countrymen. There is perhaps no nation on earth with whom we would not rather quarrel than with America.
>
> (cited in Campbell, 1974: 90)

There had definitely been movement toward the convergence of regime types. In the late eighteenth and early part of the nineteenth century, British élites had seen the United States as a revolutionary challenger to the status quo, both internationally and potentially within British domestic politics. The Americans, for their part did not see the British political system of the same period as particularly democratic. After the mid-century political reforms, Britain had become a more open political system. So, too, had the United States, at least in the abstract sense, after the abolition of slavery. Just how important this political convergence was is difficult to assess in view of all the other changes that occurred roughly at the same time. The most difficult position to defend would seem to be the extreme argument that democratization was primarily responsible for the decline in Anglo-American conflict. Doyle (1986), for instance, contends that British–US crises were more likely to be negotiated after the British liberalized their domestic political system in the early 1830s. Yet a reciprocal reluctance to transform disputes into trials of strength characterize all Anglo-American crises, and not just a later segment of them. Some credit may go to parallel democratization but it is not likely to be the only factor of significance, nor even necessarily the most significant factor. Suffice it to say, for the moment, that institutional convergence may have facilitated the later *rapprochement*, but it was probably neither a necessary nor a sufficient factor.

Nor is there any need to dismiss altogether ethnic–racial sentiments as another positive or facilitating factor. However, there are some highly idiosyncratic features of the Anglo-US sentimental ties in the late nineteenth century. On the one hand, these ties had certainly been visible at earlier points. Crawford (1987: 9–12) describes the mutual enthusiasm for Anglo-Saxon identification, reconciliation and partnership in the 1850s as extremely high. Yet it could not head off, and may have been partly responsible for, the subsequently highly strained relations in the 1860s.

On the other hand, the emotional emphasis on the virtues of Anglo-Saxon civilization benefitted from a boost from *fin de siecle*, Darwinian racism. The "white man's" burden (and superiority) imagery was, in part, a temporary reaction to the uncertainty of structural change at the turn of the century and might conceivably have taken on a Teutonic cloak instead of an Anglo-Saxon one. It was also aided by new myths that emerged in the imperial warfare of the period. First, a number of Americans believed that Britain had prevented European intervention on the side of Spain into the Spanish–American War. British élites did express their appreciation that at long last the Americans were joining the ranks of imperialism. If nothing else, it would be more awkward for US critics to chide the British for their high-handed, expansionary tendencies if the Americans were engaged in the same activities. There was also the story that British naval observers had positioned their ships in Manila Bay to prevent German interference with the US naval bombardment. In 1898, there was thus some popular feeling that a debt was owed to the British (Bourne, 1970: 172–173).

The facts that European military intervention had always been unlikely in 1898 or that the British maneuvering in Manila Bay was due solely to a desire to see the action better are beside the point. The debt was repaid at governmental level by the US reluctance to criticize the British in their Boer War which was unpopular elsewhere, including within US public opinion. Anglo-Saxon sentimentality thus depended on a peculiar, aptly timed and presumably transitory mixture of racism and imperialistic myth. The ethnic–racial similarity had long been a characteristic of the Anglo-American relationship. It happened to take on a new twist in the 1890s that seems to have facilitated further deescalation in the rivalry.

The trial-and-error element

There is one other aspect of the *rapprochement* that deserves some comment. Diplomatic histories sometimes give the impression that *rapprochements* are similar to treaty negotiations. Two sides sit down at a table and agree, after weighing their preferences and alternatives, that their mutual interests would be benefitted by working together

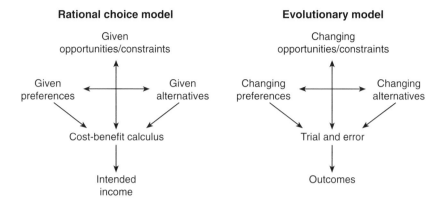

Figure 10.3 Rational choice versus evolutionary approaches to rivalry analyses

rather than at cross purposes. The left-hand side of Figure 10.3 shows this type of cost-benefit calculus. It is not inconceivable that a rivalry could be terminated in such a fashion, especially in wartime emergencies, but then the rivalry termination is likely to last only as long as the war persists. It might be thought that genuine rivalry terminations are more likely to be the result of gradually or abruptly changing contexts in which decision-makers' preferences and/or alternatives are realigned. Yesterday's enemy may be today's friend because the former opponent is seen differently, either in terms of reassessing the degree of threat associated with the opponent in question or in terms of assessing new threats on the horizon.

Both forms of threat assessment were involved in the Anglo-American *rapprochement*. The British appreciated their end-of-the century overextension made more obvious by the relative positional gains achieved by old and new rivals. Nevertheless, it is difficult to sustain the notion that British strategists sat down and worked out a plan that involved anointing Germany as the principal rival, allying with Japan, and working actively to deescalate the traditional rivalries with France, Russia, and, most importantly for our immediate purposes, the United States. All these things were done in the late 1890s and early 1900s but more on a trial-and-error basis, outlined on the right-hand side of Figure 10.3, as opposed to highly coherent, cost-benefit calculation.

British decision-makers realized that they needed to do something to protect their security and economic positions but the alternative possibilities were subject to debate and indecision. The movement toward deescalating the Anglo-American rivalry had begun seriously in the 1850s and again in the 1870s when North American superiority had been conceded to the United States. The next step along these lines came when British naval decision-makers realized that they could not maintain their formula for keeping ahead of the next two naval powers without dropping the United States from the list of contenders. Two aspects of this development deserve emphasis. One, it was done in 1901 before Germany had been christened Britain's principal rival.[7] France and Russia were still the principal rivals. Two, it was a development that took place first within British naval circles. The British army resisted the implications, when they learned of the new naval interpretation, for their own contingency planning.

So, we can neither say that the original impetus was the new German threat nor was the altered perspective on the United States entirely a product of a unitary government or a single estimate of the national interest. The British initially were responding to an uncertain environment characterized by multiple rivals with increasing capabilities. The appropriate policies to pursue were not obvious. Some selections from a variety of options was likely. The alternative was strategic paralysis. But the modification of grand strategy was not necessarily something that would be achieved in an entirely explicit or intended manner. *Rapprochement* with the United States and the increasing focus on the German threat were features of the British selections from the strategic menu. The two elements worked on parallel and reinforcing tracks, but the latter was not the original impetus for the former.

US decision-makers were also moving slowly toward the idea that Germany constituted the principal threat in the 1900s. But they earlier had rebuffed British overtures for joint diplomatic action in East Asia out of distrust of British motivations. Ironically, the British had only turned to the United States after its negotiations with Russia had broken down (Gelber, 1938/1966: 9). Rebuffed by the United States on Open Door strategy, the British next seriously contemplated aligning with Germany to coordinate Asian strategy instead. Japan and its alliance with Britain was another beneficiary of the difficulties encountered in organizing a united Anglo-Saxon front in world politics. The improved relations with France and Russia were highly dependent on French perceptions of the German threat and the lessened threat to Britain's Asian holdings due to Russian defeat in the war with Japan.

The point of these observations is not to suggest that Britain's strategy was either random or totally adrift. There was a pronounced movement toward reconcentrating forces around the home base. Exactly how this was to be done and with what impact on the British schedule of perceived rivalries seems more a matter of trial-and-error experimentation rather than a single decision or even a sequence of decisions and subsequent behaviors. One outcome of this foreign policy experimentation was Anglo-American *rapprochement*.[8] It was facilitated by some 50 years of largely unintentional laying of the foundation for the change in relationship.

CONCLUSION

Modelski (1999) suggests an interesting and innovative way to bring together some of the economic, institutional, and cultural/sentimental strands encountered in the Anglo-American rivalry story. His argument is that there is a long-term, democratic lineage process at work:

Let us define democratic lineage as the line or succession of societies that have shaped world democratization. At any given point in time in the modern world, we can identify one society, or a small set of societies, as leading examples of democratic development in the broad sense. Over time, the succession of these societies has constituted a lineage. Within that lineage, experience has developed, and has cumulated with each successive step. The democratic lineage thus constitutes a system of cultural inheritance that transmits learning in respect of social, political and economic organization, and diffuses it by example in the world system.

(Modelski, 1999: 154).

The most recent and least controversial segment of the lineage is the Netherlands–Britain–US sequence. Each, in turn, was the world system's lead economy and global naval power. For its time, each served as a type of republican–democratic exemplar. Moreover, each transition in the sequence was characterized by rivalry between the old and the new innovator. Yet while the Dutch and the English fought three wars in the seventeenth century and the Americans and the British fought two wars between 1775 and 1815, neither rivalry was as violent as might have been anticipated given what was at stake – the leadership of the world economy. In both cases, the initial rivals within the democratic lineage coalesced to deal with a greater political-economic threat emanating from outside the lineage – France in 1688–1713 and Germany in 1914–1945.

Modelski suggests that rivalries within the democratic lineage, in contrast to those outside it, are more likely to be relatively benign because these conflicts can be seen as a special type of selection process. Which actor has the best qualifications to reorganize the world's political economy? The Dutch gave way to the British and the British gave way to the Americans, partly because their successors had superior credentials (in terms of economic innovation and organization and global reach military capabilities), and had improved upon their predecessor's approach, and the declining incumbent could recognize and feel more comfortable with the similarities in their successor's regime constitution.

Less prominent in the democratic lineage model, but certainly compatible with it, are two other important elements. The "comfort" factor was enhanced by the role of the incumbent leader in shaping its successor through financial investment, trade, immigration/human capital, and the transplantation of political ideas. In this respect, the lineage pattern is amplified through the inheritance of economic, political, and cultural traits and maintained through close interaction. Nowhere in the democratic lineage which Modelski is prepared to extend back in time well before the seventeenth century is this more pronounced than in the Anglo-American case.

The other characteristic that seems to fit is that the democratic lineage rivalries are less violent ultimately because the incumbent leader is distracted by a defense of the status quo that it has created. Challenges may come from several quarters. Some are likely to be more antithetical than others to the status quo. The ones that seem most menacing, ultimately, will receive the lion's share of the attention. Coping with less menacing challenges is likely to be put off to some indefinite future. But that future opportunity never comes because the effort to maintain the status quo exhausts the incumbent and creates an opportunity for its ally to gravitate into the leadership. The exhaustion of the old leader leads to a greater probability that it will face the new political economic order with resigned acquiescence. It may have been supplanted from the leadership of the world economy but, as a member of the victorious coalition, at least it has the chance to hold on to some remnants of its former position for a while.

Still, there are idiosyncratic factors that are important in the Anglo-American rivalry case. Perhaps most significant was the geopolitical context. Britain's principal rivalries of the nineteenth century were spread throughout the globe: Russia in Asia, France in western Europe and North Africa, and the United States in North and Central America. Western Europe and Asia were consistently more important to British decision-makers; North America was always a theater of secondary or tertiary importance.[9] Accordingly, while the British were viewed consistently as their principal competitor by the Americans, the United States always ranked much lower in the British rivalry schedule. If these priorities had been reversed or more symmetrical on the US pattern, the history of the Anglo-American rivalry might well have been bloodier than it was.

Nevertheless, the point to stress is that other threats loom larger in the eyes of the beleaguered incumbent leader. That feature is certainly part of the leadership lineage in that it occurs again and again. But whether this lineage should be thought of as a democratic lineage or something broader remains to be discussed. That is the topic taken up in Chapter 11.

11

PASSING THE TORCH
IN A MANNER OF SPEAKING
The system leader lineage

Among the core dynamics of long-term economic growth processes are K-waves of innovation and even longer cycles of politico-military preeminence and order. The shape of these processes are not perfectly uniform throughout time. Their periodicities are less than precise. They have a specific historical genealogy in the sense that their operations and transitions can be traced back roughly over the last millennium in a continuous fashion and seemingly no further, at least in a continuous fashion. Nor did they emerge abruptly with all of the characteristics that K-waves and leadership long cycles currently possess. On the contrary, almost 500 years went by before these processes began to assume the attributes associated with their contemporary manifestations. Similarly, we should not assume that these core dynamics must continue forever. They may but it is most unlikely that they will do so without undergoing substantial modification just as they already have done in the past.

Yet dividing 1000 or even 500 years of political-economic fluctuations into periods of sequential systemic leadership is not without its liabilities. One of these liabilities is that we tend to bestow too much attention on the succeeding eras of distinctively identified leadership and, as a consequence, give too little attention to the long-term connections between and among the successive leaders. The focus of this chapter is to explore some of the more important longitudinal interdependencies in the historical sequence of system leaders. In the future, we need to develop perspectives that give equal attention to the vertical and horizontal dimensions of change.

THE UNDERAPPRECIATED VERTICAL DIMENSION

Curiously, most approaches to the study of system leadership, long-term economic growth, and coevolving conflict processes – and the one described above is not an exception – tend to accentuate the horizontal dimension at the expense of vertical interdependencies. By horizontal dimension we have in mind the discontinuities involved in moving from one period of system leadership to the next. Not unlike the joke about rapid European tours – if it's Tuesday, this must be Belgium – we tend to equate sizable chunks of time with the specific identity of a system leader. If someone says "seventeenth century", we think Dutch. The nineteenth century connotes Pax Britannica. The second half of the twentieth century is the US "century".

We make these linkages for a variety of reasons. Since the number of system leaders is small, we are comfortable with associating intervals of time with the proper place names of the incumbent system leader. If the number of leaders was much higher, we would find such a practice exceedingly cumbersome. Another reason is that we are more comfortable with the idea of Britain as the nineteenth-century growth leader than we are with the concept of nineteenth-century Britain as a system leader. It will take more time to fully digest the implications of a hierarchical international political economy when so much of our paradigmatic apparatus in the study of international relations assumes the anarchic absence of hierarchy. A third reason for horizontal slices is that data are more readily available for more recent cases of systemic leadership than they are for the ones more distant in time. If we analyze these coevolutionary processes of economic growth, political leadership, and systemic conflict, we are most likely to do so in the context of the current century and perhaps the preceding century as well, with the probability of covering earlier centuries decaying as we move farther back in time. Even when the effort is made to look at older data, the discontinuous natures of economic growth, leadership, and conflict tend to encourage shorter series than might otherwise be the case. Precisely how (and whether) one should splice together different types of activities over time is rarely a clear-cut proposition.

Naturally, the argument is not that the horizontal associations are invalid but only that they come at a price if pursued without reference to other dimensions. Part of the price is that we tend to get bogged down in system leader idiosyncrasies. Features such as the Portuguese location on the Atlantic, shallow Dutch harbors, deforested Britain, and a continental-sized United States may distract from us generalizing about systemic leadership, and the transitions to and from one leader to the next. Worse yet, we may be content to tell descriptive stories about the rise and fall of successive leaders. Alternatively, we may focus too much on how system leaders differ from their contemporary competitors, as opposed to how they do or do not differ from their predecessors.

Another part of the price, as implied above, is that we are breaking up long serial processes into shorter ones. If, for example, we argue that the post-World War II period was characterized, among others, by an aerospace leading sector, we are easily diverted from tracing where the aerospace industry originated and how it developed into a leading sector. We tend to take it for granted as if the leading sector simply descended from the heavens (literally and figuratively in this case). But what we may be overlooking is that aerospace developments have a specific and complicated heritage that can be traced back to the development of steam engines in an earlier system leader's era. Might we not gain additional explanatory leverage if we followed the technological trajectory through different system leaders, rather than stopping and starting over each time a new system leader emerges?

A third part of the price, and one that overlaps with the previous one, has to do with the old analytical problem of continuities versus discontinuities. Are system leader transitions characterized by punctuated equilibrium or gradual changes? The paradigmatic changes associated with each shift in systemic leadership may deserve the "revolutionary" label every time they occur. It may also be the case that some shifts are more revolutionary than others. Yet, whatever the case, there is no need to dwell exclusively on the discontinuities when there are quite likely to be substantial continuities. We need not choose between punctuated equilibrium and gradual change if elements of both are present. Nor is it inconceivable that the continuities will outweigh the discontinuities. If we emphasize the horizontal dimension too much, it is difficult to even raise the question of how much credit to give to discontinuities as opposed to continuities, and the extent to which their ratio may vary over time.

There are also specific theoretical questions, as opposed to the more generic ones such as the tradeoffs between continuities and discontinuities, at stake in the way we look at leadership transitions. One ostensibly simple question has to do with how many system leaders have we had? Different analysts with different conceptualizations of systemic leadership and different thresholds argue about whether we have had none, one, two, three, or as many as ten sequential leaders. It may not matter if we ever arrive at a consensus on the exact number if we can agree on who followed whom, even if all the actors in the sequence did not attain the same heights as some of the others. Thus, agreeing on the transition process is more important than the threshold criteria.

Another specific question pertains to how transitions are accomplished. Some analysts wonder why these leadership successions are not more contested than they are. There is often an intense crisis that involves considerable bloodshed, but it does not usually involve the successor defeating the former incumbent. Instead, they are usually aligned to defeat other challengers, as suggested in Chapter 10. But can longitudinal interdependencies help account to some extent for this phenomenon?

Other analysts have different views about transitions and the transition process. One hypothesis is that new system leaders simply muddle through in their rise to the top. This does not mean that system leaders are selected at random but it does imply that ascent strategies are more trial and error than they are grand strategy. Whether trial and error or grand strategy, some analysts view the transitions of systemic leadership as predominately episodic. One episode of leadership may give way to another but it may also give way to a temporal stretch with no leader. Another hypothesis is that the declining incumbent coopts one of the more promising rising challengers as a better place to invest than the home economy. A variation on this thesis is that declining leaders hasten their decline by investing in rapid growth abroad, and, to the extent that the rapid growth is located in economies with leadership potential, the contribution to relative decline is doubled.

A final cost of overemphasizing the horizontal dimension is that it leads us to assume that the new leader seized the leadership from a declining incumbent all on its own, and due exclusively to its particular merits. The old leader somehow was no longer up to the task; the new leader demonstrated its fitness for the task by ascending to the première position. But what if the selection process is less than straightforward? What if the leadership ascendancy game is rigged or biased by earlier leaders? The general question then becomes: to what extent do acting/declining/ former system leaders influence the probability, intentionally or inadvertently, of specific new leaders arising?

What all these costs and questions have in common is the underexplored vertical or longitudinal interdependency dimension. To what extent are system leaders linked in some type of lineage pattern? Does each new leader represent something so radically novel that we can safely ignore or downplay their links to their predecessors? Or, is each successive system leader so intricately intertwined with the successes and failures of their predecessors that we do injury to the historical record by focusing on them one at a time, as opposed to treating them as components in a serial process?

The idea of leadership lineage has already been introduced toward the end of Chapter 10 in terms of Modelski's (1999) democratic lineage argument. To explore further the leadership lineage hypothesis, three types of activities will be examined in this chapter: (1) technological heritages – to what extent are significant technologies linked across time and different leadership eras?; (2) resource transfers – to what extent do old or former system leaders transfer resources (people, money, and skills) to up and coming system leaders, and why?; and (3) geopolitical community formation – to what extent are past, present, and future system leaders significantly interactive and cooperative on issues of external security? Each cluster of questions yields slightly different answers to the central lineage question. Some, but only minimal, synthetic integration of the different answers will be necessary after reviewing available information on each set of questions.

TECHNOLOGICAL HERITAGES

The essential point about technological heritages or lineages is that they exist and, in fact, are much more common than we realize. New system leaders may be responsible for relatively novel innovations. Yet no matter how novel, the innovations usually have a developmental trajectory that can be traced back to the technological efforts of earlier system leaders. Table 11.1 highlights three examples: sugar, propulsion engines, and information technology. Other hard and soft technological examples that might have been examined include ship construction, spice routes, maritime networks, slavery, textiles, multinational corporations, public debts, iron and steel production, and chemicals/plastics.

As was the case with a number of "European" technological innovations, sugar production originated in Asia and India. European Crusaders learned about the techniques in the Middle East, and from there, sites for sugar production for European consumption gradually moved westward from the eastern Mediterranean to parts of southern Europe and North Africa and then into the Atlantic islands such as the Madeiras. The Genoese and Venetians were important agents in this westward

Table 11.1 An illustration of selected technological
lineages

	Sugar	*Engines*	*IT*
Genoa	x		
	x		
Venice	x		
	x		
Portugal	x		
	x		
Netherlands	x		
	x		
Britain I	x	x	
	x	x	
Britain II	?	x	x
		x	x
United States		x	x
			x

movement, both as producers and distributors. From the Portuguese Atlantic islands, the next movement west was to Brazil and the intensified development of the tropical plantation system with its implications for slave labor. The Dutch initially became major distributors of Brazilian sugar and then attempted to seize the source of production. Ejected from Brazil after several decades of attempting to rule the northeastern corner of South America, Dutch specialists in sugar production transferred their knowledge to the British island of Barbados which quickly became the center of a new revolution in sugar production and one of the technological jewels in Britain I's economic leadership. Some authors even see Britain I's sugar plantations as the forerunners of Britain II's factory systems, while others claim that Caribbean and North American profits underwrote the late eighteenth-century industrial revolution. Without passing judgment on these latter assertions, the idea of a technological lineage, encompassing five or six consecutive periods of systemic leadership, is certainly evident in the development of sugar production techniques.

The other two examples involve shorter lineages but they have been chosen because their genealogies may seem more obscure to many. The dependence of the twentieth century aerospace industry on jet engines hardly requires documentation. Perhaps the quickest way to demonstrate its technological roots is to reproduce Constant's (1980) schematic diagram for the partial heritage of the turbojet (Figure 11.1). The development of the turbojet was not simply a straightforward and gradual improvement of an engine that produced more speed and power but it did depend on earlier developments in steam and gas engines, along with coevolving contributions from thermodynamics, hydrodynamics, and aerodynamics. For our purposes, the point of Constant's diagram is that it traces a technological evolution at least back to Britain I's early steam engines (and water wheels raise the possibility of pushing the lineage back even further), through Britain II's breakthrough in steam engines, the

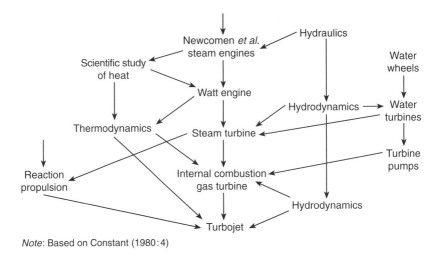

Note: Based on Constant (1980:4)

Figure 11.1 Constant's turbojet partial heritage

subsequent development of internal combustion engines in the late nineteenth century, and up to the jet engine in the mid to late twentieth century.

Information technology (IT) is all the rage as the next K-wave carrier. Even more so than the case of jet engines, it may seem not only revolutionary but also completely novel. However, Hall and Preston (1988) make a strong case to the contrary. They portray IT emerging through the last four K-waves, as demonstrated in Table 11.2, and beginning with the development of the telegraph in the 1830s. The telephone and electrical power generation were important to the next K-wave, followed by the radio, and then the introduction of transistors and microprocessors.

The argument is not that IT was a major carrier in each of the four successive K-waves. Rather, its significance as the main carrier grew over time. In the early-mid-nineteenth century, it first emerged as an auxiliary of railroadization; by the late twentieth century, it was at the center of technological change. But that centrality depended on a variety of earlier developments, including the innovation of mechanical office machines that were not initially related to electrical power. With the advantages of hindsight, then, it is possible to trace the technological lineage of IT at least back through four successive K-waves.

Observations on technological lineages may seem rather mundane to historians of technological change. However, they do or should make some difference to how we go about explaining the rise and fall of successive system leaders and their impact on the functioning of the world's political economy. Viewed horizontally, the technological mainsprings of each system leader seem as if they were orphans without a mother or father. Viewed longitudinally, we can trace their roots across multiple K-waves and periods of economic leads. The longitudinal view should not detract

Table 11.2 Information technology dealt with horizontally and longitudinally

1780s–1840s	1840s–1890s	1890s–1940s	1940s–2000
	IT handled horizontally		
Telegraph	Cable	Radio	Television
	Telephone	Record player	Transistors
	Typewriter	Radar	Computers
	Phonograph		Integrated circuits
	Lighting systems		Microprocessors
	Power generators		
	IT handled longitudinally		
1830s	Electrical telegraph		
1840s	Submarine cable		
1870s–1880s	Telephone, typewriter, phonograph		
1880s	Lighting systems		
1890s	Electrical power generators		
1910s	Wireless radio		
1920s	Radio broadcasting, record player		
1940s	Television, radar		
1950s	Transistors, computers		
1960s	Integrated circuits		
1970s	Microprocessors, personal computers		

Source: based on the discussion in Hall and Preston (1988)

from the revolutionary transformations in technology that have occurred. Discontinuities are definitely there, but so are ample elements of continuity.

RESOURCE TRANSFERS

Do incumbent and declining system leaders provide significant resources to their successors? Are these resources necessary and/or sufficient to the subsequent rise of the next leader? If old leaders do assist new leaders, why do they do it when it would seem to only hasten their own demise? The answers to these questions tend to vary somewhat over time.[1]

Genoa, Venice → Portugal

Venetian gains and Genoese losses in the eastern Mediterranean encouraged the intensification of Genoese activities in the western Mediterranean. Even before this shift in focus became apparent, Genoese participation in Portugal's economy and politics can be traced back to the opening of the Gibraltar Straits in the last quarter of the thirteenth century and the development of Portugal as a stopping point on the Atlantic run from the Mediterranean to the Baltic. Portuguese involvement in this western circuit dominated initially by the Italians, thus, was less a matter of choice than it was thrust upon a natural stopping point. But the Portuguese élite were quick to take advantage of their involvement by engaging in trade themselves and by encouraging the application of foreign expertise and capital for Portuguese ends.

As early as 1317, a Genoese was appointed as Portugal's chief admiral in exchange for 20 crewed warships. However, Genoese involvement in Portugal became even more widespread in the fifteenth century. Genoese were prominent in the exploration of the Atlantic islands (the Canaries and Madeiras), the development of sugar production in the Madeiras, and general financial support for exploring expeditions and export transactions. Since the Genoese had been active in seeking a way to eliminate the Venetian–Mamluk spice intermediation from the end of the thirteenth century, it is perhaps not surprising that the Portuguese gradually moved away from their initial concern with North African expansion and toward a search for an alternative route to the Indian Ocean. Hence, the Genoese supplied capital, key personnel, international business experience and contacts, and commercial strategies to the Portuguese expansion. This is not the same thing as saying that they showed the Portuguese how to do it, but it is clear that the Genoese participation facilitated the Portuguese expansion.

Normally, the Genoese receive all the "Italian" credit for facilitating the Portuguese expansion. Modelski (1999) credits the Venetians as well in ways that might have been discussed in the technological transfer section but deserve a brief mention here. One is that there is a great deal of similarity between the Venetian galley system and the later Carrera da India established by Portugal. What the Portuguese did was to expand the Venetian maritime network and basing system beyond its regional confines to encompass maritime Asia. In the process of doing so, they may also have captured some experimental Venetian shipping in the Indian Ocean (at the Battle of Diu) that served as the model for the galleon, an important type of ship that emerged in the Portuguese fleet only a few years later. Neither of these two "transfers" were direct or voluntary. Nevertheless, they also appeared to have greatly facilitated the Portuguese undertaking.

Portugal → the Netherlands

The Portuguese contribution to the Dutch ascent is indirect. The Portuguese contributed to the emergence of Antwerp as the leading European entrepôt by focusing the marketing of their Asian spices there and not in Lisbon. This concentration of capital and international business expertise might have remained under Spanish Hapsburg control if the capture of Antwerp by Spanish forces in 1585 had not encouraged business élites to search for more secure centers for their transactions. Although Amsterdam was not the first or immediate choice, it became the primary recipient of the migration of Antwerpian personnel, skills, and financial resources. This resource transfer fused Amsterdam's traditional preoccupation with the Baltic to the more global orientation of Antwerp at the right time to exploit the 1590s' opportunity to bypass Iberian control of Asian and Mediterranean transactions. This opportunity had been "forced" on the Dutch by the closure of Iberian ports to their trade. The basic choice was to wait more or less passively for their reopening or to bypass them and develop direct Dutch access to non-Baltic markets. The Dutch opted for the latter course of action. In doing so, the Dutch also improved on the Portuguese route to the Indian Ocean. Where the Portuguese preferred to hug the African coastline, the Dutch forged a new route across the Indian Ocean that provided a more direct approach to the source of spices. At the same time, though, the Dutch also attempted to take over all or most of the Portuguese bases on the southern Eurasian rim. Thus, the Dutch innovated while they also trod a commercial path already developed by their predecessors.

The Netherlands → Britain

Dutch–English economic relations have a long history dating back at the very least to the dependent position occupied by England as a supplier of wool and cloth to the Flemish textile industries in the thirteenth–fifteenth centuries. However, the resource that most analysts focus on in the Dutch–British case is the infusion of Dutch capital and loans into England after the invasion of William III, a rather high-level personnel resource transfer, in 1688. Specific numbers are not available but students of this process agree that the Dutch proportion of public debt funding was quite significant and remained so, subject to some decline over time, up to the 1780s. Carter (1975) asserts (see also Dehing and 'T Hart, 1997: 58) that the Dutch share declined to 25 percent by 1762 and about 12 percent by 1775. Since the size of the British public debt was expanding throughout this period, the implication is that the Dutch contribution was quite large in the first half of the eighteenth century. The basic public debt institution, for that matter, was copied from the Dutch practice (who, in turn, had borrowed the idea from the Venetians) and the very need for public debt was due to the financial demands imposed by participation in the Dutch war with France. Enlisting English participation on the Dutch side probably had been the primary reason for the Dutch invasion of England in the first place. Once they had invaded successfully, many of the élite state decision-making positions were monopolized by Dutch individuals into the mid-1690s.

Another debt owed to the Dutch among others are periodic infusions of technical skills. Continental approaches to weaving were introduced into England by Flemish migrants in the eleventh century. Later infusions of industrial skills and talents were introduced by refugees from Low Country religious persecution in the sixteenth century (Bense, 1924).

Britain → the United States

The United States had originally constituted a significant proportion of Britain's first empire. As such, much of its early economic development had been facilitated by the infusion of British labor and capital. In this sense, the Britain–US linkage comes about as close as one can imagine to corresponding to the biological process of sexual reproduction. But what became the United States was never a clone of the mother country. Meinig (1986) probably has the best take on this process. He argues that North America was the primary recipient of a thrust or thrusts from the "Northwest European Culture Hearth". This area encompassed the British Isles, the Low Countries, and the Atlantic rim of France. As such, the thrusts were characterized by their Protestant nature, their commercial orientation, and by the considerable turbulence in socio-economic, political and ideational relations that marked this region's antagonisms with centralizing France and Spain. That turbulence led to the movements of refugees and immigrants away from Europe (and Britain) and to Britain and North America. Just as Amsterdam and the Netherlands profited from the decline of Antwerp so, too, did both Britain and, ultimately, the United States, from "the reordering of the human geography of Europe" in the sixteenth–seventeenth centuries. Meinig (1986: 49) takes this one step further when he notes that the roots of American mobility and dynamism are found in Stuart England and in the Netherlands of the House of Orange.

The Revolutionary War severed the political linkages but did not permanently affect the economic linkages. The two states remained each other's primary external customer well into the nineteenth century (noted in Chapter 10). The US state retained its core English population even after that. In the investment sector, US capital formation was boosted significantly by foreign funds at particularly critical periods for industrial development. Table 11.3 draws attention, in particular to the 1816–1840 period, the 1860s, and the 1880s. During these times, foreign capital was sought by US governments and private concerns to exploit the possibilities associated with the expansion of transportation networks (canals and railroads) and the subsequent nationalization of the US economy. Shortly after the end of the 1812 War, British sources accounted for nearly half of the US federal debt. By the late 1820s, the British share had risen to 74 percent. Its overall share of foreign investment in the United States later peaked at 90 percent. But, as late as 1913, Britain's share remained as high as 59 percent. Interestingly, the number two position as principal foreign investor was held consistently by the Dutch until they were edged temporarily into third place by the Germans in 1899 before returning to the number two place in the twentieth century.

This examination is hardly exhaustive but it would appear that system leaders have provided highly significant resource transfers in terms of people, skills, and investment monies to their successors. Whether these transfers are necessary or sufficient to the rise of the successors is hard to say, especially in the absence of a fully specified model of leadership rise and decline. The British–US resource transfer comes closest to a necessary linkage. Imagine the future trajectory of the United States if it had been colonized and populated by the Iberian thrust that helped to produce Latin America. It is indeed hard to see how the US trajectory could have been the same given much different (counterfactual) origins. The Italian–Portugal and Netherlands–Britain linkages, on the other hand, seem more of a highly facilitative nature. In neither case did a former system leader create *de novo* a fertile setting for political-economic ascendancy. In both cases, it is not difficult to imagine similar outcomes in the absence of the resource assistance, albeit perhaps at a slower or more delayed pace. In

Table 11.3 US net foreign capital
input as a ratio of net
domestic capital formation

Years	Ratio
1799–1805	−0.012
1806–1815	0.005
1816–1840	0.220
1841–1850	−0.008
1851–1860	0.027
1861–1870	0.158
1871–1880	0.055
1881–1890	0.086
1891–1900	−0.028

Source: Davis and Cull (1994: 3)

none of the cases is it possible to forward the claim that the resource transfers were both necessary and sufficient.

Why do old system leaders help new ones? The shortest answer is that they provide resource assistance because it seems rational to do so and because the resource assistance is often provided on a decentralized basis. In the Portuguese case, Genoa was a factor, partly, because it had been forced to move westward. In the Dutch case, the ultimate implications of the Portuguese contribution via Antwerp could not have been foreseen in the early sixteenth century. In the English case, Dutch assistance was a factor, in part, because the Dutch feared French expansion more than they feared English expansion. In the US case, a great deal of the British input was made long before the US ascendancy began to loom on the horizon. When it did become more apparent, British–American frictions were ameliorated somewhat by a mutual fear of German expansion.

Probably even more important, though, is the fact that a great deal of the resource transfers were accomplished by individuals, syndicates and firms, and not states. The transfer of critical resources was primarily a decentralized process that the governments of the incumbent/declining/former system leaders would have been hard pressed to control even if they were so inclined to do so. One of the hallmarks of system leadership, the Portuguese notwithstanding, has been a preference for less rather than more government control of economic activities. Governmental decision-makers did (do) make efforts to deny technology, information, and resources to potential rivals. They were (are) often unsuccessful in curbing individual desires to make short-term profits and attractive investments. System leaders thus have a tendency to be hoisted by their own petards. They ascend, in part, because economic entrepreneurs have more political space to maneuver. Their eventual relative decline can be traced partially to the same attribute. Not to be overlooked is that entrepreneurs wish to invest in the new active zones because they are highly receptive to resource transfers and often more receptive than older active zones that have lost some of their taste for flexibility and risk-taking, or more simply lack the potential for high returns on their capital investments.

GEOPOLITICAL COMMUNITY FORMATION

The third area of system leader longitudinal interdependencies lies in the strategic arena. This arena works a bit differently than the first two emphases on antecedent relations. The states that have become system leaders have been unusually prominent suppliers of protection and security assistance before, during, and after the recipients' periods of systemic leadership. So much so that we cannot help speculating that this phenomena may be one of the least appreciated aspects of modern international relations history. The highlights of this proto-community formation story are found in the following chronology:

83/84	There is a long history of migration and trade between Low Countries and England extending back into prehistorical times. There is also a long history of people from the Netherlands area providing military assistance to inhabitants of the British Isles against various attackers extending back to at least 83/84 CE. At a much later point, English political élites establish habit of seeking refuge in the Low Countries.
1147	English and other northern European crusaders help capture Lisbon from Muslim control.
1190	Another intervention of English crusaders who were lost *en route* to the Crusades holds Santarem (in Portugal) against a Moroccan attack but, at the same time, other unruly English crusaders had to be evicted from Lisbon.
1200s on	England and Portugal establish trading relations in early thirteenth century – the relationship is strengthened in the fifteenthth century after England encountered increasing problems obtaining access to French and Spanish wine due to international political conflicts.
Fourteenth century	Portugal aligned on English side in Hundred Years War, as were some Burgundian (later Dutch) territories. The 1386 Portuguese–English treaty (Treaty of Windsor) has been described as the "most enduring and continuous treaty ever made". The treaty speaks of a perpetual league in which each state will assist the other against all enemies and refuse assistance to the other state's enemies as well.
Sixteenth century	English grand strategy also begins to regard Spanish, French, or German occupation of the Low Countries as a direct threat to England and a war precipitant.
1585–1604	English provision of military and financial assistance to the Dutch rebellion, including the beginning of offers of sovereignty surrender to the English crown which were, for the most part, evaded by Elizabeth I.
1588	Dutch assistance makes possible the defeat of the Spanish Armada attack on England.
Late 1620s	English and Scot mercenaries continue to constitute one-quarter of the Dutch infantry.

1625–1630	English–Dutch alliance renewed, albeit briefly, for a portion of the Thirty Years War.
1640s	Dutch facilitated Portuguese separation from Spanish empire by providing an initial period of truce.
Early 1650s	English–Dutch political union explored despite ongoing hostilities. English attacks on the Netherlands restrained by Cromwellian desire to develop Protestant alliance against Spain.
Second half of 1600s	England critical in maintaining Portuguese independence against Spanish threat after Portugal severs links with Spain in 1640.
1688	Dutch invasion of England made possible the ascension of William III to English crown; English troops are not allowed within London until the mid-1690s. One of the more important and ironic consequences of this invasion was the revival and expansion of the English Parliament as a central political institution.
1688–1713	Portugal is important to the Dutch and English as a base for naval operations in the Mediterranean. Most other bases are controlled by France or Spain. Several Methuen treaties are signed (1703), one of which involves a defensive alliance with England and the Netherlands, another binds Portugal to the Grand Alliance, and a third gives Portuguese goods preferential treatment over French goods in entering the English market.
1688–1763	American participation in intermittent British warfare with France.
1715, 1719	Dutch troops sent to Scotland to suppress Jacobite plots.
1740–1748	Britain and the Netherlands allied in opposition to France and Spain.
1788	Britain and the Netherlands allied in the Triple Alliance with Prussia.
1792–1815	Britain and Portugal are closely associated in the Peninsular War campaigns.
Early 1820s on	US Monroe Doctrine supported by British naval power.
1830–1840s	Britain and France compete over influence in the Iberian Peninsula, with Portugal gravitating toward the British sphere of influence.
1860s	After contemplating intervention, Britain discouraged European military intervention into US civil war.
Late 1890s	Britain and United States exchange governmental support for respective coercive operations in South Africa and Cuba/the Philippines.
1917–1918	US participation in British warfare with Germany.
1939–1945	US Lend Lease support to Britain.
1941–1945	US leadership in British warfare with Germany and Japan, with Dutch military participation in the Pacific theater.
Post-1945	US–Britain special relationship.
1949–	The United States, Britain, Holland, and Portugal, among others, aligned in NATO against the Soviet threat.

The fit of Portugal in this "community" may seem a bit stretched, but only because Portugal became a different sort of society than the Anglo-Saxon-Dutch variant. Portugal's links are primarily to England (see, for instance, Gibbs, 1935/1971; Lodge, 1935/1971; Prestage, 1935/1971; Williams, 1935/1971). The historical security linkages between and among the British, the Dutch, and the Americans, however, do not require much stretching.[2] They have a long history of military cooperation. Of course, the chronology listed above omits the wars, crises, and commercial rivalries between and among these same actors. It excludes the Genoese and Venetians and their four wars altogether. The Portuguese and Dutch fought each other for a number of years in the sixteenth and seventeenth centuries. The Portuguese and the English fought each other in Asia. The Dutch and British fought four wars between the 1650s and 1780s and British military intervention in the early nineteenth century ensured the success of Belgian separatism. The British and the Americans fought two wars between 1776 and 1815. So, there is no denying that relations among these actors have not always been cordial.

Yet these same wars have tended to be restrained by a variety of factors. Most importantly, they have tended to be fought at sea, and, therefore, they have been more distant affairs to the home populations and also more likely to be indecisive. They were also easier to break off. Knockout blows would require full-scale invasions of the home base which usually was not even attempted and when it was attempted, it was not very successful. System leaders, except in certain crisis situations (for example, world wars) have lacked the appropriate strategic orientation, the location, and large armies to conquer their rivals without the assistance of land powers.

What stands out most in the record of conflict and cooperation, though, is the tendency for geopolitical pressures to force these actors together before, during and after their stints as system leaders. For more than 500 years, they have had the same main enemies: Spain, France, Germany, and the Soviet Union. Intermittently at least, geopolitical circumstances, religious factors (Protestantism versus Catholicism for the English and the Dutch into the eighteenth century) and threats have encouraged them to suppress their intramural conflicts to better focus on the extramural ones. They do not seem to ally so much because they share regime types or liberal values but because they tend to find themselves under attack by the same foes. The extent to which they tend to share regime types and liberal values can be attributed in large part to the way in which their political and economic constitutions have been shaped by their commercial/industrial orientations. And it is their spectacular success at commerce and industry (in their respective eras) that has made them the targets of less successful land powers located to their east. It may be heretical to say so but it would appear that a stronger explanation for the democratic peace can be extracted from this history of system leader interactions than if one relies on more static attributes such as shared institutions and norms. Given the stakes involved – literally a preponderant position in the global system and intercontinental transactions – these states should have fought one another harder than they did. If they had done so, it is unlikely that we would be as interested in something called the democratic peace as we are. That they did not fight to the bitter end seems to have less to do directly with their political and economic attributes than it does with the peculiarly intimate history of interactions among systemic leaders confronted as they were by common foes.

CONCLUSION

Is there then a lineage of system leaders? The answer is "no" if we adhere to a rigid interpretation of lineage descent.[3] Strictly speaking, the previous system leader does not give birth to its successor, and yet it does in some ways. There are clear lineage patterns in the technological innovations that provide the foundations for systemic leadership. There is a long history of assistance and resource transfers from the old leader to the new that could be likened to parental nurturing and offspring learning. Finally, there is also an even longer history of interaction in the security realm that paints system leaders as a special community in international relations, not unlike a kin or clan relationship linked by some real or imagined bloodline. Figure 11.2 imperfectly summarizes some of these longitudinal interdependencies.

Thus it is concluded here that we can dismiss the notion of a system leader lineage as fanciful only at the risk of missing some important clues as to why some states rise

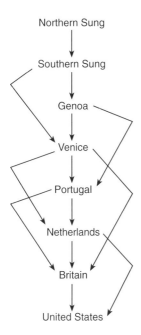

Figure 11.2 Commercial-maritime lineages

so high and fall so hard. We would also be missing some important clues as to how and why the cyclical political succession and technological escalation interact and evolve to shape world politics. Moreover, the vertical dimension underlines the fact that we are dealing with a spiraling phenomenon encompassing more and more space and increasingly stronger technology – and not just the repetitive cycling in and out of various and sundry system leaders.

One way to summarize these inheritance processes is to suggest that system leader transfers of ideas and resources take place within a slowly emerging community of people with similar ways of doing things, similar values, and similar enemies. In any given century – once this community formation process began to emerge during the last millennium – the community core is the system leader which generates innovation, resources, and protection for other members of the community. Old system leaders, for the most part (Sung China is the major exception), stay within the community once their leadership era has passed into history. Future system leaders tend to be coopted into this community before their ascent takes off.

Even so, the community is not restricted to former, present, and future system leaders. It has created clones through colonization and immigration and encouraged geographically adjacent adherents to adopt similar values and ways of doing things. Community leaders have also tried to reshape defeated foes along lines preferred by prevailing community values.

One of the consequences is that we currently operate in a two-tiered world system. One tier is relatively prosperous, technologically sophisticated, and democratic; the other is not. The question then becomes whether the subsystem and the global political economy made by the successive system leaders can continue to expand and incorporate the less prosperous, less sophisticated, and less democratic rest of the world. This will require continued and, no doubt, accelerated innovation in prevailing strategies and institutions. A second possibility is that the polarization and divergent evolution of the two worlds will persist for some time, with little or no change until (or unless) conditions really deteriorate. A third scenario, of course, is that the angry and frustrated second tier, in conjunction with other pressing political-economic problems (climate, water scarcity, overpopulation, food production and distribution, disease, and environmental degradation) will ultimately destroy the first tier's privileged existence. Conceivably, the attack on the status quo's principal beneficiaries could also be led (or precipitated?) by the next violent challenger sometime in the mid-twenty-first century.

The problem with evolutionary perspectives is that we can look back and see how the global political economy has emerged over the past several centuries and developed a number of relatively clear patterns. Less clear is how far into the future we can peer. Currently, all three of the above scenarios remain plausible. Which trajectory is selected will depend on the interaction of a number of variables but, in the end analysis, the trajectory that predominates will hinge on whether the strategies for managing the problems of the global political economy rise to the occasion. This will require evolution away from a reliance on the primitive leadership challenge sequence process. It will also depend on whether regional ascent patterns continue to shift the locus of wealth and power to new sites, in which direction, and at what pace. It will depend, moreover, on continued economic and political innovation. In short, whatever happens, it will build on past patterns and continued structural change in the global political economy, which, presumably, will continue to "emerge" into the future.

NOTES

1 K-WAVES, LEADERSHIP CYCLES, AND GLOBAL WAR: AN ORIENTATION

1 This chapter summarizes ideas expressed in more detail in Rasler and Thompson (1994) and Modelski and Thompson (1996). Other book-length works, in the same tradition, include Modelski (1987), Modelski and Modelski (1988), Modelski and Thompson (1988), Thompson (1988), Rasler and Thompson (1989), and Thompson (1998).

2 The pattern of who fights whom and why is more complicated than the image suggested by declining incumbent and rising challengers. The declining and rising leaders rarely fight one another. For a more elaborate discussion of this problem, see Rasler and Thompson (1994) and Chapter 10.

2 EVOLUTIONARY AND COEVOLUTIONARY CONSIDERATIONS

1 Another possible difference is that evolutionists in biology have had to struggle with super-natural creationist myths. The closest we come to this problem in the social sciences is the rational choice assumption that decision-makers "create" their own choice situations without reference to the constraints of structures and history. However, it is not clear that rational choice and coevolutionary perspectives need be fundamentally opposed, particularly if the former is oriented toward the short term and the latter is long run in viewpoint. Yet even this distinction is debatable. See Williams, McGinnis, and Thomas (1994) for a rational choice approach to an evolutionary process.

2 Some readers might think that Figure 2.1 resembles the traditional study of international relations, but the resemblance is only superficial. Traditional international relations tend to be ambivalent at best about the role and methods of the social sciences. In addition, Figure 2.1 assigns no separate place at the table to history and area studies. This is neither an oversight nor an attack on these approaches. The assumption is that each subsystem has its own history, as does the ensemble of parts. Thus, the history cannot be divorced from the analysis of the various causal dynamics. From a coevolutionary perspective it has, there-fore, been less than optimal to allow the social sciences to become increasingly ahistorical and to maintain, with some exceptions, the study of history as primarily a branch of the humanities. Area studies are premised on another type of understandable division of labor. But it is one thing to be interdisciplinary in perspective and quite another to be explicitly coevolutionary in one's analytical strategy. On the other hand, there is nothing that precludes a coevolutionary approach to a delimited geographical area.

3 See Pollins (1993) for a an argument about coevolutionary changes in national and inter-national financial and monetary systems.

4 This sketch of what a coevolutionary paradigm might look like has been stimulated largely but not exclusively by work in evolutionary economics. See Boulding (1981); Nelson and Winter (1982); Clark and Juma (1987); Allen (1988); Freeman and Perez (1988); Modelski (1990, 1996); David (1993); Snooks (1993a, 1993b); England (1994); Hodgson (1994); Nelson (1994); Norgaard (1994); Samuels, Schmidt, and Shaffer (1994).

3 THE 1490s: A QUESTION OF EVOLUTIONARY (DIS)CONTINUITY?

1 Britain was associated with four. The United States has had two and may have more.
2 There is an ongoing debate in world system circles about the continuity of critical processes. Ekholm and Friedman (1993), Gills and Frank (1993), Wilkinson (1993a), and Chase-Dunn and Hall (1997) argue for very long periods of continuity spanning thousands of years. Amin (1993), Wallerstein (1993), and Bergesen (1994) prefer to defend a major breakpoint around 1500. Abu-Lughod (1993) argues for an earlier emergence of the world system in the thirteenth century. Modelski and Thompson (1996) switched their position from a post-1494 stance to one that focuses on *c.* 1000 as the emergence of the paired Kondratieff-systemic crisis-global leadership processes. Future work will adopt an even longer perspective for other types of processes.
3 Palin (1992) would add monocausal, heterocausal, conjunctural, normative, and Third Worldism (in addition to exogenous, endogenous, and Eurocentric) to the adjectives describing approaches to accounting for the European "Miracle".
4 Wilkinson (1993b: 66) prefers a later date (*c.* 622 AD) for the incorporation of east Asia into the central Eurasian trading system. However, this timing seems to hinge on data limitations pertaining to urbanization thresholds on which Wilkinson relies strongly. But he acknowledges that better data might support an earlier date.
5 Pearson (1976: 15–16) notes only three instances of non-European compulsion in Indian Ocean trade: Srivijaya in the seventh and eighth centuries, Fakaner in the early fourteenth century, and Diu in the early sixteenth century. To this list should be added the Chola attacks on Srivijaya in the eleventh century and the Ming voyages of the fifteenth century.
6 McNeil (1963: 454) emphasizes the European transformation of raiders into traders.
7 Lewis (1988: 85) suggests that Amalfi was forced to drop out of this competition because they were insufficiently aggressive.

4 THE DIVERGENT COEVOLUTION OF TWO EURASION REGIONS

1 The divergent evolution idea is explored in some detail and in a much different context in Flannery and Marcus (1983).
2 Analysts who stress "blockages" in non-European regions are implying that other regions would have developed along European lines in the absence of certain constraints. But Crone (1989) makes the point that there is no compelling reason to assume that all regions were evolving in the same direction before 1500. The removal of the blockages, therefore, would not necessarily lead to an outcome similar to the west European one.
3 Adshead (1993: 120), for example, argues rather strongly that the nomadic explosions in central Asia (the Mongols through Timur the Lame) were responsible for standardizing the "global arsenal in cavalry, artillery and seapower." His argument appears to fit artillery best. The heavy cavalry response to nomadic light cavalry is a much older process than the thirteenth–fourteenth centuries and the standardization of sea power is a complicated process that was probably less dependent on central Asian osmosis than cavalry and artillery.
4 Adshead (1988: 70) notes that 20 percent of the late T'ang population resided in cities or towns.

5 The revolutionary economic growth of Sung China is dealt with at greater length in Elvin (1973), McNeill (1982), Jones (1988), and Modelski and Thompson (1996).

6 Eberhard (1977: 255) notes that the doubling of rice production led to the insertion of fish in the rice paddies to augment the fertilization process. An indirect and unplanned byproduct of this development was the reduction of malaria in southern China thanks to the fish consumption of mosquitos. Disease had long been a constraint on the economic exploitation of southern China.

7 It is estimated that Sung appeasement policies cost them about 2 percent of state revenues as opposed to 25 percent when the army was maintained at full strength (Eberhard, 1977: 211).

8 See Waldron (1994) for a discussion of what he refers to as a cyclical approach to appeasement. Each dynasty that practiced appeasement initially tended to move toward more confrontational tactics until diverted back to appeasement by failure and consideration of costs. This is another type of coevolutionary process with Chinese strategic preferences cycling within the larger cycle of Chinese nomadic interactions.

9 Another reason for moving the capital north may have been to escape epidemics that were more prevalent in the south in the aftermath of the fall of the Mongols (Abu-Lughod, 1989: 347).

10 Elvin (1973: 224) would add that the large size of the Chinese empire made withdrawal into isolation more tenable than would have been the case in smaller subsystems.

11 Adshead (1993: 124–125) provides another example of what appears to be an overly strong hypothesis that the Ming fleet voyages were intended not only to make linkages with the Muslims to the rear of Timur, but also the west Europeans.

12 Nicholas (1992:1) describes Flanders, later to become a principal center of the European ascendancy, as initially unattractive marshlands that even pirates and Vikings avoided as unworthy of their predatory attentions. Venice was another initially swampy area. It is interesting to speculate whether entrepreneurs would have been able to establish their independent, commercial niches in these places if they had been more inhabitable at an earlier stage.

13 The overrunning of Portugal and the Netherlands were transitory phenomena. Nevertheless, the problem highlights the emphasis placed on insularity (Modelski,1987; Goldstein and Rapkin, 1991) as an important ingredient in the emergence and survival of growth leaders. With the exception of Genoa (which had some protection from surrounding mountains) and Portugal (which had the Castilian buffer as long as the Castilians were preoccupied elsewhere), all growth leaders from the Southern Sung to the United States have enjoyed some form of aquatic defense. A leadership transition to Japan would maintain this tradition.

14 As usual, there are very strong, moderate, and weak ways to make this assertion. The very strong assertion would say that the Europeans could not have developed without Chinese technology. The moderate assertion would note that European development was facilitated by borrowing from, and modifying, Sung Chinese technology. The weak assertion would suggest that western ascendance may have been stimulated generally by eastern prosperity and technology. We prefer the moderate version.

15 The antimerchant bias in Chinese culture dates back at least to the time of the Han dynasty (Gernet, 1982: 145).

16 One interpretation, the Boserup thesis (Jones, 1988: 129), is that the adoption of new techniques is dependent on a rising population exhausting the available supply of inventions. This hypothesis deserves more analysis, particularly inasmuch as the relationship is likely to be complicated by some degree of reciprocity (population increase leads to innovation which, in turn, leads to prosperity and more population increase) and a likely curvilinear relationship between population growth and innovation. At the very least, North and Thomas (1973: 34) appear to be on safe historical grounds by suggesting that

"In the chronology of history, the growth of cities seems to have followed, with a lag, the expansion of population in a given area and to have been coincident with the establishment of interregional commerce."

17 Hall (1991: 229) notes that the dualism bestows more maneuverability and flexibility on the nomadic/sea power side of the equation.
18 This argument is developed in detail in Dehio (1962), Thompson (1992), and Rasler and Thompson (1994).
19 One caveat that deserves more exploration is the possibility that warfare over control of western Europe should be linked to the Hundred Years War.

5 THE MILITARY SUPERIORITY THESIS

1 For arguments about the European military revolutions, see Black (1991, 1994), the articles in Rogers (1995), and Thompson and Rasler (1999). For arguments about the application of these European military revolutions beyond Europe, in addition to Parker (1988/1996, 1995, see Guilmartin (1991, 1995), Morillo (1995), and Black (1996).
2 Nevertheless, the acknowledged lack of European interest in conquest seems problematic to an argument based on the rise of Europe via the demonstration of military superiority.
3 Parker (1988/1996: 3–4), for one, explicitly states:

> For in large measure, the "rise of the West" depended upon the exercise of force, upon the fact that the military balance between the Europeans and their adversaries overseas was steadily tilting in favor of the former; and it is the argument of this book that the key to the Westerners' success in creating the first truly global empires between 1500 and 1750 depended upon precisely these improvements in the ability to wage war which have been termed the "military revolution".

4 The treatment of the cases will not advance new historical material. The idea is to pull together very briefly and selectively the available information that seems pertinent to an evaluation of military superiority, local allies, target vulnerability, and European strategies.
5 In terms of the larger areas, Siberia and North America are ignored in this treatment. The Siberian case is less interesting given the limited opposition encountered. The North American case is complicated but by no means an exception to the arguments that will emerge for other geographical contexts. See, for instance, Steele's (1994) deemphasis of the role of European military superiority in North America.
6 It is probably inaccurate or, at least, misleading to refer to this prototypical behavior as a Venetian model *per se*. Earlier versions can be found in the behavior of Dilmun traders, Minoans, Phoenicians, Carthaginians, and, to some extent, Athenians – all of whom were influenced to various degrees by their chronological predecessors. There is also some resemblance to Baltic, Chola, and Srivajayan practices. But the Venetians perfected the model of a state run by trading interests for the benefit of expanding and protecting long-distance trade.
7 Sources for the treatment of the Portuguese experience include Wheeler and Pelissier (1971), Diffie and Winius (1977) Hess (1978), McAlister (1984), Pearson (1987), and Subrahmanyam (1993).
8 See Diffie and Winius (1977: 354–357).
9 The Portuguese were also involved in colonizing Brazil but this effort was relatively slow to develop and did not encounter highly organized indigenous opposition.
10 Macao was obtained in the mid-sixteenth century as a Portuguese base despite the naval defeats, as a matter of convenience for all concerned, and after Chinese–Portuguese cooperation in suppressing local piracy (Cady, 1964: 187–188).

11 The Spanish were evicted from trading in Japan due to Japanese fears that Spanish activity might encourage internal revolt tendencies (Cady, 1964: 241).

12 See, for example, Pearson (1987: 57).

13 The sources used for the Aztec case included Gardiner (1956), Padden (1967), Elliott (1980), Wachtel (1980), Hassig (1988, 1992), and Guilmartin (1995).

14 Inca sources were Hemming (1970), Elliott (1980), Wachtel (1980), Murra (1986), Cameron (1990), Guilmartin (1991), and Davies (1995).

15 See the testimony of several Spanish participants in Cameron (1990: 83–84). Guilmartin (1991, 1995) stresses the Spanish small group tactical cohesion displayed in Mexico and Peru as an attribute learned in European wars and, therefore, linkable to early modern European military revolutions. Still, there is a more compelling rival hypothesis. Since most of the conquistadors were not professional soldiers, sheer terror and desperation in the face of large numbers of opponents might explain group cohesion. The Spanish groups were much less cohesive when they were not faced with great odds.

16 Unfortunately, no Inca sources are available to probe the actual attitudes of the Inca army at Cajamarca.

17 For instance, Adams (1991: 401) notes that Aztec rulers would even invite enemy rulers to observe their human sacrifice of enemy captives ceremonies.

18 Sources for the Dutch Indonesian experience included Cady (1964), Hall (1964), Reid (1993), and Ricklefs (1993).

19 The Spanish did not face centralized opposition in the Philippines and tended to leave their strongest opponents there, the Moros, alone as much as possible.

20 The British involvement in India is covered in Lyall (1910), Lawford (1978), Moon (1989), Heathcote (1995), and Wolpert (1997).

21 Heathcote (1995: 26) implies that the effect may have been as much psychological as anything else.

22 These Spanish successes in America were anything but inevitable. Something similar was attempted in southeast Asia towards the end of the sixteenth century and failed miserably (Cady, 1964: 240). Forty Spanish adventurers, associated with an expedition sent from Manila, managed to capture and murder the King of Cambodia in 1596, only to be disowned by the head of their expedition who chose to exercise prudence by returning to the Philippines. Several years (1583) earlier a plan had been proposed to send an 8000-man expedition to China to gain access for Catholic missionaries, among other things. Had the plan been executed, it would have made an excellent test of the military superiority thesis. Perhaps just as well for the life expectancies of the would-be expeditionaries, the plan was rejected by authorities in Madrid.

23 There is a conventional tendency to view the European activities as incorporating parts of Asia into the world economy. This image is wholly inaccurate and overtly Eurocentric for Asia had been a rather important part of the Eurasian world economy for millennia by the 1500–1900 CE period. The "incorporation" was more a matter of coercively arranging better terms and ease of entry into markets for non-Asian commercial agents.

24 An interesting illustration is offered by Hopkins' (1978) analysis of the political economy problems encountered by the slowing down of Roman imperial expansion.

25 See, for instance, Chesneaux, Bastid, and Bergere (1976), Wakeman (1978), Jones and Kuhn (1978), and Fairbank (1978).

26 Yet, given the asymmetries in casualties within the western organized coalitions, some might argue that the Cold War wars in Korea and Indo-China restored the need for local allies if westerners expected to engage in military operations in eastern Eurasia.

27 There were, of course, variations in the extent to which external actors were interested in Chinese territorial acquisitions. The Russians and the Japanese appear to have been more interested in territory than the British.

28 This is essentially a variation on the fourteenth century Ibn Khaldun (1967) model. Lean and mean warriors with cohesion descend from the mountains to capture the sedentary and complacent towns. But Ibn Khaldun stressed both the advantages of the attackers and the vulnerability of the attacked because the sedentary town rulers had once been warriors from the mountains and had become corrupted by the process of urban rule, thereby setting up a cyclical dynamic.

29 The Mongol expansion seems to demonstrate an important variation on this principle. Barfield (1989: 198) argues that the Mongols under Ghengis Khan never intended to conquer China. Rather, their conventional strategy of border raids for extortion purposes stimulated an escalating war with the Jurchen Chin dynasty which had deviated from the typical east Asian strategy of limited resistance/appeasement. In the end, the Jurchen Chin destroyed themselves and the Mongols found themselves in control of northern China for the first time. In such a case, an explanation that emphasized only Mongol military superiority would be overlooking the critical element of the Jurchen strategy and its consequences for the vulnerability of "Chinese" defenses.

30 The Indo-European movements into India around the time of Harappan decline (early to mid-second millennium BCE) are good examples of peripheral incursions/migrations that may well have taken place after the Harappan center had already disintegrated. The Dorian movement into southern Greece (late second millennium BCE) is another.

31 It is probably considered politically incorrect, somewhere, to stress the European advantage exclusively, even if that advantage is merely the superior capability to kill people. Even so, the point of this observation is not to imply Eurocentricity or political incorrectness on anybody's part but simply to argue for a more balanced explanation of regional ascendancy. The success of militarily advantaged attackers is more comprehensible within the context of politically disadvantaged defenders, especially when the military advantages were rarely sufficient in the absence of considerable political vulnerabilities.

32 Other ingredients include population growth, urbanization, the development of food surplus, some level of insularity from attack and sufficient economic innovation to accommodate these societal changes.

33 Attempts to model these dynamics can be found in Modelski (1987, 1996), Modelski and Thompson (1988, 1996), Thompson (1988), and Rasler and Thompson (1989, 1994).

6 THE EMERGENCE OF A CHALLENGE PROCESS

1 See, for example, Gilpin (1981) who sees nineteenth-century British hegemony moving the international political economy away from a phase of competing empires.

2 Boxer (1972: 8) dates the Portuguese interest in spices as increasing after 1460.

3 Portuguese navigation in the Indian Ocean initially depended on Arab information.

4 On the role of the Baltic trade in Dutch commerce, see Steensgaard (1990); Boswell, Misra, and Brueggemann (1991); and Boswell and Misra (1997).

5 The Portuguese maintained control over Goa until 1961 and Macao almost into the twenty-first century.

7 MOUNTAINS OF GOLD AND IRON

1 English commercial companies had been first organized to deal with Turkish and Venetian markets (1580) and then the Levant (1592) before interest in the East Indies became more significant.

2 Attempts to reach Asia motivated much of the early North American explorations.

3 A small group of English and Japanese were executed by the Dutch in 1623 for conspiring to seize a Dutch fort in the Spice Islands.

4 On the Anglo-Dutch conflict, see Levy (1998) and Levy and Ali (1998).

5 The defeated Nawab had attempted to reassert the right to tax the Company's activities.
6 Black (1986) also points out that both economies were committed to textile manufacturing and their export.
7 Heckscher (1964: 52) notes that French officials had first contemplated a European union to defeat Britain's economic prowess as early as 1747.
8 The evolution toward increasingly deadly and destructive global wars underscores the fact that evolutionary processes need not be progressive in direction.

8 CHALLENGES IN THE ACTIVE ZONE

1 Attention to leading sectors dates back at least to Adam Smith. More contemporary sources include Rostow (1978), Thompson (1988), and Modelski and Thompson (1996). Note that it is not assumed that leading sectors have an exclusive monopoly on high profits.
2 See Yakovets (1994) for the application of the genotypic imagery to technological change.
3 The impact of technological clusters has been conceptualized in several ways. See among others, Schumpeter (1939), Mensch (1979), Freeman and Perez (1988), Hall and Preston (1988), Thompson (1990), Hugill (1993), and Modelski and Thompson (1996).
4 The concept of economic leadership is central to many approaches to historical-structural analyses (Thompson, 1988). However, the arguments advanced here seem most compatible with the types of approach advocated by Bousquet (1980) and Gilpin (1987). Empirical evidence on economic leadership extending back to the thirteenth century is provided in Modelski and Thompson (1996).
5 Modelski (1999) describes this lineage as a "democratic" one. I am more comfortable stressing its commercial-maritime roots as opposed to what it evolved into over time.
6 The "constitutional fitness" conceptualization is taken from D'Lugo and Rogowski (1993). This sort of conceptualization is employed gingerly given the possible misinterpretation that the argument is a revival of nineteenth century social Darwinistic thought. But this is not a straightforward "survival of the fittest" type of argument. Rather, at certain points in time, some actors possess attributes that facilitate unusual degrees of success within their political-economic environments. Winners win, in part, because they have characteristics that are not shared by the losers. As a simple illustration, consider the case of the Swiss cantons and Portugal. In the fifteenth century, Portugal was better placed (than the Swiss cantons) to find a new route to the Indian Ocean. Thus Portugal was more "fit" to do well in Asia in the sixteenth century than were the Swiss cantons. Yet in the long run, Switzerland managed to carve out a more prosperous niche for itself within the capitalist world economy than Portugal did, in part, because it was well placed to exploit the Thirty Years War and other central European conflicts. Fitness thus depends on the question being asked and, moreover, is apt to be short-lived. This is one reason why leaderships rotate.
7 The technological gradient conceptualization is taken from Galbraith (1989: 14–15).
8 The distinction between sea and land powers is quite conventional in geopolitical emphases. The way in which the distinction is applied here is developed further in Rasler and Thompson (1989, 1994).
9 What is now the mainstream position on the impact of industrialization on geopolitics is well articulated in Mackinder (1962) and Kennedy (1983).
10 Rasler and Thompson (1994) provide an elaboration of this point of view within the context of warfare.
11 No assumption is made here that breaking into or creating new markets need be strictly a function of innovation alone. Coercion can play, and has played, a major role. The Portuguese and Dutch Asian market positions in the sixteenth and seventeenth centuries, for instance, were based on a combination of commercial innovation and military force.
12 Frederick (1989, 1999) emphasizes this element in her innovative study of challenges in the nineteenth and early twentieth centuries.

13 The other side of this coin is that declining leaders sometimes anoint or at least facilitate their preferred successors via technological transfers, financial investment, and military assistance. Various types of examples can be found in the linkages between Genoa and Portugal, England and the Netherlands, and Britain and the United States.

14 Moreover, less autocratic states are more conducive to technological innovation while it is easier in more autocratic states to mobilize domestic resources for assaults on the external status quo.

15 See Chapters 3 and 4 for further discussion of the role of commercial states in the ascendancy of Europe.

16 Spain was also notorious for the extent to which its South American riches passed through the Iberian peninsula like a sieve enriching northern Europeans and Asians with little return to Spain.

17 The model outlined in Figure 8.1 does not tell us anything about when challenges should be expected. For an empirically tested model of the post-1494 period on this question, see Rasler and Thompson (1994). A periodicity calendar for challengers based on phases of long-term technological growth is found in Chapter 1 (Table 1.1).

18 See Modelski (1979) for what is now dated evidence for these generalizations. While it is suggested that most transnationals continue to have national identities that does not mean that the relationships between states and TNCs are not also becoming more complex. On the complexity issue see, for example, the arguments of Stopford and Strange (1991).

19 A different but certainly compatible argument is expressed in Sen (1984).

20 For instance, it does not rule out a period of coleadership which combined US military power with Japanese economic growth. From a historical perspective, however, such a combination, in the absence of a mutual, third party threat, is not likely to be either stable or durable. For different views on this possibility, see Gilpin (1987), Rapkin (1990), Gills (1993) and Arrighi (1994). For alternative, more general, scenarios on Japanese–American relations, see Friedman and Lebard (1991). But a variety of other possibilities are suggested by Emmott (1989), Rapkin (1990), Wallerstein (1991), Garten (1992), Thurow (1992), Katzenstein and Okawara (1993), and Modelski and Thompson (1996). Moreover, it need not be assumed that the United States will lose its economic leadership status to Japan or any other country. Britain managed to retain its leadership through two iterations and the United States may be in the process of duplicating that feat.

9 BRITAIN AS A SYSTEM LEADER IN THE NINETEENTH AND TWENTIETH CENTURIES

1 Keep in mind that global wars are an institution that emerged only after 1494 and the development of a close interdependence between global affairs and regional western European developments. Global wars occurred in the following periods: 1494–1516, 1580–1608, 1688–1713, 1792–1815, and 1914–1945.

2 For a very useful review of the issues involved, see Colin Elman and Miriam Fendius Elman (1997); Gaddis (1997); George (1997); Haber, Kennedy, and Krasner (1997); Ingram (1997); Levy (1997); and Schroeder (1997).

3 Some readers may find these distinctions regarding type A and type B political scientists counter-intuitive. What is being left out of the argument is a variable appreciation for history. Type A political scientists, given a commitment to parsimony and universal generalizations, prefer for the most part to ignore history as an inconvenient obstacle to theorizing. Structural approaches usually (but not always) entail some assumption that history matters and, therefore, are accompanied by some form of historical script or interpretation that is important to their theoretical framework. Pure type A political scientists thus will dismiss historical-structural analysis as too historicist and atheoretical for their tastes. On the other hand, some type B political scientists will also dismiss

historical structural analysis as too theoretical or not sufficiently open to countless contingencies.

4 The present focus on antistructuralist arguments is restricted primarily to Ferris (1991); Martel (1991); McKercher (1991); Neilson (1991); and Ingram (1997, 1999).

5 One explicitly stated reason for targeting Kennedy was that he had the temerity to advance the rise and fall of Britain as a paradigm for international history. While Kennedy's (1987) *The Rise and Fall of the Great Powers* is certainly compatible with Kennedy's (1976) *The Rise and Fall of British Naval Mastery* and his (1983) *Strategy and Diplomacy, 1870–1945*, we would be hardpressed to attribute paternity for structural arguments on rise and decline politics to Kennedy. Some alternative structural interpretations would include Organski (1958/1968); Frank (1978); Gilpin (1975, 1981, 1987); Waltz (1979); Organski and Kugler (1980); Braudel (1984); Wallerstein (1984); Modelski (1987, 1996); Goldstein (1988); Midlarsky (1988); Modelski and Thompson (1988, 1996); Thompson (1988); Chase-Dunn (1989); Rasler and Thompson (1989, 1994); Doran (1991), and Brawley (1993). It might be interesting to try and trace who influenced whom and how in the development of these often different arguments.

6 For those unfamiliar with the term "Granger causality", there is no implication that social scientists have discovered a way to demonstrate full-fledged causality. However, one dimension of causal arguments is that if variable X is a cause of variable Y, a change in X's values must antecede an impact on Y's values. Granger causality tests are fairly conservative statistical tests to establish whether X and Y are systematically related in a statistically significant fashion and variable X's influence really does antecede variable Y's movement over time. Currently, these types of examinations appear to be about as close as we can come to an approximation of causality. See Rasler and Thompson (1991, 1994) Reuveny and Thompson (1997).

7 The different types of frogs, as opposed to the tadpole–frog sequence was suggested by George Modelski.

8 Antistructuralists appear to use the "global" and "world" modifiers for the "power" term to signify the geographical scale of foreign policy interests. A global or world power, therefore, is one that has world-wide foreign policy interests. Some structuralists, on the other hand, tend to reserve these same terms for states with the capability to operate on a global or world scale. For instance, in leadership long-cycle vernacular, a global power is a state with the minimum global reach capability to operate beyond its local region. A world power must possess half or more of the global power capability pool at the outset of its incumbency.

9 In all fairness, Martel (1991) is attempting to suggest that capabilities that may work in one region will not necessarily work the same way or as effectively in another region. The point is well taken but it leads the author to overstate his case considerably.

10 Naval historians tend to prefer the greater detail found in Glete's (1993) naval data set over Modelski and Thompson's (1988) data which was designed entirely to examine hypotheses about naval concentration over a 500 year period. While there are problems in using Glete's data for serial purposes, the same general decay patterns can be observed in both data sets, although Glete's data stops short of addressing the question of British relative decline before 1939.

11 See Gardiner, (1956) for an example of how sea power sometimes turns up where least expected.

12 See Thompson (1992) and Rasler and Thompson (1994) for the development and application of Ludwig Dehio's arguments to European regional politics since 1494.

13 See Modelski and Thompson (1988) and Gray (1992).

14 Similarly, French challenges (for example, involving Belgium, Mohammed Ali, and Switzerland) in the first half of the nineteenth century always stopped short of going to war with Britain.

15 Structural analysts, of course, do not agree on the existence of a British first term as system leader in the eighteenth century.

16 Some might be tempted to nominate Alexander but while the Macedonian attempted to conquer a respectable proportion of his known trading world (or global system), the nature of the operation possessed a number of more traditional regional expansion aspects.

17 See the five variable model differentiating violent challenges of system leaders from non-violent challenges in the preceding chapter.

18 For more discussion of these rivalries, see Ingram (1999a) and Thompson (1999).

19 The wartime ascendance of the junior partner has occurred before, as exemplified in the Dutch-British transition in the 1688–1713 fighting.

20 World War I was also inconclusive from a regional perspective as well. The Austro-Russian and Austro-Serbian rivalries ended in 1918 but others persisted.

21 The exact institutional form of the élite actors is beside the point from a long-cycle point of view. What is important are the roles that are played in global politics (that is world power, challenger, global power). In this respect, leadership long-cycle analysis is not nation-state focused.

22 While structuralists and antistructuralists have their interplanetary communication problems, it should not be assumed that structuralists find intraplanetary communication to be a simple matter. See, for example, Thompson (1983).

10 THE ANGLO-AMERICAN RIVALRY BEFORE WORLD WAR I

1 For example, the First Lord of the Admiralty counted France, Russia, and the United States as his specific referents in 1855 when discussing the basis of British naval superiority over its nearest rivals (Bartlett, 1993: 55).

2 The peaceful transition of the United States over Britain is often thought to be a particular problem for power transition analyses (Organski, 1958/1968; Organski and Kugler, 1980; Kugler and Lemke, 1996) and leadership long-cycle analyses (Rasler and Thompson, 1994; Thompson, 1995). However, analysts working within these perspectives have, in fact, offered explanations. Organski (1958/1968) emphasizes that the inevitability of a prospective transition reduces the probability of conflict. More recently, Modelski (1999 and see the preceding chapter) has developed an argument about "democratic lineage" – a subject to which we will return in this chapter's conclusion.

3 Nearly 10,000 American sailors were impressed by the British Navy between 1793 and 1812 (Maslowski, 1994: 222).

4 Rock (1989: 17) argues that the development of more amicable relations requires a catalyst to overcome policy inertia. It is tempting to interpret the 1895 crisis in this light except that the nature of the conflict seems so similar to the earlier crises. After conceding hegemony to the United States in North and then Central America, Britain conceded to the United States in South America as well, but only after the United States had emerged from a period of reconstruction and relative isolation into a once more expansionist mode. 1895 may have come as a surprise to British decision-makers but, in retrospect, it fits the general pattern so well that it is difficult to treat it as exceptional in any way. The one difference between 1895 and the earlier crises is that US–British *rapprochement* processes accelerated shortly after the end of the crisis, and therein lies the analytical temptation.

5 The leading sector concept is developed further in Thompson (1988) and Modelski and Thompson (1996). The basic idea is to focus on sectoral indicators such as steel and automobile production that economic historians give special attention to as important lead industries, as opposed to more aggregate indicators such as gross national product. In Figure 10.2, the British share reflects the aggregation of shares of raw cotton consumption,

pig iron production, and railroad construction. The US share reflects the aggregation of shares of production in steel, sulphuric acid, motor vehicle, civilian jet airliner, and semiconductors, as well as electricity consumption.

6 The US–British case may be an exception to Rock's (1989: 14) generalization that interdependence stemming from competitive trade is less likely to generate political benefits than interdependence based on complementary trade.

7 1901 is a strong candidate for the end of the Anglo-American rivalry. Perkins (1968: 72) favors 1898 as the point after which the two states no longer saw themselves as competitors. Yet they remained competitive even after World War II, perhaps to 1956 and the Suez crisis. The question is when did they move down each other's rivalry schedules sufficiently to consider the rivalry terminated.

8 Gelber (1938/1966: 86) even describes the 1899–1901 years as a "state of experimentation" for British policy formulation.

9 This may not really be an entirely idiosyncratic factor. The low priority of North America and the virtual abandonment of the Canadians to their own defenses is a form of distancing oneself from a potential arena of conflict or, alternatively, a potential problem area of too little value to induce a continued presence. In general, it can be argued that the greater the distance between home bases, if not territorial boundaries, the less likely is militarized conflict between rivals (see Thompson, 1995). Thus, other things being equal, the pertinent distances meant that the Anglo-Dutch rivalry was more likely to become militarized than was the Venetian–Portuguese dyad.

11 PASSING THE TORCH IN A MANNER OF SPEAKING: THE SYSTEM LEADER LINEAGE

1 This study has benefitted from Kelly (1995a, 1995b) who explored some of these connections between system leaders.

2 See Bense (1924) for a detailed homage to Anglo-Dutch relations. The argument is updated by Haley (1988).

3 Although it could certainly be said that England did give birth to the United States. Nor would it be too much of a stretch to give the Dutch midwifery credit for the 1688 English revolution (see, for example, Israel, 1991).

REFERENCES

Abu-Lughod, Janet L. (1989) *Before European Hegemony: The World System, AD 1250–1350*. New York: Oxford University Press.

———(1993) "Discontinuities and Persistence: One World System or A Succession of Systems?," in Andre Gunder Frank and Barry K. Gills, eds., *The World System: Five Hundred Years or Five Thousand?* London: Routledge.

Adams, Richard E.W. (1991) *Prehistoric MesoAmerica*. rev. ed. Norman: University of Oklahoma Press.

Adams, Robert McC. (1974) "Anthropological Perspectives on Ancient Trade." *Current Anthropology* 15: 230–49.

Adshead, S.A.M. (1988) *China in World History*. New York: St. Martin's Press.

———(1993) *Central Asia in World History*. New York: St. Martin's Press.

Allen, P.M. (1988) "Evolution, Innovation, and Economics," in G. Dosi, C. Freeman, R. Nelson, G. Silverberg, and L. Soete, eds., *Technical Change and Economic Theory*. London: Pinter.

Amin, Samir (1993) "The Ancient World-Systems Versus the Modern Capitalist World-System," in Andre Gunder Frank and Barry K. Gills, eds., *The World System: Five Hundred Years or Five Thousand?*. London: Routledge.

Arrighi, Giovanni (1994) *The Long Twentieth Century*. New York: Verso Press.

Bagwell, Philip S. and G.E. Mingay (1970) *Britain and America: A Study of Economic Change, 1850–1939*. London: Routledge and Kegan Paul.

Bailey, Thomas A. (1958) *A Diplomatic History of the American People*, 7th ed. New York: Appleton-Century-Crofts.

Barfield, Thomas J. (1989) *The Perilous Frontier: Nomadic Empires and China, 221 BC to AD 1757*. Cambridge, Ma.: Blackwell.

Bartlett, C.J. (1992) *"The Special Relationship": A Political History of Anglo-American Relations Since 1945*. London: Longman.

Bartlett, Robert (1993) *The Making of Europe: Conquest, Colonization and Cultural Change, 950–1350*. Princeton, NJ: Princeton University Press.

Bayly, C.A. (1989) *Imperial Meridian: The British Empire and the World, 1780–1830*. London: Longman.

Begley, Sharon (1997) "Location, Location . . . A Real-Estate View of History's Winners and Losers". *Newsweek* June 16: 47.

Bense, Johan F. (1924) *The Anglo-Dutch Relations: From the Earliest Times to the Death of William the Third*. 'S-Gravenhage: Martinus Nijhoff.

Bentley, Jerry H. (1993) *Old World Encounters: Cross-Cultural Contacts and Exchanges in Pre-Modern Times*. New York: Oxford University Press.

Bergesen, Albert (1994) "Pre vs. Post 1500ers." *Comparative Civilizations Review* 30: 81–90.

Black, Jeremy (1986) *Natural and Necessary Enemies: Anglo-French Relations in the Eighteenth Century.* London: Duckworth.

—— (1991) *A Military Revolution? Military Change and European Society, 1550–1800.* Atlantic Highlands, NJ: Humanities Press International.

—— (1994b) *British Foreign Policy in an Age of Revolution, 1783–1793.* Cambridge: Cambridge University Press.

—— (1996) "Technology, Military Innovation, and Warfare." The First Annual Center for the Study of Force and Diplomacy Lecture, Department of History, Temple University, Philadelphia, March.

Blaut, J.M. (1992) "Fourteen Ninety-Two," in J.M. Blaut, ed., *1492: The Debate on Colonialism, Eurocentrism and History.* Trenton, NJ: African World Press.

—— (1993) *The Colonizer's Model of the World: Geographical Diffusionism and Eurocentric History.* New York: Guilford Press.

Blockmans, Wim P. (1994) "Voracious States and Obstructing Cities: An Aspect of State Formation in Preindustrial Europe," in Charles Tilly and Wim P. Blockmans, eds., *Cities and the Rise of States in Europe, AD 1000 to 1800.* Boulder, Co.: Westview.

Boswell, Terry and J. Misra (1997) "Cycles and Trends in the Early Capitalist World-Economy: An Analysis of Leading Sector Commodity Trade, 1500–1600/50–1750." *Review* 18: 45–86.

—— and J. Brueggemann (1991) "The Rise and Fall of Amsterdam and Dutch Hegemony: Evidence for the Baltic Sound Tolls, 1550–1750," in R. Kasaba, ed., *Cities in the World-System.* New York: Greenwood.

Bouchon, Genevieve and Denys Lombard (1987) "The Indian Ocean in the Fifteenth Century," in Ashin Das Gupta and M.N. Pearson, eds., *India and the Indian Ocean, 1500–1800.* Calcutta: Oxford University Press.

Boulding, K.E. (1981) *Evolutionary Economics.* Beverly Hills, CA.: Sage.

Bourne, Kenneth (1967) *Britain and the Balance of Power in North America, 1815–1908.* Berkeley: University of California Press.

—— (1970) *The Foreign Policy of Victorian England, 1830–1902.* Oxford: Clarendon Press.

Bousquet, Nicole (1980) "From Hegemony to Competition: Cycles of the Core?," in Terence K. Hopkins and Immanuel Wallerstein, eds., *Processes of the World-System.* Beverly Hills, Ca.: Sage.

Boxer, Charles R. (1972) *Four Centuries of Portuguese Expansion, 1415–1825: A Succinct Survey.* Berkeley: University of California Press.

Brady, Thomas A., Jr. (1991) "The rise of Merchant Empires, 1400–1700: A European Counterpoint," in James D. Tracy, ed., *The Political Economy of Merchant Empires.* Cambridge: Cambridge University Press.

Braudel, Fernand (1982) *The Wheels of Commerce,* translated by Sian Reynolds. New York: Harper and Row.

—— (1984) *The Perspective of the World,* translated by Sian Reynolds. New York: Harper and Row.

Brauer, K.J. (1984) "1821–1860: Economics and the Diplomacy of American Expansionism," in William H. Becker and Samuel F. Wells, Jr., eds., *Economics and World Power: An Assessment of American Diplomacy Since 1789.* New York: Columbia University Press.

Brawley, Mark R. (1993) *Liberal Leadership: Great Powers and Their Challengers in Peace and War.* Ithaca, NY: Cornell University Press.

Burt, A.L. (1961) *The United States, Great Britain and British North America*. New York: Russell and Russell.

Cady, John F. (1964) *Southeast Asia: Its Historical Development*. New York: McGraw-Hill.

Cameron, Ian (1990) *Kingdom of the Sun God: A History of the Andes and Their People*. New York: Facts on File.

Campbell, Charles S. (1974) *From Revolution to Rapprochement: The United States and Great Britain, 1783–1900*. New York: John Wiley.

Cantwell, John (1989) *Technological Innovation and Multinational Corporations*. Cambridge, Ma.: Blackwell.

Carter, Alice Clare (1975) *Getting, Spending and Investing in Early Modern TImes: Essays on Dutch, English, and Huguenot Economic History*. Assen, the Netherlands: Van Gorcum.

Chamberlain, Muriel E. (1988) *Pax Britannica? British Foreign Policy, 1789–1914*. New York: Longman.

Chase-Dunn, Christopher (1989) *Global Formation: Structures of the World-Economy*. New York: Basil Blackwell.

———— and Tom Hall (1997) *Rise and Demise: Comparing World Systems*. Boulder, Co.: Westview.

Chaudhuri, K.N. (1985) *Trade and Civilisation in the Indian Ocean: An Economic History from the Rise of Islam to 1750*. Cambridge: Cambridge University Press.

Chesneaux, Jean, Marianne Bastid, and Marie-Claire Bergere (1976) *China from the Opium Wars to the 1911 Revolution*, translated by Anne Destenay. New York: Pantheon.

Christie, Ian R. (1982) *War and Revolutions: Britain, 1760–1815*. Cambridge, Ma.: Harvard University Press.

Cipolla, Carlo M. (1965) *Guns, Sails and Empires: Technological Innovation and the Early Phases of European Expansion, 1400–1700*. New York: Minerva Press.

Clark, George N. (1931) *The Seventeenth Century*. Oxford: Clarendon Press.

Clark, N. and C. Juma (1987) *Long-Run Economics: An Evolutionary Approach to Economic Growth*. London: Pinter.

Cole, Charles W. (1939) *Colbert and a Century of French Mercantilism*, 2 vols. New York: Columbia University Press.

Constant, E.W. II (1980) *The Origins of the Turbojet Revolution*. Baltimore: The Johns Hopkins University Press.

Conybeare, John A.C. (1987) *Trade Wars: The Theory and Practice of International Commercial Rivalry*. New York: Columbia University Press.

Crawford, Martin (1987) *The Anglo-American Crisis of the Mid-Nineteenth Century: The Times and America, 1850–1862*. Athens: University of Georgia Press.

Crone, Patricia (1989) *Pre-Industrial Societies*. Cambridge, Ma.: Basil Blackwell.

Curtin, Philip D. (1984) *Cross-Sultural Trade in World History*. Cambridge: Cambridge University Press.

D'Lugo, David and Ronald Rogowski (1993) "The Anglo-German Naval Race and Comparative Constitutional 'Fitness'," in Richard Rosecrance and Arthur A. Stein, eds., *The Domestic Bases of Grand Strategy*. Ithaca: Cornell University Press.

Das Gupta, Arun (1987) "The Maritime Trade of Indonesia: 1500–1800," in Ashin Das Gupta and M.N. Pearson, eds., *India and the Indiana Ocean, 1500–1800*. Calcutta: Oxford University Press.

David, P.A. (1993) "Historical Economics in the Longrun: Some Implications of Path-Dependence," in G.D. Snooks, ed., *Historical Analysis in Economics*. London: Routledge.

Davies, Nigel (1995) *The Incas*. Niwot: University Press of Colorado.

Davis, L.E. and R.T. Cull (1994) *International Capital Markets and American Economic Growth, 1820–1914.* Cambridge: Cambridge University Press.

Dehing, Pit and Marjolein 'T Hart (1997) "Linking the Fortunes: Currency and Banking, 1550–1800," in Marjolein 'T Hart, Joost Jonker and Jan Luiten Van Zanden, eds., *A Financial History of the Netherlands.* Cambridge: Cambridge University Press.

Dehio, Ludwig (1962) *The Precarious Balance.* New York: Vintage.

Diamond, Jared (1997) *Guns, Germs and Steel: The Fates of Human Societies.* New York: Norton.

Diffie, Bailey W. and George D. Winius (1977) *Foundations of the Portuguese Empire, 1415–1580.* Minneapolis: University of Minnesota Press.

Dobson, Alan P. (1995) *Anglo-American Relations in the Twentieth Century: Of Friendship, Conflict and the Rise and Decline of Superpowers.* New York: Routledge.

Doran, Charles F. (1991) *Systems in Crisis.* Cambridge: Cambridge University Press.

Doyle, Michael (1986) "Liberalism and World Politics." *American Political Science Review* 80: 1151–69.

Eberhard, Wolfram (1977) *A History of China,* rev. 4th ed. Berkeley: University of California Press.

Ekholm, K. and J. Friedman (1993) " 'Capital' Imperialism and Exploitation in Ancient World Systems," in Andre Gunder Frank and Barry K. Gills, eds., *The World System: Five Hundred Years or Five Thousand?* London: Routledge.

Eldredge, N. (1985) *Time Frames: The Evolution of Punctuated Equilibria.* Princeton, NJ: Princeton University Press.

Elliott, John (1980) "The Spanish Conquest and Settlement of America," in Leslie Bethell, ed., *The Cambridge History of Latin America, Vol. 1: Colonial Latin America.* Cambridge: Cambridge University Press.

Elman, Colin and Miriam Fendius Elman (1997) "Diplomatic History and International Relations Theory: Respecting Difference and Crossing Boundaries." *International Security* 22: 5–21.

Elvin, Mark (1973) *The Pattern of the Chinese Past.* Stanford, Ca.: Stanford University Press.

Emmott, Bill (1989) *The Sun Also Sets: The Limits of Japan's Economic Power.* New York: Simon and Schuster.

England, R.W. (1994) "On Economic Growth and Resource Scarcity: Lessons from Non-equilibrium Thermodynamics," in R. England, ed., *Evolutionary Concepts in Contemporary Economics.* Ann Arbor: University of Michigan Press.

Fairbank, John K. (1978) "The Creation of the Treaty System," in John K. Fairbank, ed., *The Cambridge History of China, Vol. 10: Late Ch'ing, 1800–1911,* Part 1. Cambridge: Cambridge University Press.

Ferris, John R. (1991) "'The Greatest Power on Earth': Great Britain in the 1920s." *International History Review* 13: 726–50.

Field, James A. (1984) "1789–1820: All Economists, All Diplomats," in William H. Becker and Samuel F. Wells, Jr., eds., *Economics and World Power: An Assessment of American Diplomacy Since 1789.* New York: Columbia University Press.

Flannery, Kent V. and Joyce Marcus, eds. (1983) *The Cloud People: Divergent Evolution of the Zapotec and Mixtec Civilizations.* New York: Academic Press.

Fox, E.W. (1971) *History in Geographic Perspective.* New York: W.W. Norton.

Frank, Andre Gunder (1978) *World Accumulation, 1492–1789.* New York: Monthly Review Press.

———— (1998) *Global Development: The Silver Age of China, 1400–1800*. Berkeley: University of California Press.

Frederick, Suzanne Y. (1989) *Policy For Power: The Role of Foreign Economic Policy in the German and Japanese Challenges to World Leadership*. Ph.D. dissertation. Claremont, Ca.: Claremont Graduate School.

———— (1999) "The Anglo-German Rivalry, 1890–1914," in William R. Thompson, ed., *Great Power Rivalries*. Columbia: University of South Carolina Press.

Freeman, C. and C. Perez (1988) "Structural Crises of Adjustment: Business Cycles and Investment Behaviour," in G. Dosi, C. Freeman, R. Nelson, G. Silverberg, and L. Soete, eds., *Technical Change and Economic Theory*. London: Pinter.

Friedman, George and Meredith Lebard (1991) *The Coming War with Japan*. New York: St. Martin's Press.

Furber, Holden (1976) *Rival Empires of Trade in the Orient, 1600–1800*. Minneapolis: University of Minnesota Press.

Gaddis, John Lewis (1997) "History, Theory and Common Ground." *International Security* 22: 75–85.

Galbraith, James K. (1989) *Balancing Acts: Technology, Finance and the American Future*. New York: Basic Books.

Gallagher, John and Ronald Robinson (1953) "The Imperialism of Free Trade." *Economic History Review*, 2nd ser., 6: 1–25.

Gardiner, C. Harvey (1956) *Naval Power in the Conquest of Mexico*. Austin: University of Texas Press.

Garten, Jeffrey E. (1992) *A Cold Peace: America, Japan, Germany, and the Struggle for Supremacy*. New York: Random House.

Gelber, Lionel (1938/1966) *The Rise of Anglo-American Friendship: A Study in World Politics, 1898–1906*. Hamden, Ct.: Archon Books.

George, Alexander L. (1997) "Knowledge for Statecraft: The Challenge for Political Science and History." *International Security* 22: 44–52.

Gernet, Jacques (1982) *A History of Chinese Civilization*, translated by J.R. Foster. Cambridge: Cambridge University Press.

Gibbs, H.A.R. (1935/1971) "English Crusaders in Portugal," in Edgar Prestage, ed., *Chapters in Anglo-Portuguese Relations*. Westport, Ct.: Greenwood.

Gills, Barry (1993) "The Hegemonic Transition in East Asia: A Historical Perspective," in Stephen Gill, *Gramsci, Historical Materialism and International Relations*. Cambridge: Cambridge University Press.

———— (1993) "Hegemonic Transitions in the World System," in Andre Gunder Frank and Barry K. Gills, eds., *The World System: Five Hundred Years or Five Thousand?* London: Routledge.

———— and Andre Gunder Frank (1993) "World System Cycles, Crises, and Hegemonic Shifts, 1700 BC to 1700 AD," in Andre Gunder Frank and Barry K. Gills, eds., *The World System: Five Hundred Years or Five Thousand?* London: Routledge.

Gilpin, Robert (1975) *U.S. Power and the Multinational Corporation*. New York: Basic Books.

———— (1981) *War and Change in World Politics*. Cambridge: Cambridge University Press.

———— (1987) *The Political Economy of International Relations*. Princeton: Princeton University Press.

Glete, Jan (1993) *Navies and Nations: Warships, Navies and State Building in Europe and America, 1500–1860*. Stockholm: Almquist.

Goldstein, Joshua (1988) *Long Cycles: Prosperity and War in the Modern Age*. New Haven, Ct.: Yale University Press.

——— and David P. Rapkin (1991) "After Insularity: Hegemony and the Future World Order." *Futures* 23: 935–59.

Goldstone, Jack A. (1991) *Revolution and Rebellion in the Early Modern World*. Berkeley: University of California Press.

Gooch, John (1994) "The Weary Titan: Strategy and Policy in Great Britain, 1890–1918," in Williamson Murray, MacGregor Knox, and Alvin Bernstein, eds., *The Making of Strategy, Rulers, States, and War*. Cambridge: Cambridge University Press.

Gould, S.J. (1987) *Time's Arrow, Time's Cycle: Myth and Metaphor in the Discovery of Geological Time*. Cambridge, Ma.: Harvard University Press.

Gray, Colin S. (1992) *The Leverage of Sea Power*. New York: Free Press.

Guilmartin, John F., Jr. (1991) "The Cutting Edge: An Analysis of the Spanish Invasion and Overthrow of the Inca Empire, 1532–1539," in Kenneth J. Andrien and Relena Adorno, eds., *Transatlantic Encounters: Europeans and Andeans in the Sixteenth Century*. Berkeley: University of California Press.

——— (1995) "The Military Revolution: Origins and First Tests Abroad," in Clifford J. Rogers, ed., *The Military Revolution Debate: Readings on the Military Transformation of Early Modern Europe*. Boulder, Co.: Westview.

Haber, Stephen H., David M. Kennedy, and Stephen D. Krasner (1997) "Brothers Under the Skin: Diplomatic History and International Relations." *International Security* 22: 34–43.

Haley, K.H.D. (1988) *The British & the Dutch*. London: George Philip.

Hall, D.G.E. (1964) *A History of South-East Asia*. London: Macmillan.

Hall, John A. (1985) *Powers and Liberties: The Causes and Consequences of the Rise of the West*. Oxford: Blackwell.

——— (1988) "States and Societies: The Miracle in Comparative Perspective," in J. Baechler, J.A. Hall, and M. Mann, eds., *Europe and the Rise of Capitalism*. Oxford: Blackwell.

Hall, Peter and Paschal Preston (1988) *The Carrier Wave: New Information Technology and the Geography of Innovation, 1846–2003*. London: Unwin Hyman.

Hall, Thomas D. (1991) "The Role of Nomads in Core/Periphery Relations," in Christopher Chase-Dunn and Thomas D. Hall, eds., *Core-Periphery Relations in Precapitalist Worlds*. Boulder, Co.: Westview.

Hassig, Ross (1988) *Aztec Warfare: Imperial and Political Control*. Norman: University of Oklahoma Press.

Headrick, Daniel, R. (1981) *The Tools of Empire: Technology and European Imperialism in the Nineteenth Century*. New York: Oxford University Press.

Heathcote, T.A. (1995) *The Military in British India: The Development of British Land Forces in South Asia, 1600–1947*. Manchester: University of Manchester Press.

Heckscher, Eli F. (1964) *The Continental System: An Economic Interpretation*, edited by Harald Westergaard. Gloucester, Ma.: Peter Smith.

Hemming, John (1970) *The Conquest of the Incas*. London: Macmillan.

Hess, Andrew C. (1978) *The Forgotten Frontier: A History of the Sixteenth-Century Ibero-African Frontier*. Chicago: University of Chicago Press.

Hodges, Richard (1982) *Dark Age Economics: The Origins of Towns and Trade, AD 600–1000*. New York: St. Martin's Press.

——— and David Whitehouse (1983) *Mohammed, Charlemagne and the Origins of Europe: Archaeology and the Pirenne Thesis*. Ithaca, NY: Cornell University Press.

Hodgson, G.M. (1994) "Precursors of Modern Evolutionary Economics: Marx, Marshall, Veblen, and Schumpeter," in R. England, ed., *Evolutionary Concepts in Contemporary Economics*. Ann Arbor: University of Michigan Press.

Hodgson, Marshall G.S. (1974) *The Venture of Islam: Conscience and History in a World Civilization: The Expansion of Islam in the Middle Periods*, Vol. 2. Chicago, Ill.: University of Chicago Press.

——— (1993) *Rethinking World History: Essays in Europe, Islam, and World History*, edited by Edmund Burke III. Cambridge: Cambridge University Press.

Hopkins, Keith (1978) *Conquerors and Slaves*. Cambridge: Cambridge University Press.

Horsman, Reginald (1962) *The Causes of the War of 1812*. Philadelphia: University of Pennsylvania Press.

Hugill, Peter J. (1993) *World Trade Since 1431: Geography, Technology, and Capitalism*. Baltimore, Md.: Johns Hopkins University Press.

Ibn Khaldun (1967) *The Muqaddimah: An Introduction to History*, translated by Franz Rosenthal. London: Routledge and Kegan Paul.

Ingram, Edward (1997) "The Wonderland of the Political Scientist." *International Security* 22: 53–63.

——— (1999a) "Great Britain and Russia," in William R. Thompson, ed., *Great Power Rivalries*. Columbia: University of South Carolina Press.

——— (1999b) "Hegemony, Global Power and World Power: Britain II as World Leader," in Colin Elman and Miriam F. Elman, eds., *International History and International Relations Theory: Bridges and Boundarie*s. Cambridge, Ma.: MIT Press.

Israel, Jonathan I. (1989) *Dutch Primacy in World Trade, 1585–1740*. Oxford: Clarendon Press.

——— (1991) "The Dutch Role in the Glorious Revolution," in Jonathan I. Israel, ed., *The Anglo-Dutch Moment: Essays on the Glorious Revolution and Its World Impact.* Cambridge: Cambridge University Press.

Jones, E.L. (1981) *The European Miracle*. Cambridge: Cambridge University Press.

——— (1988) *Growth Recurring: Economic Change in World History*. Oxford: Clarendon Press.

Jones, Howard (1992) *Union in Peril: The Crisis Over British Intervention in the Civil War*. Chapel Hill: University of North Carolina Press.

Jones, James R. (1980) *Britain and the World, 1649–1816*. Atlantic Highlands, NJ: Humanities Press.

Jones, Susan M. and Philip A. Kuhn (1978) "Dynastic Decline and the Roots of Rebellion," in John K. Fairbank, ed., *The Cambridge History of China, Vol. 10: Late Ch'ing, 1800–1911*, Part 1. Cambridge: Cambridge University Press.

Jones, Wilbur D. (1974) *The American Problem in British Diplomacy, 1841–1861*. London: Macmillan.

Kathirithamby-Wells, Jeyamalar (1993) "Restraints on the Development of Merchant Capitalism in Southeast Asia before c. 1800," in Anthony Reid, ed., *Southeast Asia in the Early Modern Era: Trade, Power, and Belief.* Ithaca, NY: Cornell University Press.

Katzenstein, Peter J. and Nobuo Okawara (1993) "Japan's National Security: Structures, Norms, and Policies." *International Security* 17: 84–118.

Kelly, D.S. (1995a) "The Mediterranean Origins of Leadership Long Cycles: Venetian–Genoese Rivalry and the Rise of Portugal as a Global Power." Paper delivered at the annual meeting of the International Studies Association, Chicago, Illinois, February.

——— (1995b) "International Finance and Global Leadership Transitions." Unpublished manuscript, Department of Political Science, Indiana University.

Kennedy, Paul (1976) *The Rise and Fall of British Naval Mastery.* New York: Scribners' Sons.

———(1980) *The Rise of the Anglo-German Antagonism, 1860–1914.* London: Allen and Unwin.

———(1983) *Strategy and Diplomacy, 1870–1945.* London: Allen and Unwin.

———(1987) *The Rise and Fall of the Great Powers.* New York: Random House.

Knecht, R.J. (1982) *Francis I.* Cambridge: Cambridge University Press.

Kugler, Jacek and Douglas Lemke, eds. (1996) *Parity and War.* Ann Arbor: University of Michigan Press.

Ladd, Everett C. and Karlyn H. Bowman (1996) *Public Opinion in American and Japan: How We See Each Other and Ourselves.* Washington, D.C.: American Enterprise Institute Press.

Ladurie, Emmanuel Le Roy (1987) *The Royal French State, 1410–1610.* Cambridge, Ma: Blackwell.

Landes, David S. (1998) *The Wealth and Poverty of Nations: Why Some are so Rich and Some so Poor.* New York: W.W. Norton.

Lane, Frederic C. (1987) "Recent Studies in the Economic History of Venice," in B.G. Kohl and K.C. Mueller, eds., *Studies in Venetian Social and Economic History.* London: Variorum Reprints.

Lawford, James P. (1978) *Britain's Army in India: From Its Origins to the Conquest of Bengal.* London: George Allen and Unwin.

Levy, Jack S. (1997) "Too Important to Leave to the Other: History and Political Science in the Study of International Relations." *International Security* 22: 22–33.

——— and Salvatore Ali (1998) "From Commercial Competition to Strategic Rivalry to War: The Evolution of the Anglo-Dutch Rivalry, 1609–52," in Paul F. Diehl, ed., *The Dynamics of Enduring Rivalries.* Urbana: University of Illinois Press.

———(1999) "Economic Competition, Domestic Politics, and Systemic Change," in William R. Thompson, ed., *Great Power Rivalries.* Columbia: University of South Carolina Press.

Lewis, Archibald R. (1988) *Nomads and Crusaders, AD 1000–1368.* Bloomington: Indiana University Press.

Lloyd, T.O. (1984) *The British Empire, 1558–1983.* Oxford: Oxford University Press.

Lodge, Richard (1935/1971) "The Treaties of 1703," in Edgar Prestage, ed., *Chapters in Anglo-Portuguese Relations.* Westport, Ct.: Greenwood.

Long, Robert E. (1990) *Japan and the U.S.* New York: H.W. Wilson.

Lyall, Alfred C. (1910) *The Rise and Expansion of the British Dominion in India*, 5th ed. London: Routledge and Kegan Paul.

Mackinder, Halford (1962) *Democratic Ideals and Reality.* New York: Norton.

Mahan, Alfred T. (1890) *The Influence of Sea Power upon History, 1660–1783.* Boston: Little, Brown.

Mann, Michael (1986) *The Sources of Social Power*, Vol. 1. Cambridge: Cambridge University Press.

———(1988) "European Development: Approaching a Historical Explanation," in J. Baechler, J.A. Hall, and M. Mann, eds., *Europe and the Rise of Capitalism.* Oxford: Blackwell.

Martel, Gordon (1991) "The Meaning of Power: Rethinking the Decline and Fall of Great Britain." *International History Review* 13: 662–94.

Maslowski, Peter (1994) "To the Edge of Greatness: The United States, 1783–1865," in Williamson Murray, MacGregor Knox, and Alvin Bernstein, eds., *The Making of Strategy: Rulers, States, and War.* Cambridge: Cambridge University Press.

Mayr, E. (1991) *One Long Argument: Charles Darwin and the Genesis of Modern Evolutionary Thought*. Cambridge, Ma.: Harvard University Press.

McAlister, Lyle N. (1984) *Spain and Portugal in the New World, 1492–1700*. Minneapolis: University of Minnesota Press.

McEvedy, Colin and Richard Jones (1978) *Atlas of World Population History*. New York: Facts on File.

McKercher, B.J.C. (1991) "'Our Most Dangerous Enemy': Great Britain Pre-eminent in the 1930s." *International History Review* 13: 751–83.

McNeill, William H. (1963) *The Rise of the West*. Chicago, IL.: University of Chicago Press.

—— (1976) *Plagues and Peoples*. New York: Doubleday.

—— (1982) *The Pursuit of Power*. Chicago, Il.: University of Chicago Press.

—— (1992) *The Global Condition: Conquerors, Catastrophes and Community*. Princeton, NJ: Princeton University Press.

Meinig, D.W. (1986) *The Shaping of America: A Geographical Perspective on 500 Years of History: Atlantic America, 1492–1800*, Vol. 1. New Haven, Ct.: Yale University Press.

Mensch, Gerhard (1979) *Stalemate in Technology: Innovations Overcome the Depression*. Cambridge, Ma.: Ballinger.

Midlarsky, Manus (1988) *The Onset of World War*. Boston: Unwin Hyman.

Mitchell, Brian R. (1980) *European Historical Statistics, 1750–1975*. New York: Facts on File.

—— (1993) *International Historical Statistics: The Americas, 1750–1988*. New York: Stockton Press.

Modelski, George (1979) "International Content and Performance Among the World's Largest Corporations," in George Modelski, ed., *Transnational Corporations and World Order: Readings in International Political Economy*. San Francisco, Ca.: W.H. Freeman.

—— (1987) *Long Cycles in World Politics*. London: Macmillan.

—— (1990) "Is World Politics Evolutionary Learning?" *International Organization* 44: 1–24.

—— (1996) "Evolutionary Paradigm for Global Politics." *International Studies Quarterly* 40: 621–42.

—— (1999) "Enduring Rivalry in the Democratic Lineage: The Venice-Portugal Case," in William R. Thompson, ed., *Great Power Rivalries*. Columbia, University of South Carolina Press.

—— and Sylvia Modelski (1988) *Documenting Global Leadership*. London: Macmillan.

Modelski, G. and W.R. Thompson (1988) *Seapower in Global Politics, 1494–1993*. London: Macmillan.

—— (1996) *Leading Sectors and World Powers: The Coevolution of Global Politics and World Economics*. Columbia: University of South Carolina Press.

Moon, Penderel (1989) *The British Conquest and Dominion of India*. London: Duckworth.

Morillo, Stephen (1995) "Guns and Government: A Comparative Study of Europe and Japan." *Journal of World History* 6: 75–106.

Murra, John V. (1986) "The Expansion of the Inka State: Armies, War and Rebellions," John V. Murra, Nathan Wachtel, and Jacques Revel, eds., *Anthropological History of the Andean Polities*. Cambridge: Cambridge University Press.

Neilson, Keith (1991) "'Greatly Exaggerated': The Myth of the Decline of Great Britain before 1914." *International History Review* 13: 695–725.

Nelson, R.R. (1994) "The Coevolution of Technologies and Institutions," in R. England, ed., *Evolutionary Concepts in Contemporary Economics*. Ann Arbor: University of Michigan Press.

———and S. Winter (1982) *An Evolutionary Theory of Economic Change.* Cambridge, Ma.: Harvard University Press.

Nicholas, David (1992) *Medieval Flanders.* London: Longman.

Norgaard, R.B. (1994) "The Coevolution of Economics and Environmental Systems and the Emergence of Unsustainability," in R. England, ed., *Evolutionary Concepts in Contemporary Economics.* Ann Arbor: University of Michigan Press.

North, Douglas C. and Robert P. Thomas (1973) *The Rise of the Western World: A New Economic History.* Cambridge: Cambridge University Press.

Orde, Anne (1996) *The Eclipse of Great Britain: The United States and the British Imperial Decline, 1895–1956.* New York: St. Martin's Press.

Organski, A.F.K. (1958/1968) *World Politics.* New York: Alfred Knopf.

———and Jacek Kugler (1980) *The War Ledger.* Chicago, Il.: University of Chicago Press.

Padden, R.C. (1967) *The Hummingbird and the Hawk: Conquest and Sovereignty in the Valley of Mexico, 1503–1541.* Columbus: Ohio State University Press.

Palin, R. (1992) "The European Miracle of Capital Accumulation," in J.M. Blaut, ed., *The Debate on Colonialism, Eurocentrism, and History.* Trenton, NJ: African World Press.

Parker, Geoffrey (1988/1996) *The Military Revolution: Military Innovation and the Rise of the West, 1500–1800.* Cambridge: Cambridge University Press.

———(1995) "In Defense of the Military Revolution," in Clifford J. Rogers, ed., *The Military Revolution Debate: Readings in the Military Transformation of Early Modern Europe.* Boulder, Co.: Westview.

Parry, John H. (1966) *The Establishment of the European Hegemony, 1415–1715,* rev. 3rd ed. New York: Harper and Row.

———(1971) *Trade and Dominion: The European Overseas Empires in the Eighteenth Century.* New York: Praeger.

Pearson, M.N. (1976) *Merchants and Rulers in Gujerat: The Response to the Portuguese in the Sixteenth Century.* Berkeley: University of California Press.

———(1987) *The New Cambridge History of India: The Portuguese in India.* Cambridge: Cambridge University Press.

———(1987) "India and the Indian Ocean in the Sixteenth Century," in Ashin Das Gupta and M.N. Pearson, eds., *India and the Indian Ocean, 1500–1800.* Calcutta: Oxford University Press.

———(1991) "Merchants and States," in James D. Tracy, ed., *The Political Economy of Merchant Empires: State Power and World Trade, 1350–1750.* Cambridge: Cambridge University Press.

Perkins, Bradford (1968) *The Great Rapprochement: England and the United States, 1895–1914.* New York: Atheneum.

Pollins, B. (1993) "Global Capital: Two Financial Booms Compared." Unpublished paper, Mershon Center, Ohio State University.

Powelson, John P. (1994) *Centuries of Economic Endeavor.* Ann Arbor: University of Michigan Press.

Prestage, Edgar (1935/1971) "The Treaties of 1642, 1654 and 1661," in Edgar Prestage, ed., *Chapters in Anglo-Portuguese Relations.* Westport, Ct.: Greenwood.

Rapkin, David P. (1990) "Japan and World Leadership?," in David P. Rapkin, ed., *World Leadership and Hegemony.* Boulder, Co.: Lynne Rienner.

Rasler, K.A. and W.R. Thompson (1989) *War and State Making: The Shaping of the Global Powers.* Boston: Unwin Hyman/London: Routledge.

———— (1991) "Technological Innovation, Capability Positional Shifts and Systemic War." *Journal of Conflict Resolution* 35: 273–294.

———— (1994) *The Great Powers and Global Struggle, 1490–1990.* Lexington: University Press of Kentucky.

Reid, Anthony (1993) *Southeast Asia in the Age of Commerce, 1450–1680, Vol. 2: Expansion and Crisis.* New Haven, Ct.: Yale University Press.

Reuveny, Raphael and William R. Thompson (1997) "War, Systemic Leadership and Economic Growth: The United States Case." Paper delivered at the annual meeting of the Peace Science Society (International), Indianapolis, Indiana, November.

Richards, John F. (1993) *The New Cambridge History of India: The Mughal Empire.* Cambridge: Cambridge University Press.

Ricklefs, M.C. (1993) *A History of Modern Indonesia Since c. 1300,* 2nd ed. Stanford: Stanford University Press.

Rock, Stephen (1989) *Why Peace Breaks Out: Great Power Rapprochement in Historical Perspective.* Chapel Hill: University of North Carolina Press.

Rogers, Clifford J. (1995) *The Military Revolution Debate: Readings on the Military Transformation of Early Modern Europe.* Boulder: Westview Press.

Rosecrance, Richard N. (1986) *The Rise of the Trading State.* New York: Basic Books.

Rosenberg, Nathan and L.E. Birdzell, Jr. (1986) *How the West Grew Rich: The Economic Transformation of the Industrial World.* New York: Basic Books.

Rostow, Walt W. (1978) *The World Economy: History and Prospects.* Austin: University of Texas Press.

Russett, Bruce (1963) *Community and Contention: Britain and America in the Twentieth Century.* Cambridge, Ma.: MIT Press.

Samuels, W.J., A.A. Schmidt, and J.D. Shaffer (1994) "An Evolutionary Approach to Law and Economics," in R. England, ed., *Evolutionary Concepts in Contemporary Economics.* Ann Arbor: University of Michigan Press.

Sanderson, Stephen K. (1994) "Expanding World Commercialization: The Link Between World-Systems and Civilizations." *Comparative Civilizations Review* 30: 91–103.

Scammell, G.V. (1981) *The World Encompassed: The First European Maritime Empires, c. 800–1650.* Berkeley: University of California Press.

Schneider, Jane (1977) "Was There a Precapitalist World-System?" *Peasant Studies* 6: 20–29.

Schroeder, Paul W. (1997) "History and International Relations Theory: Not Use or Abuse, but Fit or Misfit." *International Security* 22: 64–74.

Schumpeter, Joseph (1939) *Business Cycles: A Theoretical, Historical and Statistical Analysis of the Capitalist Process,* 2 vols. New York: McGraw Hill.

Schweinitz, Karl de (1983) *The Rise and Fall of British India: Imperialism as Inequality.* New York: Methuen.

Sen, Gautam (1984) *The Military Origins of Industrialization and International Trade Rivalry.* London: Frances Pinter.

Small, Melvin (1980) *Was War Necessary?: National Security and U.S. Entry into War.* Beverly Hills, Ca.: Sage.

Snooks, G.D. (1993a) *Economics Without Time: A Science Blind to the Forces of Historical Change.* Ann Arbor: University of Michigan Press.

———— (1993b) "The Lost Dimension: Limitations of a Timeless Economics," in G.D. Snooks, ed., *Historical Analysis in Economics.* London: Routledge.

———— (1996) *The Dynamic Society: Exploring the Sources of Global Change.* New York: Routledge.

Steele, Ian K. (1994) *Warpaths: Invasions of North America*. New York: Oxford University Press.

Steensgaard, Niels (1990) "The Growth and Composition of the Long-Distance Trade of England and the Dutch Republic Before 1750," in James D. Tracy, ed., *The Rise of Merchant Empires: Long-Distance Trade in the Early Modern World, 1350–1750*. Cambridge: Cambridge University Press.

Stopford, John M. and Susan Strange with John S. Henley (1991) *Rival States, Rival Firms: Competition for World Market Shares*. Cambridge: Cambridge University Press.

Subrahmanyam, Sanjay (1993) *The Portuguese Empire in Asia, 1500–1700: A Political and Economic History*. London: Longman.

Swanson, Bruce (1982) *Eighth Voyage of the Dragon: A History of China's Quest for Seapower*. Annapolis, Md.: Naval Institute Press.

Taagepera, Rein (1997) "Expansion and Contraction Patterns of Large Polities: Context for Russia." *International Studies Quarterly* 41: 475–504.

Tapie, Victor -L. (1984) *France in the Age of Louis XIII and Richelieu*, translated and edited by D. McN. Lockie. Cambridge: Cambridge University Press.

Thomaz, Luis F.F.R. (1993) "The Malay Sultanate of Melaka," in Anthony Reid, ed., *Southeast Asia in the Early Modern Era: Trade, Power, and Belief*. Ithaca, NY: Cornell University Press.

Thompson, William R. (1983) "Interstate Wars, Global Wars, and the Cool Hand Luke Syndrome: A Reply to Chase-Dunn and Sokolovsky." *International Studies Quarterly* 27: 369–74.

———— (1988) *On Global War: Historical-Structural Perspectives on World Politics*. Columbia: University of South Carolina Press.

———— (1990) "Long Waves, Technological Innovation, and Relative Decline." *International Organization* 35: 201–233.

———— (1992) "Long Cycles and the Geohistorical Context of Structural Transitions." *World Politics* 43: 195–223.

———— (1995) "Principal Rivalries." *Journal of Conflict Resolution* 39: 195–223.

———— (1997/1998) "The Anglo-German Rivalry and the 1939 Failure-of-Deterrence." *Security Studies* 7: 58–97.

———— (1999) "The Evolution of a Great Power Rivalry: The Anglo-American Case," in William R. Thompson, ed., *Great Power Rivalries*. Columbia: University of South Carolina Press.

———— and Karen Rasler (1999) "War, The Military Revolution(s) Controversy, and Army Expansion: A Test of Two Explanations of Historical Influences on European State Making." *Comparative Political Studies* 32: 3–31.

Thompson, William R. and Gary Zuk (1986) "World Power and the Strategic Trap of Territorial Commitments." *International Studies Quarterly* 30: 249–67.

Thurow, Lester (1992) *Head to Head: The Coming Economic Battle Among Japan, Europe, and America*. New York: Warner Books.

Tilly, Charles (1990) *Coercion, Capital and European States, AD 990–1990*. Cambridge, Ma: Blackwell.

Totman, Conrad (1993) *Early Modern Japan*. Berkeley: University of California Press.

Wachtel, Nathan (1980) "The Indian and the Spanish Conquest," in Leslie Bethell, ed., *The Cambridge History of Latin America, Vol. 1: Colonial Latin America*. Cambridge: Cambridge University Press.

Wakeman, Frederic, Jr. (1978) "The Canton Trade and the Opium War," in John K. Fairbank, ed., *The Cambridge History of China, Vol. 10: Late Ch'ing, 1800–1911*, Part I. Cambridge: Cambridge University Press.

Waldron, Arthur (1994) "Chinese Strategy from the Fourteenth to the Seventeenth Centuries," in Williamson Murray, McGregor Knox, and Alvin Bernstein, eds., *The Making of Strategy: Rulers, States and War*. Cambridge: Cambridge University Press.

Wallerstein, Immanuel (1984) *The Politics of the World-Economy*. Cambridge: Cambridge University Press.

——— (1989) *The Modern World-System III: The Second Era of Great Expansion of the Capitalist World-Economy, 1730–1840s*. Sand Diego: Academic Press.

——— (1991) "Japan and the Future Trajectory of the World-System: Lessons From History," in Immanuel Wallerstein, ed., *Geopolitics and Geoculture*. Cambridge: Cambridge University Press.

——— (1993) "World System Versus World-Systems: A Critique," in Andre Gunder Frank and Barry K. Gills, eds., *The World System: Five Hundred Years or Five Thousand*. London: Routledge.

Waltz, Kenneth N. (1979) *Theory of International Politics*. Reading, Ma.: Addison-Wesley.

Weber, Max (1958) *The Protestant Ethic and the Spirit of Capitalism*. New York: Scribners'.

Wernham, R.B. (1966) *Before the Armada: The Emergence of the English Nation, 1485–1588, 1588–1595*. Oxford: Oxford University Press.

Wheeler, Douglas L. and Rene Pelissier (1971) *Angola*. New York: Praeger.

Wilkinson, David (1993a) "Civilizations, Cores, World Economies, and Oikemenes," in Andre Gunder Frank and Barry K. Gills, eds., *The World System: Five Hundred Years or Five Thousand*. London: Routledge.

——— (1993b) "Cities, Civilizations and Oikumenes: II." *Comparative Civilizations Review* 28: 41–73.

Williams, C.H. (1935/1971) "The Expedition of John of Gaunt to the Peninsula," in Edgar Prestage, ed., *Chapters in Anglo-Portuguese Relations*. Westport, Ct.: Greenwood.

Williams, J., M.D. McGinnis, and J.C. Thomas (1994) "Breaking the War-Economy Link," *International Interactions* 20: 169–88.

Wilson, Charles H. (1957) *Profit and Power: A Study of England and the Dutch Wars*. London: Longmans, Green and Co.

——— (1970) *Queen Elizabeth and the Revolt of the Netherlands*. Berkeley: University of California Press.

Wolpert, Stanley (1997) *A New History of India*, 5th ed. New York: Oxford University Press.

Wright, Leitch, Jr. (1975) *Britain and the American Frontier, 1783–1815*. Athens: University of Georgia Press.

Yakovets, Yuri V. (1994) "Scientific and Technical Cycles: Analysis and Forecasting of Technological Cycles and Upheavals," in Ove Granstand, ed., *Economics of Technology*. Amsterdam: North-Holland.

INDEX

Williams, J., 218,222n
Wilson, Charles H., 70, 120–122, 124
Windsor, Treaty of, 216
Winius, George D., 111, 225n
Winter, S., 223n
Wolpert, Stanley, 226n
World power, 7; qualifications 15
World power (phase), 8

World War I, 14, 18, 159, 162, 180–183, 231
World War II, 14, 17, 18, 104, 162, 169, 175, 182, 196, 232

Yakovets, Yuri V., 228n

Zaitun, 113
Zuk, Gary, 80